EVERYDAY
SlowCooker
& ONE DISH RECIPES

2013

Taste *of* **Home** BOOKS

For other *Taste of Home* books and products, visit **www.ShopTasteofHome.com**.

EDITORIAL
EDITOR-IN-CHIEF Catherine Cassidy
CREATIVE DIRECTOR Howard Greenberg
EDITORIAL OPERATIONS DIRECTOR Kerri Balliet

MANAGING EDITOR/PRINT & DIGITAL BOOKS Mark Hagen
ASSOCIATE CREATIVE DIRECTOR Edwin Robles Jr.

EDITOR Christine Rukavena
ART DIRECTOR Raeann Sundholm
LAYOUT DESIGNERS Catherine Fletcher, Nancy Novak
EDITORIAL PRODUCTION MANAGER Dena Ahlers
COPY CHIEF Deb Warlaumont Mulvey
COPY EDITOR Alysse Gear
GRAPHIC DESIGN INTERN Siya Motamedi

CHIEF FOOD EDITOR Karen Berner
FOOD EDITORS James Schend; Peggy Woodward, RD
ASSOCIATE FOOD EDITOR Krista Lanphier
ASSOCIATE EDITOR/FOOD CONTENT Annie Rundle
RECIPE EDITORS Mary King; Jenni Sharp, RD; Irene Yeh
CONTENT OPERATIONS MANAGER Colleen King

TEST KITCHEN AND FOOD STYLING MANAGER Sarah Thompson
TEST COOKS Matthew Hass, Lauren Knoelke
FOOD STYLISTS Kathryn Conrad (senior),
Shannon Roum, Leah Rekau
PREP COOKS Megumi Garcia, Nicole Spohrleder,
Bethany VanOpdorp

PHOTOGRAPHERS Dan Roberts, Jim Wieland
PHOTOGRAPHER/SET STYLIST Grace Natoli Sheldon
SET STYLING MANAGER Stephanie Marchese
SET STYLISTS Melissa Haberman, Dee Dee Jacq

BUSINESS ANALYST Kristy Martin
BILLING SPECIALIST Mary Ann Koebernik

BUSINESS
VICE PRESIDENT, PUBLISHER Jan Studin, jan_studin@rd.com

GENERAL MANAGER, TASTE OF HOME COOKING SCHOOLS
Erin Puariea

VICE PRESIDENT, BRAND MARKETING Jennifer Smith
VICE PRESIDENT, CIRCULATION AND CONTINUITY MARKETING
Dave Fiegel

READER'S DIGEST NORTH AMERICA
VICE PRESIDENT, BUSINESS DEVELOPMENT Jonathan Bigham
PRESIDENT, BOOKS AND HOME ENTERTAINING Harold Clarke
CHIEF FINANCIAL OFFICER Howard Halligan
VICE PRESIDENT, GENERAL MANAGER, READER'S DIGEST MEDIA
Marilynn Jacobs
CHIEF MARKETING OFFICER Renee Jordan
VICE PRESIDENT, CHIEF SALES OFFICER Mark Josephson
VICE PRESIDENT, GENERAL MANAGER, MILWAUKEE
Frank Quigley
VICE PRESIDENT, CHIEF CONTENT OFFICER Liz Vaccariello

THE READER'S DIGEST ASSOCIATION, INC.
PRESIDENT AND CHIEF EXECUTIVE OFFICER
Robert E. Guth

COVER PHOTOGRAPHY
PHOTOGRAPHER Jim Wieland
FOOD STYLIST Shannon Roum
SET STYLIST Sissy Lamerton

© 2013 Reiman Media Group, INC.
5400 S. 60th St., Greendale WI 53129

INTERNATIONAL STANDARD BOOK NUMBER:
978-1-61765-232-5

LIBRARY OF CONGRESS CONTROL NUMBER:
1944-6382

COMPONENT NUMBER:
119400025H00

PICTURED ON THE FRONT COVER:
Slow-Simmering Pasta Sauce (p. 53);
Herbed Chicken & Spinach Soup (p. 75);
Mexican Beef-Stuffed Peppers (p. 16);
Chocolate Peanut Drops (p. 94).

PICTURED ON THE BACK COVER:
Slow & Easy Baby Back Ribs (p. 46);
Fire Island Ziti (p. 135);
Big Kahuna Pizza (p. 209).

Table of Contents

Slow Cooking 101

The original slow cooker was introduced in 1971 by Rival®. They called it the Crock-Pot®, and it's still so successful that the term "slow cooker" and the name Crock-Pot® are often used interchangeably—but Crock-Pot® is a brand, and a slow cooker is the beloved appliance.

Most slow cookers have two or more settings. Food cooks faster on the high setting, but the low setting is ideal for all-day cooking or turning less-tender cuts of meat into juicy delights. The warm setting keeps food hot and tasty until it's ready to serve. Slow cooker recipes in this book refer to cooking on either high or low settings.

As a general guide, one hour of cooking on high equals roughly two hours of cooking on low. Read on for more useful tips and soon you'll be slow-cooker savvy.

Advantages of Slow Cooking

CONVENIENCE. Slow cookers provide people with the ease of safely preparing meals while being away from home. The appliances are readily available and budget-friendly.

HEALTH. As more people turn to better, more nutritious food choices to improve their health, slow cooking has gained popularity. Low-temperature cooking retains more vitamins in foods, and leaner cuts of meat become tender in the slow cooker without added fats. Many slow cooker recipes call for condensed soups, but lower-sodium and lower-fat versions can also be used. And, for many busy folks, knowing that a healthy meal is waiting at home helps them avoid the temptation of the drive-thru after work.

EAT SMART Mediterranean Pork and Orzo

PER SERVING: *372 cal., 11 g fat (4 g sat. fat), 71 mg chol., 306 mg sodium, 34 g carb., 3 g fiber, 31 g pro.* **Diabetic Exchanges:** *3 lean meat, 2 starch, 1 vegetable, 1 fat.*

EAT SMART Gingered Beef Stir-Fry

PER SERVING: *347 cal., 12 g fat (2 g sat. fat), 27 mg chol., 645 mg sodium, 41 g carb., 2 g fiber, 18 g pro.* **Diabetic Exchanges:** *2 starch, 2 fat, 1 lean meat, 1 vegetable.*

FINANCIAL SAVINGS. A slow cooker uses very little electricity because of its low wattage. For instance, it would cost roughly 21 cents to operate a slow cooker for a total of 10 hours. If you roast a pork roast for only 2 hours in the oven instead of using the slow cooker for 10 hours, you would spend $2.51 to operate an electric oven or $1.49 to operate a gas one. Also, slow cookers do not heat up the kitchen as ovens do, which saves on summertime home-cooling costs.

TIPS FOR TASTY OUTCOMES

■ Be sure the lid is well-placed over the ceramic insert, not tilted or askew. The steam during cooking creates a seal.

■ Refrain from lifting the lid while using the slow cooker, unless you're instructed in a recipe to stir or add ingredients. The loss of steam each time you lift the lid can mean an extra 20 to 30 minutes of cooking time.

■ Remember that slow cooking may take longer at higher altitudes.

■ When food is finished cooking, remove it from the slow cooker within an hour. Promptly refrigerate any leftovers.

■ Use a slow cooker on a buffet table to keep soup, stew, savory dips or mashed potatoes hot.

■ Don't forget your slow cooker when you go camping, if electricity is available. When space is limited and you want "set-it-and-forget-it" meals, it's a handy appliance.

■ Heat cooked food on the stovetop or in the microwave and then put it into a slow cooker to keep it hot for serving. Reheating food in a slow cooker isn't recommended.

know when it's DONE!

→ 145°F

- Medium-rare beef and lamb roasts
- Fish

→ 160°F

- Medium beef and lamb roasts
- Pork
- Egg Dishes

→ 165°F

- Ground chicken and turkey

→ 170°F

- Well-done beef and lamb roasts
- Chicken and turkey that is whole or in pieces

Purchasing a Slow Cooker

Slow cookers range in price from $20 to more than $200 and are available in sizes from 1½ to 7 quarts. Decide on a price range that fits your budget and choose a size appropriate for your family (see chart below).

Most slow cooker inserts are ceramic, but some pricier models have aluminum inserts that let you brown meats in them before slow cooking. For convenience, look for inserts that are dishwasher-safe.

Slow cookers are available in round and oval shapes. If you plan to prepare roasts in the slow cooker, you may wish to consider an oval shape. If stews and soups are your forte, then a round slow cooker is perfect for your cooking needs.

SLOW COOKER SIZES

HOUSEHOLD SIZE	SLOW COOKER CAPACITY
1 to 2 people	2 to 3½ quarts
3 to 4 people	3½ to 4½ quarts
4 to 5 people	4½ to 5 quarts
6 or more people	5 to 7 quarts

Cooking Basics

- While slow cooker models vary, they usually have at least two settings, low (about 180°) and high (about 280°). Some models also have a keep-warm setting.

- The keep-warm setting is useful if you plan to use the slow cooker to serve hot foods while entertaining. Some slow cookers will automatically switch to a keep-warm setting after cooking. This provides added convenience and helps you avoid overcooking the food while you're away from home.

- A range in cooking time is provided to account for variables such as thickness of meat, fullness of the slow cooker and desired finished temperature of the food being cooked. As you grow familiar with your slow cooker, you'll be able to judge which end of the range to use.

- New slow cookers tend to heat up more quickly than older ones. If you have an older model and your recipe directs to cook on low, you may wish to cook on high for the first hour to ensure food safety.

- Old slow cookers can lose their efficiency and may not achieve proper cooking temperatures. To confirm safe cooking temperatures, review the steps of "Slow Cooker Temperature Check" on page 9.

- To learn more about specific models, check online or in reputable consumer magazines for product reviews.

Preparing Foods for the Slow Cooker

BEANS. Dried beans can be tricky to cook in a slow cooker. Minerals in the water and variations in voltage affect various type of beans in different ways. Always soak dried beans prior to cooking. Soak them overnight or place them in a Dutch oven and add enough water to cover by 2 inches. Bring to a boil and boil for 2 minutes. Remove from the heat, cover and let stand for 1 to 4 hours or until softened. Drain and rinse beans, discarding liquid. Sugar, salt and acidic ingredients, such as vinegar, interfere with the beans' ability to cook and become tender. Add these ingredients only after the beans are fully cooked. Lentils and split peas do not need soaking.

COUSCOUS. Couscous is best cooked on the stovetop rather than in the slow cooker.

DAIRY. Milk-based products tend to break down during slow cooking. Items like milk, cream, sour cream or cream cheese are best added during the last hour of cooking. Cheeses don't generally hold up during the slow cooker's extended cooking time and should be added near the end of cooking. Condensed cream soups generally hold up well in the slow cooker..

FISH & SEAFOOD. Fish and seafood cook quickly and can break down if cooked too long. They are generally added to the slow cooker toward the end of the cooking time to keep them at optimal quality.

MEATS. Meat may be browned before adding to the slow cooker. While browning is not necessary, it adds to the flavor and appearance of the meat and allows you to drain off the fat. Cut roasts over 3 pounds in half before placing in the slow cooker to ensure even cooking. Trim off any excess fat. Fat retains heat, and large amounts of fat could raise the temperature of the cooking liquid, causing the meat to overcook.

OATS. Quick-cooking and old-fashioned oats are often interchangeable in recipes. However, old-fashioned oats hold up better in the slow cooker.

PASTA. If added to a slow cooker when dry, pasta tends to become very sticky. It's better to cook it according to the package directions and stir it into the slow cooker just before serving. Small pastas, such as orzo and

ditalini, may be cooked in the slow cooker. To keep them from becoming mushy, add during the last hour of cooking.

RICE. Converted rice is ideal for all-day cooking. If using instant rice, add it during the last 30 minutes of cooking.

VEGETABLES. Firm vegetables like potatoes and carrots tend to cook more slowly than meat. Cut these foods into uniform pieces and place on the bottom and around the sides of the slow cooker. Place the meat over the vegetables. During the last 15 to 60 minutes of cooking, add tender vegetables, like peas and zucchini, or ones you'd prefer to be crisp-tender.

COOK TIMES

Conventional Oven
15 to 30 minutes

Slow Cooker
Low: 4 to 6 hours
High: 1½ to 2 hours

Conventional Oven
35 to 45 minutes

Slow Cooker
Low: 6 to 8 hours
High: 3 to 4 hours

Conventional Oven
50 minutes or more

Slow Cooker
Low: 8 to 10 hours
High: 4 to 6 hours

Thickening
Stews & Sauces

Quick-cooking tapioca can be used as a thickener for stews. Add it along with other ingredients at the beginning of cooking.

To thicken juices at the end of cooking, use flour or cornstarch. Mix flour or cornstarch with some cold water until smooth. Stir into the slow cooker. Cover and cook on high for 30 minutes or until the cooking juices are thickened.

Or, strain cooking juices and place in a saucepan. Mix flour or cornstarch with some cold water until smooth. Stir into juices. Bring to a boil; cook and stir for 2 minutes or until thickened.

Converting Recipes for the
Slow Cooker

Almost any recipe that bakes in the oven or simmers on the stovetop can be converted for the slow cooker. Here are some guidelines.

- Before converting recipes, check the manufacturer's guidelines for your particular slow cooker. Find a recipe that is similar to the one you want to convert and use it as a guide. Note the amount and size of meat and vegetables, heat setting, cooking time and liquid.

- Since there is no evaporation, adjusting the amount of liquid in your recipe may be necessary. If a recipe calls for 6 to 8 cups of water, try starting with 5 cups. Conversely, recipes should include at least a little liquid. If a recipe does not include liquid, add 1/2 cup of water or broth.

- In general, 1 hour of simmering on the range or baking at 350°F in the oven is equal to 8-10 hours on low or 4-6 hours on high in a slow cooker. Check the chart, top left.

- Cornstarch, flour and tapioca are often used thicken stews and sauces in the slow cooker. See the information at left for more details.

Useful Handles for Lifting Food

Layered dishes or meat loaves are easier to get out of the slow cooker using foil handles. Here's how:

1. For a 3-qt. slow cooker, cut three 20x3-in. strips of heavy-duty foil (or 25x3-in. for larger slow cookers). Or cut 6-in.-wide strips from regular foil and fold in half lengthwise. Crisscross the strips so they resemble the spokes of a wheel.

2. Place the strips on the bottom and up the sides of the slow cooker insert. Let strips hang over the edge of the slow cooker. Coat strips with cooking spray.

3. Place food in the center of the strips and lower until the food rests on the bottom of the slow cooker.

4. After cooking, grasp the foil strips and carefully lift food up. Remove food from foil strips and serve.

Slow Cooker Temperature Check

To be considered safe, a slow cooker must be able to cook slowly enough that it can be left unattended, yet it must be fast enough to keep the food at a proper temperature. Here's how to check your slow cooker:

1. Fill the slow cooker ½ to ⅔ full with room-temperature water.

2. Cover and heat on low for 8 hours.

3. Using a thermometer, check the temperature of the water quickly since the temperature can drop once the lid is removed.

4. The temperature should be at least 185°. If it's too hot, a meal cooked for 8 hours would likely be overdone. If the temperature is below 185°, the slow cooker is not safe to use and should be discarded.

Power Outage Solutions

If the power goes out while you are using a slow cooker, the USDA provides the following recommendations:

- Fully cooked foods are safe at room temperature for up to 2 hours. If the food has sat for 2 hours or longer, or if the time is unknown, it should be discarded.

- If the food is not fully cooked and you're home when the power goes out, immediately finish cooking the food by another method, such as with a gas stove or grill.

CLEANING TIPS

- Removable inserts make cleanup a breeze. Be sure to cool the insert before rinsing or cleaning with water to avoid cracking or warping. Do not immerse the metal base in water. Clean it with a damp sponge.

- If dishwasher-safe, place the insert in the dishwasher. Otherwise, wash in warm soapy water. Avoid using abrasive cleansers, since they may scratch the surface.

- To remove mineral stains on a ceramic insert, fill the cooker with hot water and 1 cup of white vinegar; cover. Turn the heat to high for 2 hours, then empty. When cool, wash the insert with hot soapy water and a cloth or sponge. Rinse well and dry with a towel.

- To remove water marks from a highly glazed ceramic insert, rub the surface with canola oil and allow to stand for 2 hours before washing with hot soapy water.

MEXICAN BEEF-STUFFED PEPPERS, PAGE 16

"I grew up eating stuffed peppers and thought my husband would immediately like them as well. He didn't at first, but then I created this slow-cooked recipe. He loves fajitas and tacos, so I created these tasty peppers with all of his favorite flavors tucked inside."

—NICOLE SULLIVAN ARVADA, COLORADO
about her recipe, Mexican Beef-Stuffed Peppers, on page 16

Slow Cooker

Beef & Ground Beef

16   15   24

From **brisket and stew to stuffed peppers, meat loaf and shepherd's pie**, nothing highlights the versatility of the slow cooker like **satisfying recipes featuring beef**. Simmer up a **stick-to-your-ribs** winner today!

COFFEE-BRAISED SHORT RIBS

> When the leaves start falling, I crave comfort foods like hearty slow-cooked stews and braised meats. Short ribs that cook until tender smell and taste impressive, but they're easy to make—that's why I love these! —CAROL WOHLGEMUTH RIDING MOUNTAIN, MANITOBA

Slow-Cooked Tamale Casserole

I've been making this recipe for many years because my family really likes it. It's great for busy days because you make it earlier in the day and let it cook.
—DIANA BRIGGS VENETA, OREGON

PREP: 15 MIN. **COOK:** 4 HOURS
MAKES: 6 SERVINGS

- 1 **pound ground beef**
- 1 **egg, beaten**
- 1½ **cups milk**
- ¾ **cup cornmeal**
- 1 **can (15¼ ounces) whole kernel corn, drained**
- 1 **can (14½ ounces) diced tomatoes, undrained**
- 1 **can (2¼ ounces) sliced ripe olives, drained**
- 1 **envelope chili seasoning**
- 1 **teaspoon seasoned salt**
- 1 **cup (4 ounces) shredded cheddar cheese**

1. In a skillet, cook beef over medium heat until no longer pink; drain. In a large bowl, combine the egg, milk and cornmeal until smooth. Add corn, tomatoes, olives, chili seasoning, seasoned salt and beef.
2. Transfer to a greased 3-qt. slow cooker. Cover and cook on high for 3 hours and 45 minutes. Sprinkle with cheese; cover and cook 15 minutes longer or until cheese is melted.

Coffee-Braised Short Ribs

PREP: 25 MIN. **COOK:** 6 HOURS
MAKES: 8 SERVINGS

- 4 **pounds bone-in beef short ribs**
- 1½ **teaspoons salt, divided**
- 1 **teaspoon ground coriander**
- ½ **teaspoon pepper**
- 2 **tablespoons olive oil**
- 1½ **pounds small red potatoes, cut in half**
- 1 **medium onion, chopped**
- 1 **cup reduced-sodium beef broth**
- 1 **whole garlic bulb, cloves separated, peeled and slightly crushed**
- 4 **cups strong brewed coffee**
- 2 **teaspoons red wine vinegar**
- 3 **tablespoons butter**

1. Sprinkle ribs with 1 teaspoon salt, coriander and pepper. In a large skillet, brown ribs in oil in batches. Using tongs, transfer ribs to a 6-qt. slow cooker. Add potatoes and onion.
2. Add broth to the skillet, stirring to loosen browned bits. Bring to a boil; cook until liquid is reduced by half. Stir in garlic and remaining salt; add to slow cooker. Pour coffee over top. Cover and cook on low for 6-8 hours or until meat is tender.
3. Remove ribs and potatoes to a serving platter; keep warm. Strain cooking juices into a small saucepan; skim fat. Bring to a boil; cook until liquid is reduced by half. Stir in vinegar. Remove from the heat; whisk in butter. Serve with ribs and potatoes.

Ground beef is labeled according to the fat content, or the **percentage of lean meat** to fat, such as 90 percent lean.

My great aunt used to make the most amazing braciole, but it was a laborious and time-consuming effort. I took her basic recipe and transformed it into a slow-cooker version, making it easier for today's hurried world. My great aunt always served the flank steak sliced over orzo that had been tossed with olive oil and Romano cheese. Delicioso! —**LISA RENSHAW** KANSAS CITY, MISSOURI

BEEF BRACIOLE

Beef Braciole

PREP: 30 MIN. **COOK:** 6 HOURS
MAKES: 6 SERVINGS

- 2 jars (24 ounces each) tomato basil pasta sauce
- 1 teaspoon crushed red pepper flakes
- 1 beef flank steak (1½ pounds)
- ½ teaspoon salt
- ½ teaspoon pepper
- 2 eggs, beaten
- ½ cup seasoned bread crumbs
- 8 thin slices prosciutto or deli ham
- 1 cup (4 ounces) shredded Italian cheese blend
- 2 tablespoons olive oil

1. In a 5- or 6-qt. oval slow cooker, combine pasta sauce and pepper flakes. Pound steak with a meat mallet to ½-in. thickness; sprinkle with salt and pepper.

2. In a small bowl, combine eggs and bread crumbs. Spoon over beef to within 1 in. of edges; press onto meat. Layer with prosciutto and cheese. Roll up jelly-roll style, starting with a long side; tie at 2-in. intervals with kitchen string.

3. In a large skillet, brown meat in oil on all sides. Transfer to slow cooker; spoon sauce over meat. Cover and cook on low for 6-8 hours or until beef is tender.

4. Remove meat from sauce and discard string. Cut into slices; serve with sauce.

Potatoes and other **dense foods** are often layered in the bottom of the slow cooker, where they can be closer to the heating element. This ensures that everything is done at the same time.

I like that I usually have everything on hand for this hearty stew. Throw in some peas near the end of the cook time if your family likes them.

—**MARGERY BRYAN** MOSES LAKE, WASHINGTON

Meatball Stew

PREP: 25 MIN. **COOK:** 6 HOURS
MAKES: 4 SERVINGS

- 1 pound lean ground beef (90% lean)
- 1½ teaspoons salt or salt-free seasoning blend, divided
- ½ teaspoon pepper, divided
- 4 medium potatoes, peeled and cut into chunks
- 4 medium carrots, cut into chunks
- 1 large onion, cut into chunks
- ½ cup water
- ½ cup ketchup
- 1½ teaspoons cider vinegar
- ½ teaspoon dried basil

1. In a bowl, combine the beef, 1 teaspoon salt and ¼ teaspoon pepper. Shape into 1-in. balls. In a skillet over medium heat, brown meatballs on all sides; drain.

2. Place the potatoes, carrots and onion in a 3-qt. slow cooker; top with meatballs. Combine the water, ketchup, vinegar, basil, and the remaining salt and pepper; pour over meatballs.

3. Cover and cook on low for 6-8 hours or until the vegetables are tender.

LOUISIANA ROUND STEAK

> This beefy main dish is always a big hit with the men in our family. After simmering in a slow cooker, the steak takes on a robust flavor, and we just love the filling portions. —MEGAN ROHLCK VERMILLION, SO UTH DAKOTA

Louisiana Round Steak

PREP: 20 MIN. **COOK:** 7 HOURS
MAKES: 6 SERVINGS

- 2 **pounds sweet potatoes, peeled and cut into 1-inch pieces**
- 1 **large onion, chopped**
- 1 **medium green pepper, sliced**
- 2 **beef top round steaks (¾ inch thick and 2 pounds)**
- 1 **teaspoon salt, divided**
- 2 **tablespoons olive oil**
- 1 **garlic clove, minced**
- 3 **tablespoons all-purpose flour**
- 1 **can (28 ounces) diced tomatoes, undrained**
- ½ **cup beef broth**
- 1 **teaspoon sugar**
- ½ **teaspoon dried thyme**
- ½ **teaspoon pepper**
- ¼ **teaspoon hot pepper sauce**

1. Place the sweet potatoes, onion and green pepper in a 6-qt. slow cooker. Cut each steak into three serving-size pieces; sprinkle with ½ teaspoon salt. In a large skillet over medium heat, brown steaks in oil in batches on both sides. Place steaks over vegetables, reserving drippings in pan.
2. Add garlic to drippings; cook and stir for 1 minute. Stir in flour until blended. Stir in the remaining ingredients and remaining salt. Bring to a boil, stirring constantly. Cook and stir for 4-5 minutes or until thickened. Pour over meat. Cover and cook on low for 7-9 hours or until beef is tender.

Mexican Beef-Stuffed Peppers

I grew up eating stuffed peppers and thought my husband would immediately like them as well. He didn't at first, but then I created this slow-cooked recipe. He loves fajitas and tacos, so I created these tasty peppers with all of his favorite flavors tucked inside.

—**NICOLE SULLIVAN** ARVADA, COLORADO

PREP: 15 MIN. **COOK:** 5 HOURS
MAKES: 4 SERVINGS

- 4 **medium green or sweet red peppers**
- 1 **pound ground beef**
- 1 **package (8.8 ounces) ready-to-serve Spanish rice**
- 2 **cups (8 ounces) shredded Colby-Monterey Jack cheese, divided**
- 1½ **cups salsa**
- 1 **tablespoon hot pepper sauce**
- 1 **cup water**
- 2 **tablespoons minced fresh cilantro**

1. Cut tops off peppers and remove seeds; set aside. In a large skillet, cook beef over medium heat until no longer pink; drain.
2. Stir in the rice, 1½ cups cheese, salsa and pepper sauce. Spoon into peppers. Transfer to a 5-qt. slow cooker. Pour water around peppers.
3. Cover and cook on low for 5-6 hours or until peppers are tender and filling is heated through. Top with remaining cheese; sprinkle with cilantro.

Slow-Cooked Shepherd's Pie

Shepherd's pie is to the British as meat loaf is to Americans, so as a young child living in the UK, it was a weekly staple. This meal-in-one specialty is my go-to recipe when I'm longing for the sights and smells of my mother's kitchen.

—MARI SITKIEWICZ
DOWNERS GROVE, ILLINOIS

PREP: 35 MIN. **COOK:** 5¼ HOURS
MAKES: 5 SERVINGS

- 2 **pounds medium Yukon Gold potatoes, peeled and quartered**
- 2 **tablespoons butter**
- ¼ **to ⅓ cup 2% milk**
- ¾ **teaspoon salt, divided**
- ½ **teaspoon pepper, divided**
- 1 **pound ground beef**
- 1 **large onion, chopped**
- 2 **garlic cloves, minced**
- 3 **tablespoons tomato paste**
- 1¾ **cups sliced fresh mushrooms**
- 2 **medium carrots, chopped**
- 1 **cup beef broth**
- ¼ **cup dry white wine**
- 2 **teaspoons Worcestershire sauce**
- ½ **teaspoon dried thyme**
- ⅓ **cup frozen peas**
- ½ **cup shredded Monterey Jack cheese**
- 1 **tablespoon minced fresh parsley**

1. Place potatoes in a large saucepan and cover with water. Bring to a boil. Reduce heat; cover and cook for 10-15 minutes or until tender. Drain, then shake potatoes over low heat for 1 minute to dry. Mash potatoes, gradually adding butter and enough milk to reach desired consistency. Stir in ½ teaspoon salt and ¼ teaspoon pepper.

2. Meanwhile, in a large skillet, cook the beef, onion, and garlic over medium heat until meat is no longer pink; drain.

3. Add tomato paste; cook for 2 minutes. Add the mushrooms, carrots, broth, wine, Worcestershire sauce and thyme. Bring to a boil. Reduce heat; simmer, uncovered, until most of the liquid is evaporated. Stir in peas. Season with remaining salt and pepper.

4. Transfer beef mixture to a greased 4-qt. slow cooker. Spread mashed potatoes over top. Cover and cook on low for 5-6 hours or until bubbly. Sprinkle with cheese. Cover and cook 10 minutes longer or until cheese is melted. Just before serving, sprinkle with parsley.

BAKE OPTION *Transfer cooked beef mixture to a greased 8-in. square baking dish. Spread mashed potatoes over top. Sprinkle with cheese. Bake, uncovered, at 350° for 30-40 minutes or until bubbly and topping is lightly browned. Sprinkle with parsley.*

My sister shared an India-inspired dish with me, and I made a few modifications to fit my tastes. I love the smell of the spices as the ribs slow cook all day!

—LORRAINE CARLSTROM NELSON, BRITISH COLUMBIA

BEEF SHORT RIBS VINDALOO

Beef Short Ribs Vindaloo

PREP: 30 MIN. + MARINATING
COOK: 8¼ HOURS **MAKES:** 4 SERVINGS

- 1 tablespoon cumin seeds
- 2 teaspoons coriander seeds
- 1 tablespoon butter
- 1 medium onion, finely chopped
- 8 garlic cloves, minced
- 1 tablespoon minced fresh gingerroot
- 2 teaspoons mustard seed
- ½ teaspoon ground cloves
- ¼ teaspoon kosher salt
- ¼ teaspoon ground cinnamon
- ¼ teaspoon cayenne pepper
- ½ cup red wine vinegar
- 4 bay leaves
- 2 pounds bone-in beef short ribs
- 1 cup fresh sugar snap peas, halved
  Hot cooked rice and plain yogurt

1. In a small dry skillet over medium heat, toast cumin and coriander seeds until aromatic, stirring frequently. Cool. Coarsely crush seeds in a spice grinder or with a mortar and pestle.

2. In a large saucepan, heat butter over medium heat. Add the onion, garlic and ginger; cook and stir for 1 minute. Add the mustard seed, cloves, salt, cinnamon, cayenne pepper and crushed seeds; cook and stir 1 minute longer. Cool mixture completely.

3. In a large resealable plastic bag, combine the vinegar, bay leaves and onion mixture. Add ribs; seal bag and turn to coat. Refrigerate overnight.

4. Transfer rib mixture to a 4-qt. slow cooker. Cover and cook on low for 8-10 hours or until meat is tender. Stir in peas; cook 8-10 minutes longer or until peas are crisp-tender. Skim fat; discard bay leaves. Serve rib mixture with rice and yogurt.

GUINNESS CORNED BEEF AND CABBAGE

Passed down through multiple generations in our family, this robust corned beef and cabbage recipe is requested often in our house. The Irish stout beer adds excellent richness to the corned beef. Just throw the ingredients together in the slow cooker and let them simmer until delicious!

—KARIN BRODBECK RED HOOK, NEW YORK

Guinness Corned Beef and Cabbage

PREP: 20 MIN. **COOK:** 8 HOURS
MAKES: 9 SERVINGS

- 2 pounds red potatoes, quartered
- 1 pound carrots, cut into 3-inch pieces
- 2 celery ribs, cut into 3-inch pieces
- 1 small onion, quartered
- 1 corned beef brisket with spice packet (3 to 3½ pounds)
- 8 whole cloves
- 6 whole peppercorns
- 1 bay leaf
- 1 bottle (12 ounces) Guinness (dark beer) or beef broth
- ½ small head cabbage, thinly sliced
  Prepared horseradish

1. In a 6-qt. slow cooker, combine the potatoes, carrots, celery and onion. Add brisket (discard spice packet from corned beef or save for another use). Place the cloves, peppercorns and bay leaf on a double thickness of cheesecloth; bring up corners of cloth and tie with string to form a bag. Place in slow cooker. Pour beer over top.

2. Cover and cook on low for 8-10 hours or until meat and vegetables are tender, adding cabbage during the last hour of cooking. Discard spice bag.

3. Thinly slice corned beef across the grain. Serve with vegetables and prepared horseradish.

FRENCH BEEF STEW

French Beef Stew

When it comes to making a thick and hearty, classic beef stew, I let my slow cooker do the work. I simply toss a green side salad and dinner is ready.
—IOLA EGLE BELLA VISTA, ARKANSAS

PREP: 20 MIN. **COOK:** 9 HOURS
MAKES: 8-10 SERVINGS

- 3 **medium potatoes, peeled and cubed**
- 2 **pounds beef stew meat**
- 4 **medium carrots, sliced**
- 2 **medium onions, sliced**
- 3 **celery ribs, sliced**
- 2 **cups tomato juice**
- 1 **cup water**
- ⅓ **cup quick-cooking tapioca**
- 1 **tablespoon sugar**
- 1 **tablespoon salt**
- 1 **teaspoon dried basil**
- ½ **teaspoon pepper**

1. Place the potatoes in a greased 5-qt. slow cooker. Top with the beef, carrots, onions and celery.

In a large bowl, combine the remaining ingredients. Pour over the vegetables.
2. Cover and cook on low for 9-10 hours or until meat and vegetables are tender.

Beef Tips

This recipe was given to my mother when I was young, and the entire family loved it. Now I often make it for my own family.
—DIANE BENSKIN LEWISVILLE, TEXAS

PREP: 20 MIN. **COOK:** 6¼ HOURS
MAKES: 4 SERVINGS

- 1 **pound beef sirloin tips, cut into 1-inch cubes**
- 2 **medium carrots, chopped**
- 2 **medium celery ribs, chopped**
- 1 **cup chopped onion**
- 1 **can (10¾ ounces) condensed golden mushroom soup, undiluted**
- ⅔ **cup white wine or beef broth**
- 2 **teaspoons cornstarch**
- ¼ **cup cold water**
  Hot cooked egg noodles

1. In a 3-qt. slow cooker, combine the beef, carrots, celery, onion, soup and wine. Cover and cook on low for 6-7 hours or until meat is tender.
2. Combine cornstarch and water until smooth; gradually stir into cooking juices. Cover and cook on high for 15 minutes or until thickened. Serve with noodles.

Grandma Schwartz's Rouladen

PREP: 35 MIN. **COOK:** 6 HOURS
MAKES: 6 SERVINGS

- 3 **bacon strips, chopped**
- 1½ **pounds beef top round steak**
- 2 **tablespoons Dijon mustard**
- 3 **medium carrots, quartered lengthwise**
- 6 **dill pickle spears**
- ¼ **cup finely chopped onion**
- 1 **cup sliced fresh mushrooms**
- 1 **small parsnip, peeled and chopped**
- 1 **celery rib, chopped**
- 1 **can (10¾ ounces) condensed golden cream of mushroom soup, undiluted**
- ⅓ **cup dry red wine**
- 2 **tablespoons Worcestershire sauce**
- 2 **tablespoons minced fresh parsley**

1. In a large skillet, cook bacon over medium heat until crisp. Remove to paper towels with a slotted spoon; drain, reserving drippings.
2. Meanwhile, cut steak into 6 serving-size pieces; pound with a meat mallet to ¼-in. thickness. Spread tops with mustard. Top each with two carrot pieces and one pickle spear; sprinkle with onion. Roll up from a short side and secure with toothpicks.
3. In a large skillet, brown roll-ups in bacon drippings over medium-high heat. Place roll-ups in a 4-qt. slow cooker. Top with mushrooms, parsnip, celery and cooked bacon.
4. In a small bowl, whisk the soup, wine and Worcestershire sauce. Pour over top. Cover and cook on low for 6-8 hours or until beef is tender. Sprinkle with parsley.

This was one of my Grandma Schwartz's recipes. Grandpa Schwartz was a German butcher and this was one of his (and our) favorite meals. It makes an extra-special dinner served with mashed potatoes made with butter and sour cream.

—**LYNDA SHARAI** SUMMER LAKE, OREGON

GRANDMA SCHWARTZ'S ROULADEN

As part of a prize I won for a recipe contest, I received a slow cooker. I hadn't used one in years so had no recipes on hand. This tasty beef was my first creation and is now a family favorite. —JULIE MERRIMAN COLD BROOK, NEW YORK

SAUSAGE-STUFFED FLANK STEAK

Sausage-Stuffed Flank Steak

PREP: 35 MIN. **COOK:** 6 HOURS
MAKES: 4 SERVINGS

- ¼ cup dried cherries
- ¾ cup dry red wine or beef broth, divided
- 1 beef flank steak (1½ pounds)
- ¾ teaspoon salt, divided
- ½ teaspoon pepper, divided
- 1 medium onion, finely chopped
- 3 tablespoons olive oil, divided
- 4 garlic cloves, minced
- ½ cup seasoned bread crumbs
- ¼ cup pitted Greek olives, halved
- ¼ cup grated Parmesan cheese
- ¼ cup minced fresh basil
- ½ pound bulk hot Italian sausage
- 1 jar (24 ounces) marinara sauce
   Hot cooked pasta

1. In a bowl, combine cherries and ¼ cup wine; let stand 10 minutes. Meanwhile, cut steak into four serving-size pieces; flatten to ¼-in. thickness. Sprinkle both sides with ½ teaspoon salt and ¼ teaspoon pepper.
2. In a skillet, saute onion in 1 tablespoon oil until tender. Add garlic; cook 1 minute longer. Transfer to a large bowl; stir in bread crumbs, olives, cheese, basil, cherry mixture and remaining salt and pepper. Crumble sausage over mixture and mix well.
3. Spread ½ cup sausage mixture over each steak piece. Roll up jelly-roll style, starting with a long side; tie with kitchen string.
4. In the same skillet, brown meat in remaining oil on all sides. Transfer to a greased 3-qt. slow cooker. Top with marinara sauce and remaining wine. Cook and cook on low for 6-8 hours or until beef is tender. Serve with pasta.

SO-EASY SWISS STEAK

EAT SMART So-Easy Swiss Steak

Let your slow cooker simmer up this fuss-free and flavorful Swiss steak. It's perfect for busy days—the longer it cooks, the better it tastes!
—**SARAH BURKS** WATHENA, KANSAS

PREP: 10 MIN. **COOK:** 6 HOURS
MAKES: 2 SERVINGS

- 1 tablespoon all-purpose flour
- ¼ teaspoon salt
- ⅛ teaspoon pepper
- ¾ pound beef top round steak, cut in half
- ½ medium onion, cut into ¼-inch slices
- ⅓ cup chopped celery
- 1 can (8 ounces) tomato sauce

1. In a large resealable plastic bag, combine the flour, salt and pepper. Add beef; seal bag and shake to coat.
2. Place onion in a 3-qt. slow cooker coated with cooking spray. Layer with the beef, celery and tomato sauce. Cover and cook on low for 6-8 hours or until meat is tender.
PER SERVING *272 cal., 5 g fat (2 g sat. fat), 96 mg chol., 882 mg sodium, 13 g carb., 2 g fiber, 41 g pro.* **Diabetic Exchanges:** *5 lean meat, 2 vegetable, 1 fat.*

Onion Meat Loaf

My husband and I really enjoy this delicious meat loaf. It's so simple to make with just five ingredients from the pantry. The leftovers are good in sandwiches.
—**RHONDA COWDEN** QUINCY, ILLINOIS

PREP: 15 MIN. **COOK:** 5 HOURS
MAKES: 8 SERVINGS

- 2 eggs, beaten
- ¾ cup quick-cooking oats
- ½ cup ketchup
- 1 envelope onion soup mix
- 2 pounds ground beef

1. Cut three 20-in. x 3-in. strips of heavy-duty foil; crisscross so they resemble spokes of a wheel. Place strips on the bottom and up the sides of a 3-qt. slow cooker. Coat strips with cooking spray.
2. In a large bowl, combine the eggs, oats, ketchup and soup mix. Crumble beef over mixture and mix well. Shape into a loaf. Place loaf in the center of the strips. Cover and cook on low for 5-6 hours or until a thermometer reads 160°.
3. Using foil strips as handles, remove meat loaf to a platter.

MEAT LOAF FROM THE SLOW COOKER

> This tasty, easy-to-make meat loaf is one of my personal favorites. I'm often asked for the recipe.
>
> —**LAURA BURGESS** MOUNT VERNON, SOUTH DAKOTA

EAT SMART Meat Loaf From the Slow Cooker

PREP: 25 MIN. **COOK:** 3 HOURS
MAKES: 8 SERVINGS

- ½ cup tomato sauce
- ½ cup egg substitute
- ¼ cup ketchup
- 1 teaspoon Worcestershire sauce
- 1 small onion, chopped
- ⅓ cup crushed saltines (about 10 crackers)
- ¾ teaspoon minced garlic
- ½ teaspoon seasoned salt
- ⅛ teaspoon seasoned pepper
- 1½ pounds lean ground beef (90% lean)
- ½ pound reduced-fat bulk pork sausage

SAUCE
- ½ cup ketchup
- 3 tablespoons brown sugar
- ¾ teaspoon ground mustard
- ¼ teaspoon ground nutmeg

1. Cut three 25-in. x 3-in. strips of heavy-duty foil; crisscross so they resemble spokes of a wheel. Place strips on the bottom and up the sides of a 4- or 5-qt. slow cooker. Coat strips with cooking spray.
2. In a large bowl, combine the first nine ingredients. Crumble beef and sausage over mixture and mix well (mixture will be moist). Shape into a loaf. Place meat loaf in the center of the strips.
3. In a small bowl, combine sauce ingredients. Spoon over meat loaf. Cover and cook on low 3-4 hours or until no pink remains and a thermometer reads 160°. Using foil strips as handles, remove the meat loaf to a platter.
PER SERVING *267 cal., 12 g fat (5 g sat. fat), 72 mg chol., 740 mg sodium, 16 g carb., trace fiber, 23 g pro.* **Diabetic Exchanges:** *3 lean meat, 1 starch, ½ fat.*

Beef Stew Provencal

PREP: 25 MIN. **COOK:** 6 HOURS
MAKES: 6 SERVINGS

- 4 medium carrots, chopped
- 4 celery ribs, chopped
- 1 cup beef broth
- 1 jar (7 ounces) julienned oil-packed sun-dried tomatoes, drained
- 1 can (6 ounces) tomato paste
- 1 small onion, chopped
- ⅓ cup honey
- ¼ cup balsamic vinegar
- 1 garlic clove, minced
- 1 teaspoon dried thyme
- ½ teaspoon onion powder
- ¼ teaspoon white pepper
- 1 boneless beef chuck roast (2½ pounds), cut into 2-inch cubes
- ½ cup all-purpose flour
- ½ teaspoon salt
- ½ teaspoon pepper
- 2 tablespoons olive oil
  Hot cooked mashed potatoes or egg noodles

1. In a 4-qt. slow cooker, combine the first 12 ingredients. In a large bowl, combine the beef, flour, salt and pepper; toss to coat. In a large skillet, brown beef in oil in batches. Transfer to slow cooker.
2. Cover and cook on low for 6-8 hours or until beef is tender. Serve with mashed potatoes.

To give limp celery **a second chance** to season soups and stews, cut the ends from the stalks and place the stalks in a glass of cold water in the refrigerator. You'll be surprised how **rejuvenated** the celery will be.

When I was young, my favorite food to order in a restaurant was beef stew. My mother and I decided to create our own and experimented with different ingredients until we came up with this recipe. Everyone liked this slow-cooker version so much that now it's a tradition every time the whole family is together.

—**CHELSEY LARSEN** SPARKS, NEVADA

BEEF STEW PROVENCAL

We loved how tender this brisket came out of the slow cooker. The sauce has a robust, beefy flavor with a slight tang from the balsamic vinegar, and the rich caramelized onions complete the dish. —TASTE OF HOME TEST KITCHEN

SUNDAY DINNER BRISKET

EAT SMART Sunday Dinner Brisket

PREP: 45 MIN. **COOK:** 8 HOURS
MAKES: 10 SERVINGS

- 4 **cups sliced onions**
- 3 **tablespoons olive oil, divided**
- 4 **garlic cloves, minced**
- 1 **tablespoon brown sugar**
- ⅓ **cup all-purpose flour**
- 1 **fresh beef brisket (4 to 5 pounds)**
- 1 **teaspoon salt**
- 1 **teaspoon coarsely ground pepper**
- ¼ **cup balsamic vinegar**
- 1 **can (14 ounces) reduced-sodium beef broth**
- 2 **tablespoons tomato paste**
- 2 **teaspoons Italian seasoning**
- 1 **teaspoon Worcestershire sauce**
- ½ **teaspoon paprika**
- 1 **tablespoon cornstarch**
- 2 **tablespoons cold water**

1. In a skillet, saute onions in 1 tablespoon oil until softened. Sprinkle with garlic and brown sugar. Reduce heat to medium-low; cook for 10 minutes or until onions are golden brown, stirring occasionally. Transfer to a 4- or 5-qt. slow cooker.

2. Sprinkle flour over both sides of brisket; shake off excess. In the same skillet, brown beef in remaining oil on all sides. Remove from the heat; sprinkle with salt and pepper. Place beef on top of onions. Add balsamic vinegar to skillet; increase heat to medium-high. Cook, stirring to loosen browned bits from pan. Pour over beef.

3. In a small bowl, combine the broth, tomato paste, Italian seasoning, Worcestershire sauce and paprika; pour over beef. Cover and cook on low for 8-10 hours or until meat is tender.

4. Remove roast to a serving platter and keep warm. Pour cooking juices into a small saucepan; skim fat and bring to a boil. Combine cornstarch and cold water until smooth; stir into cooking juices. Return to a boil; cook and stir for 1-2 minutes or until thickened. Thinly slice beef across the grain; serve with sauce.

NOTE *This is a fresh beef brisket, not corned beef.*

PER SERVING *319 cal., 12 g fat (4 g sat. fat), 78 mg chol., 381 mg sodium, 12 g carb., 1 g fiber, 39 g pro.* **Diabetic Exchanges:** *5 lean meat, 1 starch, 1 fat.*

Zesty Beef Stew

Preparation couldn't be simpler for this hearty no-fuss stew! I created the recipe when I didn't have some of my usual ingredients for vegetable beef soup. My husband says it's the best I ever made!

—MARGARET TURZA
SOUTH BEND, INDIANA

PREP: 10 MIN. **COOK:** 3½ HOURS
MAKES: 6 SERVINGS

- 1 **pound beef stew meat, cut into 1-inch cubes**
- 1 **package (16 ounces) frozen mixed vegetables, thawed**
- 1 **can (15 ounces) pinto beans, rinsed and drained**
- 1½ **cups water**
- 1 **can (8 ounces) pizza sauce**
- 2 **tablespoons medium pearl barley**
- 1 **tablespoon dried minced onion**
- 2 **teaspoons beef bouillon granules**
- ¼ **teaspoon crushed red pepper flakes**

1. In a 3-qt. slow cooker, combine all of the ingredients.

2. Cover and cook on low for 3½ to 4½ hours or until meat is tender.

Poultry

Discover **tender, perfectly cooked** turkey breast.
Succulent chicken thighs in a rich gravy. Even hearty
chili with a corn bread topping! On the following pages,
you're sure to find **delectable choices** for family dinners,
potlucks and company.

CHICKEN THIGHS WITH GINGER-PEACH SAUCE

Butter & Herb Turkey

My kids love turkey for dinner, and this easy recipe lets me make it whenever I want. No special occasion required! The meat is so tender that it comes right off the bone.

—ROCHELLE POPOVIC
SOUTH BEND, INDIANA

PREP: 10 MIN. **COOK:** 5 HOURS
MAKES: 12 SERVINGS (3 CUPS GRAVY)

- 1 bone-in turkey breast (6 to 7 pounds)
- 2 tablespoons butter, softened
- ½ teaspoon dried rosemary, crushed
- ½ teaspoon dried thyme
- ¼ teaspoon garlic powder
- ¼ teaspoon pepper
- 1 can (14½ ounces) chicken broth
- 3 tablespoons cornstarch
- 2 tablespoons cold water

1. Rub turkey with butter. Combine the rosemary, thyme, garlic powder and pepper; sprinkle over turkey. Place in a 6-qt. slow cooker. Pour broth over top. Cover and cook on low for 5-6 hours or until tender.
2. Remove turkey to a serving platter; keep warm. Skim fat from cooking juices; transfer to a small saucepan. Bring to a boil. Combine cornstarch and water until smooth. Gradually stir into the pan. Bring to a boil; cook and stir for 2 minutes or until thickened. Serve with turkey.

> My peachy sweet and sour chicken has become a Sunday dinnertime favorite. It's easy to prepare and requires very little cleanup, plus the slow cooker leaves me plenty of time to tackle other tasks.
>
> **—LISA RENSHAW** KANSAS CITY, MISSOURI

Chicken Thighs With Ginger-Peach Sauce

PREP: 15 MIN. **COOK:** 4 HOURS
MAKES: 10 SERVINGS

- 10 boneless skinless chicken thighs (about 2½ pounds)
- 1 cup sliced peeled fresh or frozen peaches
- 1 cup golden raisins
- 1 cup peach preserves
- ⅓ cup chili sauce
- 2 tablespoons minced crystallized ginger
- 1 tablespoon reduced-sodium soy sauce
- 1 tablespoon minced garlic
  Hot cooked rice, optional

1. Place chicken in a 4-qt. slow cooker coated with cooking spray. Top with peaches and raisins. In a small bowl, combine the preserves, chili sauce, ginger, soy sauce and garlic. Spoon over top.
2. Cover and cook on low for 4-5 hours or until the chicken is tender. Serve with rice if desired.

You wouldn't believe this golden-brown chicken was made in the slow cooker. Packed with flavor, the meat is moist, the carrots are tender and the juices make a nice gravy. —TASTE OF HOME TEST KITCHEN

SLOW COOKER ROTISSERIE-STYLE CHICKEN

Slow Cooker Rotisserie-Style Chicken

PREP: 30 MIN.
COOK: 6 HOURS + STANDING
MAKES: 6 SERVINGS

- 4 teaspoons seasoned salt
- 4 teaspoons poultry seasoning
- 1 tablespoon paprika
- 1½ teaspoons onion powder
- 1½ teaspoons brown sugar
- 1½ teaspoons salt-free lemon-pepper seasoning
- ¾ teaspoon garlic powder
- 1 broiler/fryer chicken (4 pounds)
- 1 pound carrots, halved lengthwise and cut into 1½-inch lengths
- 2 large onions, chopped
- 2 tablespoons cornstarch

1. In a small bowl, combine the first seven ingredients. Carefully loosen skin from chicken breast; rub 1 tablespoon spice mixture under the skin. Rub remaining spice mixture over chicken. In another bowl, toss carrots and onions with cornstarch; transfer to a 5-qt. slow cooker. Place chicken on vegetables.

2. Cover and cook on low for 6-7 hours or until a thermometer inserted in thigh reads 180°. Remove chicken and vegetables to a serving platter; cover and let stand for 15 minutes before carving. Skim fat from cooking juices. Serve with chicken and vegetables.

If you don't have **fresh rosemary** sprigs, substitute ½ to ¾ teaspoon of **crushed dried rosemary.**

TUSCAN CHICKEN

Tuscan Chicken

I found this Italian-style chicken recipe in a magazine and tweaked it to my family's tastes. I have taken it to potlucks and served it at dinner parties and no one ever guesses that it's made in the slow cooker. I serve this chicken entree with bread and a spinach salad with lemon vinaigrette.
—**MARY WATKINS** LITTLE ELM, TEXAS

PREP: 25 MIN. **COOK:** 6 HOURS
MAKES: 4 SERVINGS

- 2 cans (14½ ounces each) Italian stewed tomatoes, undrained
- 10 small red potatoes (about 1 pound), quartered
- 1 medium onion, chopped
- 1 can (6 ounces) tomato paste
- 2 fresh rosemary sprigs
- 4 garlic cloves, minced
- 1 teaspoon olive oil
- ½ teaspoon dried basil
- 1 teaspoon Italian seasoning, divided
- 1 broiler/fryer chicken (3 to 4 pounds), cut up and skin removed
- ½ teaspoon salt
- ½ teaspoon pepper
- 1 jar (5¾ ounces) pimiento-stuffed olives, drained

1. In a 5-qt. slow cooker, combine the first eight ingredients. Stir in ½ teaspoon Italian seasoning. Place chicken on top. Sprinkle with salt, pepper and remaining Italian seasoning. Top with olives.

2. Cover and cook on low for 6-7 hours or until chicken is tender. Discard rosemary sprigs before serving.

CHICKEN & MUSHROOM ALFREDO

Amazing Slow Cooker Orange Chicken

Orange chicken is my favorite Chinese takeout food, but I know that it's high in sodium and fat. So I got to work at home and created a healthier version. Now I have peace of mind knowing what ingredients are in it and that it's better for my family.

—BARBARA J. MILLER
OAKDALE, MINNESOTA

PREP: 25 MIN. **COOK:** 4½ HOURS
MAKES: 8 SERVINGS

- 1 cup chicken stock
- 1 cup orange juice
- 1 cup orange marmalade
- ½ cup ketchup
- ¼ cup Dijon mustard
- 2 tablespoons brown sugar
- 2 tablespoons rice vinegar
- 2 tablespoons reduced-sodium soy sauce
- 1 tablespoon minced fresh gingerroot
- 1 teaspoon garlic powder
- ¾ teaspoon crushed red pepper flakes
- 2 tablespoons molasses, optional
- 2 pounds boneless skinless chicken breasts, cut into ¾-inch pieces
- ½ cup cornstarch
- ¾ teaspoon salt
- ½ teaspoon pepper
- 1 large sweet red pepper, cut into 1-inch pieces
- 2 cups fresh broccoli florets
  Hot cooked rice
  Optional toppings: chopped green onions, peanuts and fresh cilantro

1. In a small bowl, combine the first 11 ingredients; stir in molasses if desired. In a large bowl, combine chicken, cornstarch, salt and pepper; toss to coat. Transfer chicken to a 4-qt. slow cooker. Top with red pepper. Pour stock mixture over top. Cover and cook on low for 4 hours or until chicken is tender.
2. Stir in broccoli. Cover and cook on high 30-40 minutes longer or until broccoli is crisp-tender. Serve with rice. Sprinkle with toppings of your choice.

> Everyone in my family loves when I make this dinner...even my kids! What's great about this recipe is that you can add vegetables you have on hand to make it heartier, such as corn, peas or diced red bell pepper. **—MONICA WERNER** TEMECULA, CALIFORNIA

Chicken & Mushroom Alfredo

PREP: 20 MIN. **COOK:** 4 HOURS
MAKES: 4 SERVINGS

- 4 bone-in chicken breast halves (12 ounces each), skin removed
- 2 tablespoons canola oil
- 1 can (10¾ ounces) condensed cream of chicken soup, undiluted
- 1 can (10¾ ounces) condensed cream of mushroom soup, undiluted
- 1 cup chicken broth
- 1 small onion, chopped
- 1 jar (6 ounces) sliced mushrooms, drained
- ¼ teaspoon garlic salt
- ¼ teaspoon pepper
- 8 ounces fettuccine
- 1 package (8 ounces) cream cheese, softened and cubed
  Shredded Parmesan cheese, optional

1. In a large skillet, brown chicken in oil in batches. Transfer to a 4- or 5-qt. slow cooker. In a large bowl, combine the soups, broth, onion, mushrooms, garlic salt and pepper; pour over meat. Cover and cook on low for 4-5 hours or until the chicken is tender.
2. Cook fettuccine according to package directions; drain. Remove chicken from slow cooker and keep warm. Turn slow cooker off and stir in cream cheese until melted. Serve with fettucine. Top with Parmesan cheese if desired.

Mediterranean Chicken in Eggplant Sauce

Spice-coated chicken thighs simmer in a rich red pepper-eggplant sauce. This savory entree is perfect for an everyday meal or potluck. It's an easy slow-cooker dish to prepare in the morning so that dinner is ready at the end of the day.

—JUDY ARMSTRONG
PRAIRIEVILLE, LOUISIANA

PREP: 45 MIN. **COOK:** 5 HOURS
MAKES: 8 SERVINGS

- ⅓ cup all-purpose flour
- 2 teaspoons paprika
- 2 teaspoons ground cumin
- 1 teaspoon salt
- 1 teaspoon freshly ground pepper
- 3 pounds boneless skinless chicken thighs, cut into 2-inch pieces
- 2 tablespoons olive oil
- 1¼ cups white wine or chicken broth
- 1 small eggplant (1 pound), peeled and cubed
- 1 jar (12 ounces) roasted sweet red peppers, drained
- 1 medium onion, chopped
- 1 jalapeno pepper, seeded and chopped
- 2 tablespoons tomato paste
- 1 tablespoon brown sugar
- 3 garlic cloves, minced
- 1 cup pitted ripe olives, halved
- ¼ cup minced fresh Italian parsley
- 1 cup (4 ounces) crumbled feta cheese
- 8 naan flatbreads, quartered

1. In a large bowl, combine the first five ingredients. Add chicken; toss to coat. In a large skillet, brown chicken in oil in batches. Transfer to a 4-qt. slow cooker.

2. Add wine to the skillet, stirring to loosen browned bits from pan. Stir in the eggplant, red peppers, onion, jalapeno, tomato paste, brown sugar and garlic. Bring to a boil. Reduce heat; simmer, uncovered, for 5 minutes. Cool slightly. Transfer to a blender; cover and process until pureed. Pour over chicken.

3. Cover and cook on low for 5-6 hours or until chicken is tender, adding olives and parsley during the last 30 minutes. Just before serving, sprinkle with feta cheese. Serve with naan.

NOTE *Wear disposable gloves when cutting hot peppers; the oils can burn skin. Avoid touching your face.*

CORN BREAD-TOPPED CHICKEN CHILI

After seeing a recipe for a slow-cooker chicken potpie, I knew I had to try it. I loved the no-fuss idea, but I also wanted a Southwestern flair. I added peppers, spices and a crust that's like corn bread.

—NICOLE FILIZETTI, GRAND MARAIS, MICHIGAN

Corn Bread-Topped Chicken Chili

PREP: 20 MIN. **COOK:** 4 HOURS
MAKES: 6 SERVINGS

- 1 can (16 ounces) kidney beans, rinsed and drained
- 2 cans (2¼ ounces each) sliced ripe black olives, drained
- 1 cup frozen whole kernel corn, thawed and drained
- 1 cup tomato juice
- 1 can (4 ounces) chopped green chilies, drained
- 2 tablespoons minced fresh cilantro
- 1 tablespoon chili powder
- ½ teaspoon ground chipotle pepper
- 1 small onion, finely chopped
- 1 small sweet red pepper, chopped
- 2 tablespoons canola oil, divided
- 2 garlic cloves, minced
- 1¼ pounds boneless skinless chicken breasts, cubed
- 2 tablespoons cornstarch
- ½ teaspoon salt, divided
- 1 cup cornmeal
- 2 teaspoons baking powder
- ½ teaspoon baking soda
- ½ cup 2% milk

1. In a 4-qt. slow cooker, combine the first eight ingredients. In a large skillet, saute onion and red pepper in 1 tablespoon oil until tender. Add garlic; cook 1 minute longer. Transfer to slow cooker. In a small bowl, toss chicken with cornstarch and ¼ teaspoon salt; stir into bean mixture. Cover and cook on low for 3-4 hours or until chicken is tender.

2. In a small bowl, combine the cornmeal, baking powder, baking soda and remaining salt. Stir in milk and remaining oil. Drop by tablespoonfuls over chicken mixture. Cover and cook 1 hour longer or until a toothpick inserted in center of topping comes out clean.

Momma's Turkey Stew With Dumplings

My mother used to make turkey stew every year with our Thanksgiving leftovers. It's straightforward and really celebrates the natural flavors of good, simple ingredients. To this day, it's one of my favorite meals.

—STEPHANIE RABBITT-SCHAPP
CINCINNATI, OHIO

PREP: 20 MIN. **COOK:** 6½ HOURS
MAKES: 6 SERVINGS

- 3 cups shredded cooked turkey
- 1 large sweet onion, chopped
- 1 large potato, peeled and cubed
- 2 large carrots, chopped
- 2 celery ribs, chopped
- 2 bay leaves
- 1 teaspoon salt
- ½ teaspoon poultry seasoning
- ½ teaspoon dried thyme
- ¼ teaspoon pepper
- 1 carton (32 ounces) chicken broth
- ⅓ cup cold water
- 3 tablespoons cornstarch
- ½ cup frozen corn, thawed
- ½ cup frozen peas, thawed
- 1 cup biscuit/baking mix
- ⅓ cup 2% milk

1. In a 6-qt. slow cooker, combine the first 10 ingredients; stir in broth. Cover and cook on low for 6-7 hours.

2. Remove bay leaves. In a small bowl, mix water and cornstarch until smooth; stir into turkey mixture. Add corn and peas. Cover and cook on high until mixture reaches a simmer.

3. Meanwhile, in a small bowl, mix baking mix and milk just until moistened. Drop by rounded tablespoonfuls on top of simmering liquid. Reduce heat to low; cover and cook for 20-25 minutes or until a toothpick inserted a dumpling comes out clean.

Turkey Leg Pot Roast

Well-seasoned turkey legs and tender veggies make an ideal dinner for a crisp fall day. Tender and satisfying, this old-fashioned meal couldn't be easier!

—RICK AND VEGAS PEARSON
CADILLAC, MICHIGAN

PREP: 15 MIN. **COOK:** 5 HOURS
MAKES: 3 SERVINGS

- 3 medium potatoes, peeled and quartered
- 2 cups fresh baby carrots
- 2 celery ribs, cut into 2½-inch pieces
- 1 medium onion, peeled and quartered
- 3 garlic cloves, peeled and quartered
- ½ cup chicken broth
- 3 turkey drumsticks (12 ounces each), skin removed
- 2 teaspoons seasoned salt
- 1 teaspoon dried thyme
- 1 teaspoon dried parsley flakes
- ¼ teaspoon pepper

In a greased 5-qt. slow cooker, combine the first six ingredients. Place drumsticks over vegetables. Sprinkle with the seasoned salt, thyme, parsley and pepper. Cover and cook on low for 5 to 5½ hours or until turkey is tender.

Slow Cooker Buffalo Chicken Lasagna

I make this tasty chicken lasagna with a whole bottle of buffalo wing sauce because my family likes it nice and spicy. Use less if you prefer, and increase the pasta sauce.

—HEIDI PEPIN SYKESVILLE, MARYLAND

PREP: 25 MIN. **COOK:** 4 HOURS +
STANDING **MAKES:** 8 SERVINGS

- 1½ pounds ground chicken
- 1 tablespoon olive oil
- 1 bottle (12 ounces) buffalo wing sauce
- 1½ cups meatless spaghetti sauce
- 1 carton (15 ounces) ricotta cheese
- 2 cups (8 ounces) shredded part-skim mozzarella cheese
- 9 no-cook lasagna noodles
- 2 medium sweet red peppers, chopped
- ½ cup crumbled blue cheese or feta cheese
- Chopped celery and additional crumbled blue cheese, optional

1. In a Dutch oven, cook chicken in oil over medium heat until no longer pink; drain. Stir in wing sauce and spaghetti sauce. In a small bowl, mix ricotta and mozzarella cheeses.

2. Spread 1 cup sauce onto the bottom of an oval 6-qt. slow cooker. Layer with three noodles (breaking noodles to fit), 1 cup sauce, a third of the peppers and a third of the cheese mixture. Repeat layers twice. Top with remaining sauce; sprinkle with blue cheese.

3. Cover and cook on low for 4-5 hours or until noodles are tender. Let stand 15 minutes before serving. Top with celery and additional blue cheese if desired.

SLOW COOKER BUFFALO CHICKEN LASAGNA

ZESTY CHICKEN MARINARA

A friend served this delicious Italian-style chicken before a church social, and I fell in love with it. My husband says it tastes like something you'd get at a restaurant. —LINDA BAUMANN RICHFIELD, WISCONSIN

Zesty Chicken Marinara

PREP: 15 MIN. **COOK:** 4 HOURS
MAKES: 4 SERVINGS

- 4 bone-in chicken breast halves (12 to 14 ounces each), skin removed
- 2 cups marinara sauce
- 1 medium tomato, chopped
- ½ cup Italian salad dressing
- 1½ teaspoons Italian seasoning
- 1 garlic clove, minced
- ½ pound uncooked angel hair pasta
- ½ cup shredded part-skim mozzarella cheese

1. Place chicken in a 4-qt. slow cooker. In a small bowl, combine the marinara sauce, tomato, salad dressing, Italian seasoning and garlic; pour over chicken. Cover and cook on low for 4-5 hours or until chicken is tender.
2. Cook pasta according to package directions; drain. Serve chicken and sauce with pasta; sprinkle with cheese.

Stuffed Turkey With Mojo Sauce

PREP: 30 MIN. **COOK:** 5 HOURS + STANDING **MAKES:** 8 SERVINGS

- 1 medium green pepper, finely chopped
- 1 medium onion, finely chopped
- 2 garlic cloves, minced
- 2 teaspoons ground coriander
- 1 teaspoon ground cumin
- ⅛ teaspoon cayenne pepper
- 1 pound uncooked chicken sausage links, casings removed
- 1 fresh boneless turkey breast (4 pounds)
- ¼ teaspoon salt
- ¼ teaspoon pepper

MOJO SAUCE
- 1 cup orange juice
- ½ cup fresh cilantro leaves
- ¼ cup minced fresh oregano or 4 teaspoons dried oregano
- ¼ cup lime juice
- 4 garlic cloves, minced
- 1 teaspoon ground cumin
- ½ teaspoon pepper
- ¼ teaspoon salt
- ⅛ teaspoon cayenne pepper
- 1 cup olive oil

1. In a bowl, combine the first six ingredients. Crumble sausage over mixture and mix well.
2. With skin side down, pound turkey breast with a meat mallet to ½-in. thickness. Sprinkle with salt and pepper. Spread sausage mixture over turkey to within 1 in. of edges. Roll up jelly-roll style, starting with a short side; tie at 1½-in. to 2-in. intervals with kitchen string. Place in a 5-qt. oval slow cooker.
3. In a blender, combine the first nine sauce ingredients; cover and process until blended. While processing, gradually add oil in a steady stream. Pour over turkey.
4. Cover and cook on low for 5 hours or until a thermometer inserted in center reads 165°. Remove from slow cooker; cover and let stand for 10 minutes before slicing. Discard string.
5. Meanwhile, skim fat from cooking juices; transfer juices to a small saucepan. Bring to a boil; cook until liquid is reduced by half. Serve with turkey.
BAKE OPTION *Place turkey roll in a 13-in. x 9-in. baking dish. Pour sauce over top. Bake, uncovered, at 400° for 70-80 minutes or until a thermometer inserted in center of stuffing reads 165°. (Cover loosely with foil during the last 20 minutes if turkey browns too quickly.) Remove from oven; cover and let stand for 10 minutes before slicing. Discard string. Skim fat from cooking juices; serve juices with turkey.*

Serve the turkey with a green salad and cold limeade for a **refreshing summer meal** that doesn't heat up the kitchen.

I love Latin food, so I created this recipe that combines wonderful spices and fresh ingredients. My traditional turkey has a healthier twist because it uses chicken sausage instead of chorizo. —**MELISSA LAUER** SAN ANTONIO, TEXAS

STUFFED TURKEY WITH MOJO SAUCE

Soy-Garlic Chicken

Because I'm a full-time mom and help my husband on our ranch, I'm always looking for simple yet hearty meals for the slow cooker. My family really likes this one.
—**COLLEEN FABER** BUFFALO, MONTANA

PREP: 10 MIN. **COOK:** 4 HOURS
MAKES: 6 SERVINGS

- 6 **chicken leg quarters, skin removed**
- 1 **can (8 ounces) tomato sauce**
- ½ **cup reduced-sodium soy sauce**
- ¼ **cup packed brown sugar**
- 2 **teaspoons minced garlic**

1. With a sharp knife, cut leg quarters at the joints if desired. Place in a 4-qt. slow cooker. In a small bowl, combine the tomato sauce, soy sauce, brown sugar and garlic; pour over chicken.
2. Cover and cook on low for 4-5 hours or until chicken is tender.

Saucy Chicken Thighs

Everyone raves about the delectable sauce with these tender slow-cooked chicken thighs. Add your favorite side dish for a terrific meal.
—**KIM PUCKETT** REAGAN, TENNESSEE

PREP: 20 MIN. **COOK:** 4 HOURS
MAKES: 9 SERVINGS

- 9 **bone-in chicken thighs (about 3¼ pounds)**
- ½ **teaspoon salt**
- ¼ **teaspoon pepper**
- 1½ **cups barbecue sauce**
- ½ **cup honey**
- 2 **teaspoons prepared mustard**
- 2 **teaspoons Worcestershire sauce**
- ⅛ **to ½ teaspoon hot pepper sauce**

1. Sprinkle chicken with salt and pepper. Place on a broiler pan. Broil 4-5 in. from the heat for 3-4 minutes on each side or until lightly browned. Transfer to a 5-qt. slow cooker.
2. In a small bowl, combine the barbecue sauce, honey, mustard, Worcestershire sauce and pepper sauce. Pour over chicken; stir to coat. Cover and cook on low for 4-5 hours or until chicken is tender.

APPLE BALSAMIC CHICKEN

I just love the sweet and tart flavor that balsamic vinegar gives to this dish. It's easy to prepare, and after spending time in the slow cooker, the chicken thighs are tender and flavorful. —**JULI SNAER** ENID, OKLAHOMA

Apple Balsamic Chicken

PREP: 15 MIN. **COOK:** 4 HOURS
MAKES: 4 SERVINGS

- 4 **bone-in chicken thighs (about 1½ pounds), skin removed**
- ½ **cup chicken broth**
- ¼ **cup apple cider or juice**
- ¼ **cup balsamic vinegar**
- 2 **tablespoons lemon juice**
- ½ **teaspoon salt**
- ½ **teaspoon garlic powder**
- ½ **teaspoon dried thyme**
- ½ **teaspoon paprika**
- ½ **teaspoon pepper**
- 2 **tablespoons butter**
- 2 **tablespoons all-purpose flour**

1. Place chicken in a 1½-qt. slow cooker. In a small bowl, combine the broth, cider, vinegar, lemon juice and seasonings; pour over meat. Cover and cook on low for 4-5 hours or until chicken is tender.
2. Remove chicken; keep warm. Skim fat from cooking liquid. In a small saucepan, melt butter; stir in flour until smooth. Gradually add cooking liquid. Bring to a boil; cook and stir for 2-3 minutes or until thickened. Serve with chicken.

Mango-Pineapple Chicken Tacos

I lived in the Caribbean as a child. Fresh tropical fruits in these delightful chicken tacos really bring me back to my sunny childhood!

—**LISSA NELSON** PROVO, UTAH

PREP: 25 MIN. **COOK:** 5 HOURS
MAKES: 16 SERVINGS

- 2 medium mangoes, peeled and chopped
- 1½ cups cubed fresh or canned pineapple
- 2 medium tomatoes, chopped
- 1 medium red onion, finely chopped
- 2 small Anaheim peppers, seeded and chopped
- 2 green onions, finely chopped
- 1 tablespoon lime juice
- 1 teaspoon sugar
- 4 pounds bone-in chicken breast halves, skin removed
- 3 teaspoons salt
- ¼ cup packed brown sugar
- 32 taco shells, warmed
- ¼ cup minced fresh cilantro

1. In a large bowl, combine the first eight ingredients. Place chicken in a 6-qt. slow cooker; sprinkle with salt and brown sugar. Top with mango mixture. Cover and cook on low for 5-6 hours or until chicken is tender.
2. Remove chicken; cool slightly. Strain cooking juices, reserving mango mixture and ½ cup juices. Discard remaining juices. When cool enough to handle, remove chicken from bones; discard bones.
3. Shred chicken with two forks. Return chicken and reserved mango mixture and cooking juices to slow cooker; heat through. Serve in taco shells; sprinkle with cilantro.
FREEZE OPTION *Freeze cooled meat mixture in freezer containers. To use, partially thaw in refrigerator overnight. Heat through in a saucepan, stirring occasionally and adding a little broth if necessary.*
PER SERVING *246 cal., 7 g fat (2 g sat. fat), 51 mg chol., 582 mg sodium, 25 g carb., 2 g fiber, 21 g pro.* **Diabetic Exchanges:** *3 lean meat, 1½ starch.*

MANGO-PINEAPPLE CHICKEN TACOS

Apricot-Orange Salsa Chicken

An easy chicken entree is just five ingredients away! Sweet oranges and apricots blend effortlessly with easy, zippy salsa. Keep the heat to your liking with mild, medium or hot salsa.

—**LADONNA REED**
PONCA CITY, OKLAHOMA

PREP: 10 MIN. **COOK:** 2½ HOURS
MAKES: 2 SERVINGS

- ¾ cup salsa
- ⅓ cup apricot preserves
- ¼ cup orange juice
- 2 boneless skinless chicken breast halves (5 ounces each)
- 1 cup hot cooked rice

1. In a small bowl, combine the salsa, preserves and orange juice. In a 1½-qt. slow cooker coated with cooking spray, layer ⅓ cup salsa mixture and a chicken breast. Repeat layers. Top with remaining salsa.
2. Cover and cook on low for 2½ to 3 hours or until chicken is tender. If desired, thicken pan juices. Serve with rice.

TURKEY MEATBALLS AND SAUCE

> My sweetie and I have fought the battle of the bulge forever. This is my less-fattening take on meatballs. They're slow-cooker simple—and so flavorful!
>
> —JANE MCMILLAN DANIA BEACH, FLORIDA

Turkey Meatballs and Sauce

PREP: 30 MIN. **COOK:** 6 HOURS
MAKES: 8 SERVINGS

- ¼ cup egg substitute
- ½ cup seasoned bread crumbs
- ⅓ cup chopped onion
- ½ teaspoon pepper
- ¼ teaspoon salt-free seasoning blend
- 1½ pounds lean ground turkey

SAUCE

- 1 can (15 ounces) tomato sauce
- 1 can (14½ ounces) diced tomatoes, undrained
- 1 small zucchini, chopped
- 1 medium green pepper, chopped
- 1 medium onion, chopped
- 1 can (6 ounces) tomato paste
- 2 bay leaves
- 2 garlic cloves, minced
- 1 teaspoon dried oregano
- 1 teaspoon dried basil
- 1 teaspoon dried parsley flakes
- ¼ teaspoon crushed red pepper flakes
- ¼ teaspoon pepper
- 1 package (16 ounces) whole wheat spaghetti

1. In a large bowl, combine the egg substitute, bread crumbs, onion, pepper and seasoning blend. Crumble turkey over mixture and mix well. Shape into 1-in. balls; place on a rack coated with cooking spray in a shallow baking pan. Bake, uncovered, at 400° for 15 minutes or until no longer pink.

2. Meanwhile, in a 4- or 5-qt. slow cooker, combine the tomato sauce, tomatoes, zucchini, green pepper, onion, tomato paste, bay leaves, garlic and seasonings. Stir in meatballs. Cover and cook on low for 6 hours. Cook spaghetti according to package directions; serve with meatballs and sauce.

Chicken With Apple-Chardonnay Gravy

PREP: 20 MIN. **COOK:** 6 HOURS
MAKES: 6 SERVINGS

- 6 chicken leg quarters
- ½ teaspoon salt
- ¼ teaspoon pepper
- 2 large sweet apples, peeled and cut into wedges
- 1 large sweet onion, chopped
- 2 celery ribs, chopped
- ½ cup chardonnay
- 1 envelope brown gravy mix
- 2 large garlic cloves, minced
- 1 teaspoon each minced fresh oregano, rosemary and thyme
  Hot mashed potatoes

1. Sprinkle chicken with salt and pepper. Place half of the chicken in a 5-qt. slow cooker. In a bowl, combine the apples, onion and celery; spoon half of the mixture over chicken. Repeat layers.

2. In the same bowl, whisk wine, gravy mix, garlic and herbs until blended; pour over top. Cover and cook on low for 6-8 hours or until chicken is tender.

3. Remove chicken to a serving platter; keep warm. Cool apple mixture slightly; skim fat. In a blender, cover and process apple mixture in batches until smooth. Transfer to a saucepan and heat through over medium heat, stirring occasionally. Serve with chicken and mashed potatoes.

To **ensure tender meatballs** and meat loaf, mix the other ingredients well before crumbling the meat on top. Mix all ingredients **just until combined,** but no longer.

CHICKEN WITH APPLE-CHARDONNAY GRAVY

EAT SMART Indonesian Peanut Chicken

Here's a great make-ahead recipe! I cut up fresh chicken, put it in a bag with the remaining slow-cooker ingredients and freeze. To cook, just remove the bag a day ahead to thaw in the fridge, then pour all the contents into the slow cooker.

—SARAH NEWMAN

MAHTOMEDI, MINNESOTA

PREP: 15 MIN. **COOK:** 4 HOURS
MAKES: 6 SERVINGS

- 1½ **pounds boneless skinless chicken breasts, cut into 1-inch cubes**
- ⅓ **cup chopped onion**
- ⅓ **cup water**
- ¼ **cup reduced-fat creamy peanut butter**
- 3 **tablespoons chili sauce**
- ¼ **teaspoon salt**
- ¼ **teaspoon cayenne pepper**
- ¼ **teaspoon pepper**
- 3 **cups hot cooked brown rice**
- 6 **tablespoons chopped salted peanuts**
- 6 **tablespoons chopped sweet red pepper**

1. Place chicken in a 4-qt. slow cooker. In a small bowl, combine the onion, water, peanut butter, chili sauce, salt, cayenne and pepper; pour over chicken.

2. Cover and cook on low for 4-6 hours or until the chicken is no longer pink.

3. Shred meat with two forks and return to slow cooker; heat through. Serve with rice. Sprinkle with peanuts and red pepper.

PER SERVING *353 cal., 12 g fat (2 g sat. fat), 63 mg chol., 370 mg sodium, 31 g carb., 3 g fiber, 31 g pro.* **Diabetic Exchanges:** *3 lean meat, 2 starch, 2 fat.*

SAUSAGE PASTA STEW

I use my slow cooker to whip up a hearty pasta specialty. It's packed with turkey sausage, beans and veggies. My gang gobbles it up without realizing they're eating healthy! **—SARA BOWEN** UPLAND, CALIFORNIA

EAT SMART Sausage Pasta Stew

PREP: 20 MIN. **COOK:** 7¼ HOURS
MAKES: 8 SERVINGS

- 1 **pound turkey Italian sausage links, casings removed**
- 4 **cups water**
- 1 **jar (24 ounces) meatless spaghetti sauce**
- 1 **can (16 ounces) kidney beans, rinsed and drained**
- 1 **medium yellow summer squash, halved lengthwise and cut into 1-inch pieces**
- 2 **medium carrots, sliced**
- 1 **medium sweet red or green pepper, diced**
- ⅓ **cup chopped onion**
- 1½ **cups uncooked spiral pasta**
- 1 **cup frozen peas**
- 1 **teaspoon sugar**
- ½ **teaspoon salt**
- ¼ **teaspoon pepper**

1. In a nonstick skillet, cook sausage over medium heat until no longer pink; drain and place in a 5-qt. slow cooker. Stir in the water, spaghetti sauce, beans, summer squash, carrots, red pepper and onion.

2. Cover and cook on low for 7-9 hours or until vegetables are tender.

3. Stir in the pasta, peas, sugar, salt and pepper. Cover and cook on high for 15-20 minutes or until pasta is tender.

PER SERVING *276 cal., 6 g fat (2 g sat. fat), 30 mg chol., 1,111 mg sodium, 38 g carb., 6 g fiber, 18 g pro.* **Diabetic Exchanges:** *2 lean meat, 2 vegetable, 1½ starch.*

EAT SMART Chicken Thighs With Sausage

Whether you're serving your family or special guests, this delicious entree hits the spot on cold winter nights.

—JOANNA IOVINO KINGS PARK, NEW YORK

PREP: 25 MIN. **COOK:** 6 HOURS
MAKES: 8 SERVINGS

- 2 medium carrots, chopped
- 2 celery ribs, chopped
- 1 large onion, finely chopped
- 8 bone-in chicken thighs (about 3 pounds), skin removed
- 1 package (14 ounces) smoked turkey sausage, cut into ½-inch slices
- ¼ cup ketchup
- 6 garlic cloves, minced
- 1 tablespoon Louisiana-style hot sauce
- 1 teaspoon dried basil
- 1 teaspoon paprika
- 1 teaspoon dried thyme
- ½ teaspoon dried oregano
- ½ teaspoon pepper
- ¼ teaspoon ground allspice
- 1 teaspoon browning sauce, optional

1. In a 4- or 5-qt. slow cooker, combine the carrots, celery and onion. Top with chicken and sausage.
2. In a small bowl, combine the ketchup, garlic, hot sauce, seasonings and, if desired, browning sauce. Spoon over meats. Cover and cook on low for 6-8 hours or until chicken is tender.
PER SERVING *280 cal., 12 g fat (4 g sat. fat), 118 mg chol., 675 mg sodium, 8 g carb., 1 g fiber, 33 g pro. Diabetic Exchanges: 5 lean meat, ½ starch.*

CHICKEN THIGHS WITH SAUSAGE

EAT SMART Slow Cooker Turkey Breast

Here's an easy recipe to try when you're craving turkey. It uses simple pantry ingredients, which is handy . The turkey is very tender and tasty.

—MARIA JUCO MILWAUKEE, WISCONSIN

PREP: 10 MIN. **COOK:** 5 HOURS
MAKES: 14 SERVINGS

- 1 bone-in turkey breast (6 to 7 pounds), skin removed
- 1 tablespoon olive oil
- 1 teaspoon dried minced garlic
- 1 teaspoon seasoned salt
- 1 teaspoon paprika
- 1 teaspoon Italian seasoning
- 1 teaspoon pepper
- ½ cup water

1. Brush the turkey breast with oil. Combine the garlic, seasoned salt, paprika, Italian seasoning and pepper; rub over turkey breast. Transfer to a 6-qt. slow cooker; add the water.
2. Cover and cook on low for 5-6 hours or until tender.
PER SERVING *174 cal., 2 g fat (trace sat. fat), 101 mg chol., 172 mg sodium, trace carb., trace fiber, 37 g pro. Diabetic Exchange: 4 lean meat.*

Other Entrees

49   51   52

Your slow cooker can help you **breeze through even the busiest day**. Whether you need a **simple brunch-time favorite**, a healthy **meatless** option, or a main dish using **ham, pork, or lamb**...you'll find it in this delightful and taste-tempting chapter.

EAT SMART Carrot Cake Oatmeal

This warm breakfast cereal is a tasty way to keep a healthy diet! For added crunch and protein, I sprinkle each serving with finely chopped walnuts or pecans. You can add a sprinkling of additional cinnamon, too.
—DEBBIE KAIN
COLORADO SPRINGS, COLORADO

PREP: 10 MIN. **COOK:** 6 HOURS
MAKES: 8 SERVINGS

- 4½ cups water
- 1 can (20 ounces) crushed pineapple, undrained
- 2 cups shredded carrots
- 1 cup steel-cut oats
- 1 cup raisins
- 2 teaspoons ground cinnamon
- 1 teaspoon pumpkin pie spice
  Brown sugar, optional

In a 4-qt. slow cooker coated with cooking spray, combine the first seven ingredients. Cover and cook on low for 6-8 hours or until oats are tender and liquid is absorbed. Sprinkle with brown sugar if desired.
PER SERVING *197 cal., 2 g fat (trace sat. fat), 0 chol., 23 mg sodium, 46 g carb., 4 g fiber, 4 g pro.* **Diabetic Exchanges:** *2 starch, 1 fruit.*

SLOW COOKER BREAKFAST CASSEROLE

> I love this breakfast casserole because I can make it the night before and it's ready in the morning. What a perfect recipe while I'm out camping or when I have weekend guests! **—ELLA STUTHEIT** LAS VEGAS, NEVADA

Slow Cooker Breakfast Casserole

PREP: 25 MIN. **COOK:** 7 HOURS
MAKES: 12 SERVINGS

- 1 package (30 ounces) frozen shredded hash brown potatoes
- 1 pound bulk pork sausage, cooked and drained
- 1 medium onion, chopped
- 1 can (4 ounces) chopped green chilies
- 1½ cups (6 ounces) shredded cheddar cheese
- 12 eggs
- 1 cup 2% milk
- ½ teaspoon salt
- ½ teaspoon pepper

In a greased 5- or 6-qt. slow cooker, layer half of the potatoes, sausage, onion, chilies and cheese. Repeat layers. In a large bowl, whisk the eggs, milk, salt and pepper; pour over top. Cover and cook on low for 7-9 hours or until eggs are set.

EAT SMART Enchilada Pie

This impressive, hearty dish is perfect for vegetarians and meat eaters alike.

—JACQUELINE CORREA

LANDING, NEW JERSEY

PREP: 40 MIN. **COOK:** 4 HOURS
MAKES: 8 SERVINGS

- 1 package (12 ounces) frozen vegetarian meat crumbles
- 1 cup chopped onion
- ½ cup chopped green pepper
- 2 teaspoons canola oil
- 1 can (16 ounces) kidney beans, rinsed and drained
- 1 can (15 ounces) black beans, rinsed and drained
- 1 can (10 ounces) diced tomatoes and green chilies, undrained
- ½ cup water
- 1½ teaspoons chili powder
- ½ teaspoon ground cumin
- ¼ teaspoon pepper
- 6 whole wheat tortillas (8 inches)
- 2 cups (8 ounces) shredded reduced-fat cheddar cheese

1. Cut three 25-in. x 3-in. strips of heavy-duty foil; crisscross so they resemble spokes of a wheel. Place strips on the bottom and up the sides of a 5-qt. slow cooker. Coat strips with cooking spray.

2. In a saucepan, cook the meat crumbles, onion and green pepper in oil until vegetables are tender. Stir in both cans of beans, tomatoes, water, chili powder, cumin and pepper. Bring to a boil. Reduce heat; simmer, uncovered, for 10 minutes.

3. In prepared slow cooker, layer about a cup of bean mixture, one tortilla and ⅓ cup cheese. Repeat layers five times. Cover and cook on low for 4-5 hours or until heated through and cheese is melted.

4. Using foil strips as handles, remove the pie to a platter.

NOTE *Vegetarian meat crumbles are a nutritious protein source made from soy. Look for them in the natural foods freezer section.*

PER SERVING *367 cal., 11 g fat (4 g sat. fat), 20 mg chol., 818 mg sodium, 41 g carb., 9 g fiber, 25 g pro.* **Diabetic Exchanges:** *3 starch, 2 lean meat, 1 fat.*

If you enjoy ribs, good luck resisting these fall-off-the-bone baby back ribs. Not only are they delicious, but the recipe is easy to prepare in the slow cooker.

—BARBARA BIRK ST. GEORGE, UTAH

Slow & Easy Baby Back Ribs

PREP: 20 MIN. **COOK:** 5 HOURS
MAKES: 4 SERVINGS

- 4 pounds pork baby back ribs, cut into 2-rib portions
- 1 medium onion, chopped
- ½ cup ketchup
- ¼ cup packed brown sugar
- ¼ cup cider vinegar
- ¼ cup tomato paste or tomato sauce
- 2 tablespoons paprika
- 2 tablespoons Worcestershire sauce
- 1 tablespoon prepared mustard
- 1 teaspoon salt
- ¼ teaspoon pepper
- 2 tablespoons cornstarch
- 2 tablespoons cold water

1. Place ribs in a 5-qt. slow cooker. Combine the onion, ketchup, brown sugar, vinegar, tomato paste, paprika, Worcestershire, mustard, salt and pepper; pour over ribs. Cover and cook on low for 5-6 hours or until meat is tender.

2. Remove ribs to a serving platter; keep warm. Skim fat from cooking juices; transfer juices to a small saucepan. Bring to a boil.

3. Combine cornstarch and water until smooth. Gradually stir into the pan. Bring to a boil; cook and stir for 2 minutes or until thickened. Serve with ribs.

So-Easy Pork Chops

Everyone will enjoy fork-tender pork chops with a light and creamy gravy. I also like to prepare the recipe with boneless chicken breasts instead of pork, substituting poultry seasoning for the ground mustard.

—SUE BINGHAM

MADISONVILLE, TENNESSEE

PREP: 15 MIN. **COOK:** 3 HOURS
MAKES: 4 SERVINGS

- ¾ cup all-purpose flour, divided
- ½ teaspoon ground mustard
- ½ teaspoon garlic pepper blend
- ¼ teaspoon seasoned salt
- 4 boneless pork loin chops (4 ounces each)
- 2 tablespoons canola oil
- 1 can (14½ ounces) chicken broth

1. In a large resealable plastic bag, combine ½ cup flour, mustard, garlic pepper and seasoned salt. Add pork chops, one at a time, and shake to coat. In a large skillet, brown chops in oil on both sides.

2. Transfer to a 5-qt. slow cooker. Place remaining flour in a small bowl; whisk in broth until smooth. Pour over chops. Cover and cook on low for 3-4 hours or until meat is tender.

3. Remove pork to a serving plate and keep warm. Whisk cooking liquid until smooth; serve with pork.

Tender Teriyaki Pork

My children really loved this dish growing up: it was the only meat they would gladly eat besides hot dogs! I got the recipe from my mother.

—DEBBIE DUNAWAY KETTERING, OHIO

PREP: 10 MIN. **COOK:** 6¼ HOURS
MAKES: 6-8 SERVINGS

- 1 boneless pork shoulder butt roast (3 to 4 pounds)
- 1 cup packed brown sugar
- ⅓ cup unsweetened apple juice
- ⅓ cup reduced-sodium soy sauce
- ½ teaspoon salt
- ¼ teaspoon pepper
- 2 tablespoons cornstarch
- 3 tablespoons cold water

1. Cut roast in half; rub with brown sugar. Place in a 5-qt. slow cooker. Pour apple juice and soy sauce over roast. Sprinkle with salt and pepper. Cover and cook on low for 6 to 8 hours or until meat is tender.

2. Remove roast; cover and keep warm. Skim fat from cooking juices. Mix cornstarch and water until smooth; stir into juices. Cover and cook on high for 15 minutes or until thickened. Serve with pork.

Shoulder butt roast is flavorful but high in fat. Be sure to **skim excess fat** from the cooking liquid.

SO-EASY PORK CHOPS

I wanted to create my ideal version of stuffed manicotti, which requires fantastic filling and meat sauce to die for. This version is the final result, and I don't mind saying it's a huge success! —SHALIMAR WIECH GLASSPORT, PENNSYLVANIA

SLOW COOKER TWO-MEAT MANICOTTI

Slow Cooker Two-Meat Manicotti

PREP: 45 MIN. **COOK:** 4 HOURS
MAKES: 7 SERVINGS

- ½ **pound medium fresh mushrooms, chopped**
- 2 **small green peppers, chopped**
- 1 **medium onion, chopped**
- 1½ **teaspoons canola oil**
- 4 **garlic cloves, minced**
- ¾ **pound ground sirloin**
- ¾ **pound bulk Italian sausage**
- 2 **jars (23½ ounces each) Italian sausage and garlic spaghetti sauce**
- 1 **carton (15 ounces) ricotta cheese**
- 1 **cup minced fresh parsley**
- ½ **cup shredded part-skim mozzarella cheese, divided**
- ½ **cup grated Parmesan cheese, divided**
- 2 **eggs, lightly beaten**
- ½ **teaspoon salt**
- ¼ **teaspoon pepper**
- ⅛ **teaspoon ground nutmeg**
- 1 **package (8 ounces) manicotti shells**

1. In a large skillet, saute the mushrooms, peppers and onion in oil until tender. Add garlic; cook 1 minute longer. Remove from pan.

2. In the same skillet, cook beef and sausage over medium heat until no longer pink; drain. Stir in mushroom mixture and spaghetti sauce; set aside.

3. In a small bowl, combine the ricotta cheese, parsley, ¼ cup mozzarella cheese, ¼ cup Parmesan cheese, eggs and seasonings. Stuff into uncooked manicotti shells.

4. Spread 2¼ cups sauce onto the bottom of a 6-qt. slow cooker. Arrange five stuffed manicotti shells over sauce; repeat two times, using four shells on the top layer. Top with remaining sauce. Sprinkle with remaining cheeses. Cover and cook on low for 4-5 hours or until pasta is tender.

BAKE OPTION *Spread half of the sauce mixture into a greased 13x9-in. baking dish. Arrange stuffed manicotti shells in a single layer over sauce. Top with remaining sauce. Cover and bake at 375° for 45-55 minutes or until pasta is tender. Uncover and sprinkle with remaining cheeses. Bake 10-15 minutes longer or until cheese is melted. Let stand for 5 minutes before serving.*

SPICED LAMB STEW WITH APRICOTS

My family loves lamb, especially my son. During his first year of college, he claimed to be a vegetarian. When he came home, I had a pot of this slow-cooked lamb stew simmering on the counter. When my husband and I wanted to eat dinner, there were only a few shreds of meat left floating in the gravy—and my son confessed that he was the culprit!

—ARLENE ERLBACH MORTON GROVE, ILLINOIS

Spiced Lamb Stew with Apricots

PREP: 30 MIN. **COOK:** 5 HOURS
MAKES: 5 SERVINGS

- 2 **pounds lamb stew meat, cut into ¾-inch cubes**
- 3 **tablespoons butter**
- 1½ **cups chopped sweet onion**
- ¾ **cup dried apricots**
- ½ **cup orange juice**
- ½ **cup chicken broth**
- 2 **teaspoons paprika**
- 2 **teaspoons ground allspice**
- 2 **teaspoons ground cinnamon**
- 1½ **teaspoons salt**
- 1 **teaspoon ground cardamom**
  Hot cooked couscous
  Chopped dried apricots, optional

1. In a large skillet, brown lamb in butter in batches. Transfer to a 3-qt. slow cooker. In the same pan, saute onion in drippings until tender. Stir in the apricots, orange juice, broth and seasonings; pour over lamb.

2. Cover and cook on high for 5-6 hours or until meat is tender. Serve with couscous. Sprinkle with chopped apricots if desired.

SLOW-COOKED PORK ROAST DINNER

This delicious recipe will give you the most tender pork you've ever tasted! You can cut it with a fork, and it's just as moist the next day...if there are any leftovers. —JANE MONTGOMERY PIQUA, OHIO

EAT SMART Slow-Cooked Pork Roast Dinner

PREP: 25 MIN. **COOK:** 6 HOURS
MAKES: 8 SERVINGS

- 1 large onion, halved and sliced
- 1 boneless pork loin roast (2½ pounds)
- 4 medium potatoes, peeled and cubed
- 1 package (16 ounces) frozen sliced carrots
- 1 cup hot water
- ¼ cup sugar
- 3 tablespoons cider vinegar
- 2 tablespoons reduced-sodium soy sauce
- 1 tablespoon ketchup
- ½ teaspoon salt
- ½ teaspoon pepper
- ¼ teaspoon garlic powder
- ¼ teaspoon chili powder
- 2 tablespoons cornstarch
- 2 tablespoons cold water

1. Place onion in a 5-qt. slow cooker. Add the pork, potatoes and carrots. Whisk the hot water, sugar, vinegar, soy sauce, ketchup, salt, pepper, garlic powder and chili powder; pour over pork and vegetables.
2. Cover and cook on low for 6-8 hours or until meat is tender.
3. Remove pork and vegetables to a serving platter; keep warm. Skim fat from cooking juices; transfer to a small saucepan. Bring liquid to a boil. Combine cornstarch and cold water until smooth. Gradually stir into the pan. Bring to a boil; cook and stir for 2 minutes or until thickened. Serve with meat and vegetables.
PER SERVING *304 cal., 7 g fat (2 g sat. fat), 70 mg chol., 401 mg sodium, 30 g carb., 3 g fiber, 29 g pro.* **Diabetic Exchanges:** *4 lean meat, 1½ starch, 1 vegetable.*

Big Easy Jambalaya

Friends and family often request my jambalaya for gatherings. And I don't mind, since it's so easy to make.
—ELIZABETH RENTERIA
VANCOUVER, WASHINGTON

PREP: 25 MIN. **COOK:** 5½ HOURS
MAKES: 8 SERVINGS

- 4½ cups chicken stock
- 1 pound boneless skinless chicken thighs, cut into 1-inch pieces
- 1 can (15½ ounces) black-eyed peas, rinsed and drained
- 1 can (14½ ounces) fire-roasted diced tomatoes, undrained
- 14 ounces smoked kielbasa, sliced
- 2 fully cooked andouille sausage links, chopped
- 3 celery ribs, chopped
- 2 poblano peppers, seeded and chopped
- 1 medium onion, chopped
- 4 garlic cloves, minced
- 1 tablespoon dried oregano
- 2 teaspoons dried parsley flakes
- 2 teaspoons dried thyme
- 2 teaspoons Worcestershire sauce
- 1 teaspoon salt
- 1 teaspoon pepper
- ¼ teaspoon cayenne pepper
- 2 cups uncooked converted rice

1. In a 5-qt. slow cooker, combine all ingredients except rice. Cover and cook on low for 5-6 hours or until chicken is tender.
2. Stir in rice. Cook on high 30 minutes longer or until rice is tender.

Apple-Cinnamon Pork Loin

I love making this slow-cooked dish for chilly fall dinners with my family—the delightful apple-cinnamon aroma fills our entire house. The pork roast tastes even better served with buttery homemade mashed potatoes.

—RACHEL SCHULTZ
LANSING, MICHIGAN

PREP: 20 MIN. **COOK:** 6 HOURS
MAKES: 6 SERVINGS

- 1 **boneless pork loin roast (2 to 3 pounds)**
- ½ **teaspoon salt**
- ¼ **teaspoon pepper**
- 1 **tablespoon canola oil**
- 3 **medium apples, peeled and sliced, divided**
- ¼ **cup honey**
- 1 **small red onion, halved and sliced**
- 1 **tablespoon ground cinnamon**
   Minced fresh parsley, optional

1. Sprinkle the pork roast with salt and pepper. In a large skillet, brown the roast in oil on all sides; cool slightly. With a paring knife, cut about sixteen 3-in.-deep slits in sides of roast; insert an apple slice into each slit.

2. Place half of the remaining apples in a 4-qt. slow cooker. Place roast over apples. Drizzle with honey; top with onion and remaining apples. Sprinkle with cinnamon.

3. Cover and cook on low for 6-8 hours or until meat is tender. Remove pork and apple mixture; keep warm.

4. Transfer cooking juices to a small saucepan. Bring to a boil; cook until liquid is reduced by half. Serve with pork and apple mixture. Sprinkle with parsley if desired.

PER SERVING *290 cal., 10 g fat (3 g sat. fat), 75 mg chol., 241 mg sodium, 22 g carb., 2 g fiber, 29 g pro.* **Diabetic Exchanges:** *4 lean meat, 1 starch, ½ fruit, ½ fat.*

BLACK-EYED PEAS & HAM

> Every New Year's Day we have these slow-cooked black-eyed peas to bring good luck for the coming year. —**DAWN FRIHAUF** FORT MORGAN, COLORADO

Black-Eyed Peas & Ham

PREP: 20 MIN. **COOK:** 6 HOURS
MAKES: 9 SERVINGS

- 1 package (16 ounces) dried black-eyed peas, rinsed and sorted
- ½ pound fully cooked boneless ham, finely chopped
- 1 medium onion, finely chopped
- 1 medium sweet red pepper, finely chopped
- 5 bacon strips, cooked and crumbled
- 1 large jalapeno pepper, seeded and finely chopped
- 2 garlic cloves, minced
- 1½ teaspoons ground cumin
- 1 teaspoon reduced-sodium chicken bouillon granules
- ½ teaspoon salt
- ½ teaspoon cayenne pepper
- ¼ teaspoon pepper
- 6 cups water
  Minced fresh cilantro, optional
  Hot cooked rice

In a 6-qt. slow cooker, combine the first 13 ingredients. Cover and cook on low for 6-8 hours or until peas are tender. Sprinkle with cilantro if desired. Serve with rice.

NOTE *Wear disposable gloves when cutting hot peppers; the oils can burn skin. Avoid touching your face.*

EAT SMART Baja Pork Tacos

Here's my copycat version of the best Mexican food we ever tasted. The original recipe used beef, but we love these succulent tacos made with tender shredded pork.
—**ARIELLA WINN** MESQUITE, TEXAS

PREP: 10 MIN. **COOK:** 8 HOURS
MAKES: 12 SERVINGS

- 1 boneless pork sirloin roast (3 pounds)
- 5 cans (4 ounces each) chopped green chilies
- 2 tablespoons reduced-sodium taco seasoning
- 1 tablespoon ground cumin
- 24 corn tortillas (6 inches), warmed
- 3 cups shredded lettuce
- 1½ cups (6 ounces) shredded part-skim mozzarella cheese

1. Cut roast in half; place in a 3- or 4-qt. slow cooker. In a small bowl, combine the chilies, taco seasoning and cumin; pour over pork. Cover and cook on low for 8-10 hours or until meat is tender.

2. Remove pork; cool slightly. Skim fat from cooking juices. Shred meat with two forks; return to the slow cooker and heat through. Spoon ¼ cup onto each tortilla; top each with 2 tablespoons lettuce and 1 tablespoon cheese.

PER SERVING *326 cal., 10 g fat (4 g sat. fat), 76 mg chol., 469 mg sodium, 28 g carb., 4 g fiber, 30 g pro. **Diabetic Exchanges:** 3 lean meat, 2 starch, 1 fat.*

Sweet 'n' Sour Pork Chops

These slightly tangy pork chops are tender, moist and simply delicious. And they couldn't be much simpler to make with only five ingredients!

—LAURIE STAFFORD
WATERVILLE, NEW YORK

PREP: 5 MIN. **COOK:** 4 HOURS
MAKES: 4 SERVINGS

- 1 can (8 ounces) crushed pineapple, undrained
- 1 cup honey barbecue sauce
- ⅓ cup finely chopped onion
- 2 tablespoons chili sauce
- 4 bone-in pork loin chops (8 ounces each)

1. In a small bowl, combine the pineapple, barbecue sauce, onion and chili sauce. Pour half into a greased 3-qt. slow cooker. Top with pork chops and remaining sauce.
2. Cover and cook on low for 4-5 hours or until meat is tender.

Cranberry Pork Chops

My husband and kids rave over these pork chops. The mild sauce is delicious served with mashed potatoes or rice. Just add salad and you have a satisfying meal that didn't keep you in the kitchen for hours.

—ROBIN CZACHOR
APPLETON, WISCONSIN

PREP: 15 MIN. **COOK:** 7 HOURS
MAKES: 6 SERVINGS

- 6 bone-in pork loin chops (8 ounces each)
- 1 can (14 ounces) jellied cranberry sauce
- ½ cup cranberry or apple juice
- ¼ cup sugar
- 2 tablespoons spicy brown mustard
- 2 tablespoons cornstarch
- ¼ cup cold water
- ½ teaspoon salt
  Dash pepper

1. Place chops in a 3-qt. slow cooker. Combine the cranberry sauce, juice, sugar and mustard until smooth; pour over chops. Cover and cook on low for 7-8 hours or until tender.
2. Remove chops and keep warm. In a small saucepan, combine the cornstarch and cold water until smooth; gradually stir in cooking juices. Bring to a boil; cook and stir for 2 minutes or until thickened. Stir in salt and pepper. Serve with chops.

Slow-Simmering Pasta Sauce

Spaghetti with sauce is my kids' favorite dinner, so through trial and error, I came up with my own signature recipe. This is the winning result. I love that it's made in a slow cooker.

—SAMANTHA VICARS
KENOSHA, WISCONSIN

PREP: 20 MIN. **COOK:** 6 HOURS
MAKES: 6 SERVINGS

- 1 pound bulk Italian sausage
- 1 medium onion, chopped
- 3 garlic cloves, minced
- 2 cans (14½ ounces each) diced tomatoes, undrained
- 1 can (8 ounces) tomato sauce
- 1 can (6 ounces) tomato paste
- 1 tablespoon brown sugar
- 2 bay leaves
- 2 teaspoons dried oregano
- 2 teaspoons dried basil
- 1 teaspoon salt
- ½ teaspoon dried thyme
- ¼ cup minced fresh basil, divided
  Hot cooked pasta

1. In a large skillet, cook sausage and onion over medium heat for 7-8 minutes or until sausage is no longer pink and onion is tender. Add garlic; cook 1 minute longer. Drain. Transfer to a 3-qt. slow cooker.
2. Stir in the tomatoes, tomato sauce, tomato paste, brown sugar, bay leaves, oregano, dried basil, salt and thyme. Cover and cook on low for 6-8 hours.
3. Discard bay leaves; stir in half of the fresh basil. Serve with pasta. Top with remaining basil.

SLOW-SIMMERING PASTA SAUCE

PORK WITH PEACH PICANTE SAUCE

When fresh peaches are in season, I cook these pork ribs up for family and friends. I love the recipe because I only need six ingredients, the slow cooker does the work for me and the ribs turn out tender and tasty. —**CONNIE JENISTA** VALRICO, FLORIDA

Pork With Peach Picante Sauce

PREP: 20 MIN. + CHILLING
COOK: 5½ HOURS **MAKES:** 6 SERVINGS

- 2 **pounds boneless country-style pork ribs**
- 2 **tablespoons taco seasoning**
- ½ **cup mild salsa**
- ¼ **cup peach preserves**
- ¼ **cup barbecue sauce**
- 2 **cups chopped fresh peeled peaches or frozen unsweetened sliced peaches, thawed and chopped**

1. In a large bowl, toss ribs with taco seasoning. Cover and refrigerate overnight.
2. Place pork in a 3-qt. slow cooker. In a small bowl, combine the salsa, preserves and barbecue sauce. Pour over ribs. Cover and cook on low for 5-6 hours or until meat is tender.
3. Add peaches; cover and cook 30 minutes longer or until peaches are tender.

Polish Kraut and Apples

My family loves this hearty meal on cold winter nights. The tender apples, kraut and smoked sausage give it a heartwarming Old World flavor. I like making it because the prep time is very short.

—**CAREN MARKEE** CARY, ILLINOIS

PREP: 10 MIN. **COOK:** 4 HOURS
MAKES: 4 SERVINGS

- 1 **can (14 ounces) sauerkraut, rinsed and well drained**
- 1 **pound smoked Polish sausage or kielbasa, cut up**
- 3 **medium tart apples, peeled and cut into eighths**
- ½ **cup packed brown sugar**
- ½ **teaspoon caraway seeds, optional**
- ⅛ **teaspoon pepper**
- ¾ **cup apple juice**

1. Place half of the sauerkraut in an ungreased 3-qt. slow cooker. Top with sausage, apples, brown sugar, caraway seeds if desired and pepper.

Top with remaining sauerkraut. Pour apple juice over all.
2. Cover and cook on low for 4-5 hours or until apples are tender.

Tangy Lamb Tagine

PREP: 40 MIN. **COOK:** 8 HOURS
MAKES: 8 SERVINGS

- 3 **pounds lamb stew meat, cut into 1½-inch cubes**
- 1 **teaspoon salt**
- 1 **teaspoon pepper**
- 4 **tablespoons olive oil, divided**
- 6 **medium carrots, sliced**
- 2 **medium onions, chopped**
- 6 **garlic cloves, minced**
- 2 **teaspoons grated lemon peel**
- ¼ **cup lemon juice**
- 1 **tablespoon minced fresh gingerroot**
- 1½ **teaspoons ground cinnamon**
- 1½ **teaspoons ground cumin**
- 1½ **teaspoons paprika**
- 2½ **cups reduced-sodium chicken broth**
- ¼ **cup sweet vermouth**
- ¼ **cup honey**
- ½ **cup pitted dates, chopped**
- ½ **cup sliced almonds, toasted**

1. Sprinkle lamb with salt and pepper. In a Dutch oven, brown meat in 2 tablespoons oil in batches. Using a slotted spoon, transfer to a 4- or 5-qt. slow cooker.
2. In the same skillet, saute the carrots, onions, garlic and lemon peel in remaining oil until crisp-tender. Add the lemon juice, ginger, cinnamon, cumin and paprika; cook and stir 2 minutes longer. Add to slow cooker.
3. Stir in the broth, vermouth, honey and dates. Cover and cook on low for 8-10 hours or until lamb is tender. Sprinkle with almonds.
STOVETOP OPTION *Combine browned lamb and carrot mixture in Dutch oven. Stir in broth, vermouth, honey and dates; bring to a boil. Reduce heat; simmer, covered, for about 1 hour or until lamb is tender.*

TANGY LAMB TAGINE

Zesty Ham

Entertaining doesn't get much easier than when you serve this tasty five-ingredient ham from the slow cooker. Leftovers are delicious in casseroles.

—HEATHER SPRING

SHEPPARD AIR FORCE BASE, TEXAS

PREP: 5 MIN. **COOK:** 6 HOURS
MAKES: 15-20 SERVINGS

- ½ **cup packed brown sugar**
- 1 **teaspoon ground mustard**
- 1 **teaspoon prepared horseradish**
- 2 **tablespoons plus ¼ cup cola, divided**
- 1 **fully cooked boneless ham (5 to 6 pounds), cut in half**

In a small bowl, combine the brown sugar, mustard, horseradish and 2 tablespoons cola. Rub over ham. Transfer to a 5-qt. slow cooker; add remaining cola to slow cooker. Cover and cook on low for 6-8 hours or until a thermometer reads 140°.

Sweet and Savory Ribs

My husband, Randy, and I love barbecue ribs, but with our busy schedules, we rarely have time to fire up the grill. So we let the slow cooker do the work for us. By the time we get home from work, the ribs are succulent, juicy and ready to devour.

—KANDY BINGHAM

GREEN RIVER, WYOMING

PREP: 10 MIN. **COOK:** 8 HOURS
MAKES: 8 SERVINGS

- 1 **large onion, chopped**
- 4 **pounds boneless country-style pork ribs**
- 1 **bottle (18 ounces) honey barbecue sauce**
- ⅓ **cup maple syrup**
- ¼ **cup spicy brown mustard**
- ½ **teaspoon salt**
- ¼ **teaspoon pepper**

Place onion in a 5-qt. slow cooker. Top with ribs. In a small bowl, combine remaining ingredients; pour over ribs. Cook, covered, on low 8-9 hours or until meat is tender.

CREAMY MUSHROOM HAM & POTATOES

Everyone loves these potatoes and always comes back for more. I like the comforting main dish because it uses only seven ingredients and cooks up easily in the slow cooker. **—TRACI MEADOWS** MONETT, MISSOURI

Creamy Mushroom Ham & Potatoes

PREP: 25 MIN. **COOK:** 4 HOURS
MAKES: 4 SERVINGS

- 1 **can (10¾ ounces) condensed cream of mushroom soup, undiluted**
- ½ **cup 2% milk**
- 1 **tablespoon dried parsley flakes**
- 6 **medium potatoes, peeled and thnly sliced**
- 1 **small onion, chopped**
- 1½ **cups cubed fully cooked ham**
- 6 **slices process American cheese**

In a small bowl, combine the soup, milk and parsley. In a greased 3-qt. slow cooker, layer half of the potatoes, onion, ham, cheese and soup mixture. Repeat layers. Cover and cook on low for 4-5 hours or until potatoes are tender.

EAT SMART Pork and Apple Curry

Here's a gentle curry dish that's sure to please American palates. For fun, try varying the garnishes. Add some chopped peanuts or a spoonful of chutney.

—NANCY RECK

MILL VALLEY, CALIFORNIA

PREP: 15 MIN. **COOK:** 5½ HOURS
MAKES: 8 SERVINGS

- 2 **pounds boneless pork loin roast, cut into 1-inch cubes**
- 1 **medium apple, peeled and chopped**
- 1 **small onion, chopped**
- ½ **cup orange juice**
- 1 **tablespoon curry powder**
- 1 **teaspoon chicken bouillon granules**
- 1 **garlic clove, minced**
- ½ **teaspoon salt**
- ½ **teaspoon ground ginger**
- ¼ **teaspoon ground cinnamon**
- 2 **tablespoons cornstarch**
- 2 **tablespoons cold water**
  Hot cooked rice, optional
- ¼ **cup raisins**
- ¼ **cup flaked coconut, toasted**

1. In a 3-qt. slow cooker, combine the first 10 ingredients. Cover and cook on low for 5-6 hours or until meat is tender.
2. Increase heat to high. In a small bowl, combine cornstarch and water until smooth; stir into slow cooker. Cover and cook for 30 minutes or until thickened, stirring once.
3. Serve with rice if desired. Sprinkle with raisins and coconut.
PER SERVING *235 cal., 9 g fat (4 g sat. fat), 68 mg chol., 341 mg sodium, 13 g carb., 1 g fiber, 25 g pro.* **Diabetic Exchanges:** *3 lean meat, 1 fruit.*

PORK AND APPLE CURRY

EAT SMART Vegetarian Stuffed Peppers

What an easy way to fix stuffed peppers without parboiling! Light and packed with Southwest flavor, they also come with 8 grams of fiber per serving. How can you go wrong?

—MICHELLE GURNSEY

LINCOLN, NEBRASKA

PREP: 15 MIN. **COOK:** 3 HOURS
MAKES: 4 SERVINGS

- 4 **medium sweet red peppers**
- 1 **can (15 ounces) black beans, rinsed and drained**
- 1 **cup (4 ounces) shredded pepper jack cheese**
- ¾ **cup salsa**
- 1 **small onion, chopped**
- ½ **cup frozen corn**
- ⅓ **cup uncooked converted long grain rice**
- 1¼ **teaspoons chili powder**
- ½ **teaspoon ground cumin**
  Reduced-fat sour cream, optional

1. Cut tops off peppers and remove seeds; set aside. In a large bowl, combine the beans, cheese, salsa, onion, corn, rice, chili powder and cumin; spoon into peppers. Place in a 5-qt. slow cooker coated with cooking spray.
2. Cover and cook on low for 3-4 hours or until peppers are tender and filling is heated through. Serve with sour cream if desired.
PER SERVING *317 cal., 10 g fat (5 g sat. fat), 30 mg chol., 565 mg sodium, 43 g carb., 8 g fiber, 15 g pro.* **Diabetic Exchanges:** *2 starch, 2 lean meat, 2 vegetable, 1 fat.*

Soups, Sides & Sandwiches

65　　75　　80

Friends and family will love the crowd-pleasing **sloppy joes, barbecues and other sandwiches** you create with the easy, delicious recipes in this chapter. Chase away the cold with **heartwarming, economical soups** and chilis. Plus, convenient **slow-cooked side dishes** free you up to focus on the main event.

SLOW COOKER PASTA FAGIOLI

Italian Pulled Pork Sandwiches

Enjoy all the flavors of classic Italian sausage sandwiches with a healthier alternative that uses pulled pork instead.
—**DELLARIO LIA** MIDDLEPORT, NEW YORK

PREP: 20 MIN. **COOK:** 8 HOURS
MAKES: 12 SERVINGS

- 1 **tablespoon fennel seed, crushed**
- 1 **tablespoon steak seasoning**
- 1 **teaspoon cayenne pepper, optional**
- 1 **boneless pork shoulder butt roast (3 pounds)**
- 1 **tablespoon olive oil**
- 2 **medium green or sweet red peppers, thinly sliced**
- 2 **medium onions, thinly sliced**
- 1 **can (14½ ounces) diced tomatoes, undrained**
- 12 **whole wheat hamburger buns, split**

1. In a small bowl, combine the fennel seed, steak seasoning and cayenne if desired. Cut roast in half. Rub seasoning mixture over pork. In a large skillet, brown roast in oil on all sides. Place in a 4- or 5-qt. slow cooker. Add the peppers, onions and tomatoes; cover and cook on low for 7-9 hours or until meat is tender.
2. Remove roast; cool slightly. Skim fat from cooking juices. Shred pork with two forks and return to slow cooker; heat through. Using a slotted spoon, place ½ cup meat mixture on each bun.
NOTE *This recipe was tested with McCormick's Montreal Steak Seasoning. Look for it in the spice aisle.*
PER SERVING *288 cal., 8 g fat (2 g sat. fat), 56 mg chol., 454 mg sodium, 27 g carb., 5 g fiber, 26 g pro. Diabetic Exchanges: 3 lean meat, 2 starch.*

> This is my favorite soup to make because it's so flavorful, hearty and healthy. I have served it to guests and received many compliments. Every spoonful will be thick and delicious.
>
> —**PENNY NOVY** BUFFALO GROVE, ILLINOIS

Slow Cooker Pasta Fagioli

PREP: 30 MIN. **COOK:** 7½ HOURS
MAKES: 8 SERVINGS (2½ QUARTS)

- 1 **pound ground beef**
- 1 **medium onion, chopped**
- 1 **carton (32 ounces) chicken broth**
- 2 **cans (14½ ounces each) diced tomatoes, undrained**
- 1 **can (15 ounces) white kidney or cannellini beans, rinsed and drained**
- 2 **medium carrots, chopped**
- 1½ **cups finely chopped cabbage**
- 1 **celery rib, chopped**
- 2 **tablespoons minced fresh basil or 2 teaspoons dried basil**
- 2 **garlic cloves, minced**
- ½ **teaspoon salt**
- ½ **teaspoon pepper**
- 1 **cup ditalini or other small pasta**
  Grated Parmesan cheese, optional

1. In a large skillet, cook beef and onion over medium heat until beef is no longer pink and onion is tender; drain.
2. Transfer to a 4- or 5-qt. slow cooker. Stir in the broth, tomatoes, beans, carrots, cabbage, celery, basil, garlic, salt and pepper. Cover and cook on low for 7-8 hours or until vegetables are tender.
3. Stir in pasta. Cover and cook on high 30 minutes longer or until pasta is tender. Sprinkle with cheese if desired.

SLOW-COOKED SLOPPY JOES

> On hot summer days, this cooks without heating up the kitchen while I work on the rest of the meal. It's easy to double or triple for crowds, and if there are any leftovers, you can freeze them to enjoy later!
>
> **—CAROL LOSIER** BALDWINSVILLE, NEW YORK

Chili Coney Dogs

Everyone in our family, from smallest kids to oldest adults, loves these dogs. They're so easy to throw together and heat in the slow cooker.

—MICHELE HARRIS
VICKSBURG, MICHIGAN

PREP: 20 MIN. **COOK:** 4 HOURS
MAKES: 8 SERVINGS

- 1 **pound lean ground beef (90% lean)**
- 1 **can (15 ounces) tomato sauce**
- ½ **cup water**
- 2 **tablespoons Worcestershire sauce**
- 1 **tablespoon dried minced onion**
- ½ **teaspoon garlic powder**
- ½ **teaspoon ground mustard**
- ½ **teaspoon chili powder**
- ½ **teaspoon pepper**
  Dash cayenne pepper
- 8 **hot dogs**
- 8 **hot dog buns, split**
  Shredded cheddar cheese, relish and chopped onion, optional

1. In a large skillet, cook beef over medium heat until no longer pink; drain. Stir in the tomato sauce, water, Worcestershire sauce, onion and spices.
2. Place hot dogs in a 3-qt. slow cooker; top with beef mixture. Cover and cook on low for 4-5 hours or until heated through. Serve on buns with cheese, relish and onion if desired.

Slow-Cooked Sloppy Joes

PREP: 20 MIN. **COOK:** 3 HOURS
MAKES: 8 SERVINGS

- 1½ **pounds ground beef**
- 1 **cup chopped celery**
- ½ **cup chopped onion**
- 1 **bottle (12 ounces) chili sauce**
- 2 **tablespoons brown sugar**
- 2 **tablespoons sweet pickle relish**
- 1 **tablespoon Worcestershire sauce**
- 1 **teaspoon salt**
- ⅛ **teaspoon pepper**
- 8 **hamburger buns, split**

1. In a large skillet, cook the beef, celery and onion over medium heat until meat is no longer pink; drain. Transfer to a 3-qt. slow cooker.
2. Stir in the chili sauce, brown sugar, pickle relish, Worcestershire sauce, salt and pepper. Cover and cook on low for 3-4 hours or until heated through and flavors are blended. Spoon ½ cup beef mixture onto each bun.

MANGO & COCONUT CHICKEN SOUP

Mango & Coconut Chicken Soup

I love preparing dinner in a slow cooker because it's carefree cooking. This Asian-style soup uses ingredients that I love, such as coconut milk, edamame and fresh ginger. It's perfect for a potluck or special party.

—ROXANNE CHAN ALBANY, CALIFORNIA

PREP: 25 MIN. **COOK:** 6 HOURS
MAKES: 6 SERVINGS

- 1 broiler/fryer chicken
  (3 to 4 pounds), skin removed
  and cut up
- 2 tablespoons canola oil
- 1 can (15 ounces) whole baby corn,
  drained
- 1 package (10 ounces) frozen
  chopped spinach, thawed
- 1 cup frozen shelled edamame,
  thawed
- 1 small sweet red pepper, chopped
- 1 can (13.66 ounces) light coconut
  milk
- ½ cup mango salsa
- 1 teaspoon minced fresh gingerroot
- 1 medium mango, peeled and
  chopped
- 2 tablespoons lime juice
- 2 green onions, chopped

1. In a large skillet, brown chicken in oil in batches. Transfer chicken and drippings to a 5-qt. slow cooker. Add the corn, spinach, edamame and pepper. In a small bowl, combine the coconut milk, salsa and ginger; pour over vegetables.

2. Cover and cook on low for 6-8 hours or until chicken is tender. Remove chicken; cool slightly. When cool enough to handle, remove meat from bones; cut or shred meat into bite-size pieces. Return meat to slow cooker.

3. Just before serving, stir in mango and lime juice. Sprinkle servings with green onions.

I love the combination of green beans and bacon, so I created a slow-cooked version. It's great for when you have company because you can start the side dish and continue preparing the rest of your dinner. —**BARBARA BRITTAIN** SANTEE, CALIFORNIA

EASY BEANS & POTATOES WITH BACON

EAT SMART Easy Beans & Potatoes with Bacon

PREP: 15 MIN. **COOK:** 6 HOURS
MAKES: 10 SERVINGS

- 8 bacon strips, chopped
- 1½ pounds fresh green beans, trimmed and cut into 2-inch pieces (about 4 cups)
- 4 medium potatoes, peeled and cubed (½ inch)
- 1 small onion, halved and sliced
- ¼ cup reduced-sodium chicken broth
- ½ teaspoon salt
- ¼ teaspoon pepper

1. In a large skillet, cook bacon over medium heat until crisp, stirring occasionally. Remove to paper towels with a slotted spoon; drain, reserving 1 tablespoon drippings. Cover and refrigerate bacon until serving.
2. In a 5-qt. slow cooker, combine the remaining ingredients; stir in reserved drippings. Cover and cook on low for 6-8 hours or until potatoes are tender. Stir in bacon; heat through.
PER SERVING *116 cal., 4 g fat (1 g sat. fat), 8 mg chol., 256 mg sodium, 17 g carb., 3 g fiber, 5 g pro.* **Diabetic Exchanges:** *1 starch, 1 fat.*

Sausage Dressing

I first used this recipe one Thanksgiving when there was no room in the oven to bake stuffing. Now it's a holiday staple!
—**MARY KENDALL** APPLETON, WISCONSIN

PREP: 20 MIN. **COOK:** 4 HOURS
MAKES: 12 SERVINGS

- 1 pound bulk pork sausage
- 1 large onion, chopped
- 2 celery ribs, chopped
- 1 package (14 ounces) seasoned stuffing croutons
- 1 can (14½ ounces) chicken broth
- 1 large tart apple, chopped
- 1 cup chopped walnuts or pecans
- ½ cup egg substitute
- ¼ cup butter, melted
- 1½ teaspoons rubbed sage
- ½ teaspoon pepper

1. In a large skillet, cook the sausage, onion and celery over medium heat until meat is no longer

CHICAGO-STYLE BEEF SANDWICHES

pink; drain. Transfer to a greased 5-qt. slow cooker. Stir in the remaining ingredients.
2. Cover and cook on low for 4-5 hours or until a thermometer reads 160°.

Chicago-Style Beef Sandwiches

I'm originally from the Windy City, so I love Chicago-style beef. These tender sandwiches have an authentic flavor.
—**LOIS SZYDLOWSKI** TAMPA, FLORIDA

PREP: 30 MIN. **COOK:** 8 HOURS
MAKES: 12 SERVINGS

- 1 boneless beef chuck roast (4 pounds)
- 1 teaspoon salt
- ¾ teaspoon pepper
- 2 tablespoons olive oil
- ½ pound fresh mushrooms
- 2 medium carrots, cut into chunks
- 1 medium onion, cut into wedges
- 6 garlic cloves, halved
- 2 teaspoons dried oregano
- 1 carton (32 ounces) beef broth
- 1 tablespoon beef base
- 12 Italian rolls, split
- 1 jar (16 ounces) giardiniera, drained

1. Cut roast in half; sprinkle with salt and pepper. In a large skillet, brown meat in oil on all sides. Transfer to a 5-qt. slow cooker.
2. In a food processor, process the mushrooms, carrots, onion, garlic and oregano until finely chopped. Transfer to slow cooker. Combine beef broth and base; pour over top. Cover and cook on low for 8-10 hours or until tender.
3. Remove meat and shred with two forks. Skim fat from cooking juices. Return meat to slow cooker; heat through. Using a slotted spoon, serve beef on buns; top with giardiniera.
NOTE *Look for beef base near the broth and bouillon.*

Shrimp Chowder

I simmer my rich and creamy shrimp soup in the slow cooker. Because the chowder is ready in less than four hours, it can be prepared in the afternoon and served to dinner guests that night.

—WILL ZUNIO GRETNA, LOUISIANA

PREP: 15 MIN. **COOK:** 3½ HOURS
MAKES: 12 SERVINGS (3 QUARTS)

- ½ cup chopped onion
- 2 teaspoons butter
- 2 cans (12 ounces each) evaporated milk
- 2 cans (10¾ ounces each) condensed cream of potato soup, undiluted
- 2 cans (10¾ ounces each) condensed cream of chicken soup, undiluted
- 1 can (7 ounces) white or shoepeg corn, drained
- 1 teaspoon Creole seasoning
- ½ teaspoon garlic powder
- 2 pounds peeled and deveined cooked small shrimp
- 1 package (3 ounces) cream cheese, cubed

1. In a small skillet, saute onion in butter until tender. In a 5-qt. slow cooker, combine the onion, milk, soups, corn, Creole seasoning and garlic powder.

2. Cover and cook on low for 3 hours. Stir in shrimp and cream cheese. Cook 30 minutes longer or until cheese is melted. Stir to blend.

NOTE *The following spices may be substituted for 1 teaspoon Creole seasoning: ¼ teaspoon each salt, garlic powder and paprika; and a pinch each of dried thyme, ground cumin and cayenne pepper.*

Sweet and Spicy Beans

My husband and I love this sweet and savory bean dish. It can be used as a side, but we normally eat it as a dip. When you fill up a tortilla-chip scoop with these beans, the party starts in your mouth! I've shared the recipe many times.

—SONDRA POPE
MOORESVILLE, NORTH CAROLINA

PREP: 10 MIN. **COOK:** 5 HOURS
MAKES: 12 SERVINGS (⅔ CUP EACH)

- 1 can (16 ounces) kidney beans, rinsed and drained
- 1 can (15¼ ounces) whole kernel corn, drained
- 1 can (15 ounces) garbanzo beans or chickpeas, rinsed and drained
- 1 can (15 ounces) black beans, rinsed and drained
- 1 can (15 ounces) chili with beans
- 1 cup barbecue sauce
- 1 cup salsa
- ⅓ cup packed brown sugar
- ¼ teaspoon hot pepper sauce
  Chopped green onions, optional

In a 4- or 5-qt. slow cooker, combine the first nine ingredients. Cover and cook on low for 5-6 hours. Top with green onions if desired.

To make the bean dish even **heartier**, stir in some ham or **crumbled cooked bacon** near the end of cooking time. Or cook two meaty **ham hocks** along with the beans. Discard the bones before serving.

White Bean Chicken Chili

My sister shared this chili recipe with me. I usually double it and add one extra can of beans. The jalapeno adds just enough heat to notice but not too much for my children.
—KRISTINE BOWLES
RIO RANCHO, NEW MEXICO

PREP: 35 MIN. **COOK:** 3 HOURS
MAKES: 6 SERVINGS

- ¾ pound boneless skinless chicken breasts, cubed
- ½ teaspoon salt
- ¼ teaspoon pepper
- 2 tablespoons olive oil
- 1 medium onion, chopped
- 4 garlic cloves, minced
- 1 jalapeno pepper, seeded and chopped
- 2 teaspoons dried oregano
- 1 teaspoon ground cumin
- 2 cans (15 ounces each) white kidney or cannellini beans, rinsed and drained, divided
- 3 cups chicken broth, divided
- 1½ cups (6 ounces) shredded cheddar cheese
  Sour cream and minced fresh cilantro, optional

1. Sprinkle chicken with salt and pepper. In a large skillet over medium heat, cook chicken in oil for 2 minutes.

2. Stir in the onion, garlic and jalapeno; cook 2 minutes longer. Sprinkle with oregano and cumin; cook 1 minute longer or until chicken is browned and vegetables are tender. Transfer to a 3-qt. slow cooker.

3. In a small bowl, mash 1 cup of beans; add ½ cup broth and stir until blended. Add to the slow cooker with the remaining beans and broth.

4. Cover and cook on low for 3 to 3½ hours or until chicken is tender. Stir before serving. Sprinkle with cheese. Garnish with sour cream and cilantro if desired.
NOTE *Wear disposable gloves when cutting hot peppers; the oils can burn skin. Avoid touching your face.*

Rich & Creamy Mashed Potatoes

PREP: 15 MIN. **COOK:** 2 HOURS
MAKES: 10 SERVINGS

- 3¾ cups boiling water
- 1½ cups 2% milk
- 1 package (8 ounces) cream cheese, softened
- ½ cup butter, cubed
- ½ cup sour cream
- 4 cups mashed potato flakes
- 1 teaspoon garlic salt
- ¼ teaspoon pepper
  Minced fresh parsley, optional

In a greased 4-qt. slow cooker, whisk the boiling water, milk, cream cheese, butter and sour cream until smooth. Stir in the potato flakes, garlic salt and pepper. Cover and cook on low for 2-3 hours or until heated through. Sprinkle with parsley if desired.

> It's a cinch to jazz up instant mashed potatoes with sour cream and cream cheese, then cook and serve them from a slow cooker. For a special touch, sprinkle them with chives, French-fried onions or Parmesan cheese. **—DONNA BARDOCZ** HOWELL, MICHIGAN

RICH & CREAMY MASHED POTATOES

VEGETABLE BEEF SOUP

Convenient frozen veggies and hash browns make this meaty soup a snap to mix up. Simply brown the ground beef, then stir everything together to simmer all day. It's wonderful served with bread and a salad. —CAROL CALHOUN SIOUX FALLS, SOUTH DAKOTA

Boston Baked Beans

Simmered in molasses, these beans are perfect to take to your next potluck. The sauce is sweet, dark and rich. The beans complement anything you serve with them.

—DARLENE DUNCAN

LANGHORNE, PENNSYLVANIA

PREP: 20 MIN. + SOAKING
COOK: 10 HOURS **MAKES:** 10 SERVINGS

- 1 pound dried navy beans
- 6 cups water, divided
- ¼ pound diced salt pork or 6 bacon strips, cooked and crumbled
- 1 large onion, chopped
- ½ cup packed brown sugar
- ½ cup molasses
- ¼ cup sugar
- 1 teaspoon ground mustard
- 1 teaspoon salt
- ½ teaspoon ground cloves
- ½ teaspoon pepper

1. Sort beans and rinse in cold water. Place beans in a 3- or 4-qt. slow cooker; add 4 cups water. Cover and let stand overnight.
2. Drain and rinse beans, discarding liquid. Return beans to slow cooker; add salt pork.
3. In a small bowl, combine the onion, brown sugar, molasses, sugar, mustard, salt, cloves, pepper and remaining water. Pour mixture over beans; stir to combine. Cover and cook on low for 10-12 hours or until beans are tender.

Vegetable Beef Soup

PREP: 10 MIN. **COOK:** 8 HOURS
MAKES: 10 SERVINGS (2½ QUARTS)

- 1 pound ground beef
- 1 can (46 ounces) tomato juice
- 1 package (16 ounces) frozen mixed vegetables, thawed
- 2 cups frozen cubed hash brown potatoes, thawed
- 1 envelope onion soup mix

1. In a large skillet, cook beef over medium heat until no longer pink; drain. Transfer to a 5-qt. slow cooker. Stir in the tomato juice, mixed vegetables, potatoes and soup mix.
2. Cover and cook on low for 8-10 hours or until heated through.

Ginger Applesauce

This is my favorite way to prepare applesauce. It's simple to do and makes the whole house smell like fall.

—RENEE PAJESTKA BRUNSWICK, OHIO

PREP: 25 MIN. **COOK:** 4 HOURS
MAKES: ABOUT 5 CUPS

- 4 pounds apples (about 12 medium), peeled and cubed
- ¼ cup water
- 2 tablespoons brown sugar
- 2 teaspoons ground cinnamon
- 2 teaspoons minced fresh gingerroot
- 2 teaspoons vanilla extract

1. Place all ingredients in a 4-qt. slow cooker; stir until combined.
2. Cover and cook on low for 4-5 hours or until apples are tender. Mash if desired. Refrigerate leftovers.

EAT SMART **Healthy Tomato Soup**

To trim the sodium in my slow-cooked soup, I season it with herbs and spices instead of salt. It's delicious served with fresh bread for dipping.

—HEATHER CAMPBELL
LAWRENCE, KANSAS

PREP: 10 MIN. **COOK:** 5 HOURS
MAKES: 6 SERVINGS

- 1 **can (46 ounces) tomato juice**
- 1 **can (8 ounces) tomato sauce**
- ½ **cup water**
- ½ **cup chopped onion**
- 1 **celery rib with leaves, chopped**
- 2 **tablespoons sugar**
- ½ **teaspoon dried basil**
- 3 **to 5 whole cloves**
- 1 **bay leaf**

In a 3-qt. slow cooker, combine all ingredients. Cover and cook on low for 5-6 hours or until heated through. Discard cloves and bay leaf.
PER SERVING *69 cal., trace fat (trace sat. fat), 0 chol., 964 mg sodium, 17 g carb., 2 g fiber, 2 g pro.* **Diabetic Exchange:** *1 starch.*

EAT SMART **Black Bean 'n' Pumpkin Chili**

Our family loves this slow-cooked recipe, especially on cold days. It's a wonderful variation on standard chili that freezes well and tastes even better as leftovers.

—DEBORAH VLIET
HOLLAND, MICHIGAN

PREP: 20 MIN. **COOK:** 4 HOURS
MAKES: 10 SERVINGS (2½ QUARTS)

- 2 **tablespoons olive oil**
- 1 **medium onion, chopped**
- 1 **medium sweet yellow pepper, chopped**
- 3 **garlic cloves, minced**
- 2 **cans (15 ounces each) black beans, rinsed and drained**
- 1 **can (15 ounces) solid-pack pumpkin**
- 1 **can (14-½ ounces) diced tomatoes, undrained**
- 3 **cups chicken broth**
- 2½ **cups cubed cooked turkey**
- 2 **teaspoons dried parsley flakes**
- 2 **teaspoons chili powder**
- 1½ **teaspoons ground cumin**
- 1½ **teaspoons dried oregano**
- ½ **teaspoon salt**

1. In a large skillet, heat oil over medium-high heat. Add onion and pepper; cook and stir until tender. Add garlic; cook 1 minute longer.
2. Transfer to a 5-qt. slow cooker; stir in the remaining ingredients. Cook, covered, on low 4-5 hours or until heated through.
PER SERVING *192 cal., 5 g fat (1 g sat. fat), 28 mg chol., 658 mg sodium, 21 g carb., 7 g fiber, 16 g pro.* **Diabetic Exchanges:** *2 lean meat, 1½ starch, ½ fat.*

Fresh basil is a natural with **tomato** soup. Add as much as you like of the **garden star** to your favorite soup!

For a vegetarian chili that meat lovers would also like, this recipe is healthy and tastes great. It takes just a few minutes to prepare, then the chili simmers in the slow cooker leaving me free to do something else. I top bowls with shredded cheddar cheese. —**CONNIE BARNETT** ATHENS, GEORGIA

VEGETARIAN RED BEAN CHILI

Vegetarian Red Bean Chili

PREP: 10 MIN. **COOK:** 5 HOURS
MAKES: 6 SERVINGS (2 QUARTS)

- 1 can (16 ounces) red beans, rinsed and drained
- 2 cans (8 ounces each) no-salt-added tomato sauce
- 2 cups water
- 1 can (14½ ounces) diced tomatoes, undrained
- 1 package (12 ounces) frozen vegetarian meat crumbles
- 1 large onion, chopped
- 1 to 2 tablespoons chili powder
- 1 tablespoon ground cumin
- 2 garlic cloves, minced
- 1 teaspoon pepper
- ½ teaspoon salt
- ½ teaspoon cayenne pepper
- Sour cream and shredded cheddar cheese, optional

In a 4-qt. slow cooker, combine all ingredients. Cover and cook on low for 5-6 hours or until heated through. Serve with sour cream and cheddar cheese if desired.

NOTE *Vegetarian meat crumbles are a nutritious protein source made from soy. Look for them in the natural foods freezer section.*

Barbecue Chicken Sandwiches

I love to use my slow cooker. In fact, I have three of them in various sizes! These saucy chicken sandwiches are real crowd pleasers.

—LYNN IRELAND LEBANON, WISCONSIN

PREP: 20 MIN. **COOK:** 5 HOURS
MAKES: 10 SERVINGS

- 3 pounds boneless skinless chicken thighs
- 1 cup ketchup
- 1 small onion, chopped
- ¼ cup water
- ¼ cup cider vinegar
- 2 tablespoons Worcestershire sauce
- 1 tablespoon brown sugar
- 1 garlic clove, minced
- 1 bay leaf
- 2 teaspoons paprika
- 1 teaspoon dried oregano
- 1 teaspoon chili powder

- ½ teaspoon salt
- ½ teaspoon pepper
- 10 kaiser rolls, split

1. Place chicken in a 5-qt. slow cooker. In a small bowl, combine the ketchup, onion, water, vinegar, Worcestershire sauce, brown sugar, garlic, bay leaf and seasonings. Pour over chicken. Cover and cook on low for 5 hours or until tender.

2. Discard bay leaf. Remove chicken; shred with two forks and return to slow cooker. Heat through. Serve on rolls.

EAT SMART Hoisin Pork Wraps

PREP: 25 MIN. **COOK:** 7 HOURS
MAKES: 15 SERVINGS

- 1 boneless pork loin roast (3 pounds)
- 1 cup hoisin sauce, divided
- 1 tablespoon minced fresh gingerroot
- 6 cups shredded red cabbage

- 1½ cups shredded carrots
- ¼ cup thinly sliced green onions
- 3 tablespoons rice vinegar
- 4½ teaspoons sugar
- 15 flour tortillas (8 inches), warmed

1. Cut roast in half. Combine ⅓ cup hoisin sauce and ginger; rub over pork. Transfer to a 3-qt. slow cooker. Cover and cook on low for 7-8 hours or until pork is tender.

2. Meanwhile, in a large bowl, combine the cabbage, carrots, onions, vinegar and sugar. Chill until serving.

3. Shred meat with two forks and return to the slow cooker; heat through. Place 2 teaspoons remaining hoisin sauce down the center of each tortilla; top with ⅓ cup shredded pork and ⅓ cup coleslaw. Roll up.

PER SERVING *314 cal., 8 g fat (2 g sat. fat), 46 mg chol., 564 mg sodium, 37 g carb., 1 g fiber, 23 g pro.* **Diabetic Exchanges:** *2½ starch, 2 lean meat.*

This flavorful pork with its tasty slaw is fun to serve at a buffet because it lets guests make their own wraps. Even my grandchildren like it.
—LINDA WOO DERBY, KANSAS

HOISIN PORK WRAPS

Hot Fruit Salad

My old-fashioned fruit salad is convenient to make in the slow cooker when your oven and stovetop are occupied with other dishes. It's delicious alongside roasted meats, or even served over pound cake for dessert.

—DEBBIE KIMBROUGH
LEXINGTON, MISSISSIPPI

PREP: 10 MIN. **COOK:** 2 HOURS
MAKES: 10 SERVINGS

- ¾ cup sugar
- ½ cup butter, melted
- ¼ teaspoon ground cinnamon
- ¼ teaspoon ground nutmeg
- ⅛ teaspoon salt
- 2 cans (15¼ ounces each) sliced peaches, drained
- 2 cans (15¼ ounces each) sliced pears, undrained
- 1 jar (23 ounces) chunky applesauce
- ½ cup dried apricots, chopped
- ¼ cup dried cranberries

In a 3-qt. slow cooker, combine the sugar, butter, cinnamon, nutmeg and salt. Stir in the remaining ingredients. Cover and cook on high for 2 hours or until heated through.

Seasoned Pork Sandwiches

This is one of the time-honored dishes that my husband never seems to tire of. The bonus for me is that it's quick, easy to make and even easier to clean up!

—JACQUE THOMPSON HOUSTON, TEXAS

PREP: 20 MIN. **COOK:** 5 HOURS
MAKES: 8 SERVINGS

- 1 boneless pork loin roast (2 to 3 pounds)
- 1 tablespoon fajita seasoning mix
- ¼ teaspoon garlic powder
- ½ cup Italian salad dressing
- ¼ cup Worcestershire sauce
- 8 sandwich rolls, split

1. Cut roast in half; place in a 5-qt. slow cooker. Sprinkle with fajita seasoning and garlic powder. Pour salad dressing and Worcestershire sauce over meat. Cover and cook on low for 5-6 hours or until the meat is tender.

2. Remove roast; shred meat with two forks. Return to cooking juices; heat through. Using a slotted spoon, serve pork on rolls.

Hominy Pork Soup

Here's a deliciously different soup that's quick to make. Serve lots of toppings so each person can customize their bowl.

—RAQUEL WALKUP SAN PEDRO, CALIFORNIA

PREP: 15 MIN. **COOK:** 6 HOURS
MAKES: 7 SERVINGS

- 1 pound pork chop suey meat
- 2 cans (15 ounces each) chili without beans
- 1 can (15½ ounces) hominy, drained
- 1 can (8 ounces) tomato sauce
- 1 medium onion, chopped
- 1 bay leaf
- 1 tablespoon chili powder
- 1 teaspoon each dried basil, oregano and parsley flakes
- 1 teaspoon ground cumin
    Warmed flour tortillas, shredded Monterey Jack cheese, sliced green onions and lime wedges, optional

1. In a 3-qt. slow cooker, combine the pork, chili, hominy, tomato sauce, onion and seasonings.

2. Cover and cook on low for 6 to 8 hours or until meat is tender. Discard the bay leaf. Serve soup with tortillas, cheese, onions and lime wedges if desired.

Spicy Chicken and Hominy Soup

PREP: 15 MIN. **COOK:** 4 HOURS
MAKES: 4 SERVINGS

- 1 pound boneless skinless chicken breasts, cubed
- 2 tablespoons olive oil
- 1 medium onion, chopped
- 3 garlic cloves, minced
- 2 chipotle peppers in adobo sauce
- 2 cans (14½ ounces each) chicken broth, divided
- 1 can (15 ounces) hominy, rinsed and drained
- 1 can (4 ounces) chopped green chilies
- 1 teaspoon dried oregano
- 1 teaspoon ground cumin
- ¼ teaspoon pepper

1. In a large skillet, brown chicken in oil.

2. With a slotted spoon, transfer chicken to a 3- or 4-qt. slow cooker. In the same skillet, saute onion and garlic in drippings until tender; add to chicken.

3. Place chipotle peppers and ¼ cup broth in a blender or food processor; cover and process until blended. Add to chicken mixture. Stir in the hominy, chilies, seasonings and remaining broth.

4. Cover and cook on low for 4-5 hours or until chicken is tender.

This slow-cooked soup is also called "posole," a traditional good luck New Year's meal in my native New Mexico. Everyone makes it differently, and my soup answers the age-old chili question—"Red or green?"—by using both!

—JANET CHRISTINE MCDANIEL ARLINGTON, TEXAS

SPICY CHICKEN AND HOMINY SOUP

SLOW COOKER MUSHROOM RICE PILAF

> A few modifications to our dear Great Aunt Bernice's easy mushroom rice pilaf recipe have made this an always-requested dish for potlucks, barbecues and family get-togethers. It'll become a slow-cooker favorite in your household, too!
>
> **—AMY WILLIAMS** RIALTO, CALIFORNIA

EAT SMART Slow Cooker Mushroom Rice Pilaf

PREP: 20 MIN. **COOK:** 3 HOURS
MAKES: 6 SERVINGS

- 1 cup medium grain rice
- ¼ cup butter
- 6 green onions, chopped
- 2 garlic cloves, minced
- ½ pound sliced baby portobello mushrooms
- 2 cups warm water
- 4 teaspoons beef base

1. In a large skillet, saute rice in butter until lightly browned. Add green onions and garlic; cook and stir until tender. Stir in mushrooms.
2. Transfer to a 1½-qt. slow cooker. In a small bowl, whisk water and beef base; pour over rice mixture. Cover and cook on low for 3 to 3½ hours or until rice is tender and liquid is absorbed. Fluff with a fork.
NOTE *Look for beef base near the broth and bouillon.*
PER SERVING *210 cal., 8 g fat (5 g sat. fat), 20 mg chol., 512 mg sodium, 30 g carb., 1 g fiber, 4 g pro.* **Diabetic Exchanges:** *2 starch, 2 fat.*

Chicken Soup With Beans

I place lime-flavored tortilla chips into the serving bowls before ladling in this Southwestern soup. Loaded with chicken, beans, corn, tomatoes and green chilies, it's so satisfying.
—PENNY PERONIA
WEST MEMPHIS, ARKANSAS

PREP: 20 MIN. **COOK:** 6 HOURS
MAKES: 12 SERVINGS (3 QUARTS)

- 1 large onion, chopped
- 1 tablespoon canola oil
- 2 garlic cloves, minced
- 1¼ pounds boneless skinless chicken breasts, cooked and cubed
- 2 cans (15½ ounces each) great northern beans, rinsed and drained
- 3 cans (7 ounces each) white or shoepeg corn, drained
- 1 can (10 ounces) diced tomatoes and green chilies, undrained
- 3 cups water
- 1 can (4 ounces) chopped green chilies
- 2 tablespoons lime juice
- 1 teaspoon lemon-pepper seasoning
- 1 teaspoon ground cumin
- ¼ teaspoon salt
- ¼ teaspoon pepper

1. In a small skillet, saute onion in oil until tender. Add garlic; cook 1 minute longer.
2. Transfer to a 5-qt. slow cooker. Stir in the chicken, beans, corn, tomatoes, water, chopped green chilies, lime juice and seasonings. Cover and cook on low for 6-7 hours or until heated through.

French Dip au Jus

I created this sandwich because so many French Dip recipes seem bland or rely on a mix. Mine is simple to make and tastes better than a restaurant version.

—LINDSAY EBERT OREM, UTAH

PREP: 30 MIN. **COOK:** 8 HOURS
MAKES: 8 SERVINGS

- 1½ teaspoons beef base
- 1 teaspoon dried thyme
- 1 beef rump roast or bottom round roast (3 pounds), cut in half
- 1 medium onion, quartered
- ½ cup reduced-sodium soy sauce
- 2 garlic cloves, minced
- 1 bay leaf
- ½ teaspoon pepper
- 8 cups water
- 2 tablespoons Dijon mustard
- 2 loaves French bread (1 pound each), split and toasted
- 12 slices part-skim mozzarella cheese
- 1 jar (4½ ounces) sliced mushrooms, drained

1. Combine beef base and thyme; rub over roast and place in a 5-qt. slow cooker. Combine the onion, soy sauce, garlic, bay leaf and pepper; pour over roast. Add water.

2. Cover and cook on low for 8-9 hours or until meat is tender. Remove roast to a cutting board; cool slightly. Strain cooking juices, reserving onion; skim fat from juices. Discard bay leaf. Thinly slice meat.

3. To assemble sandwiches, spread mustard over bread. Top each bottom with three slices cheese; layer with beef, remaining cheese, mushrooms and reserved onion. Replace tops. Cut each loaf into four slices; serve with reserved juices.

NOTE *Look for beef base near the broth and bouillon.*

HEARTY SPLIT PEA SOUP

We started a 39-day soup challenge to eat healthfully after the holidays, figuring if "Survivor" contestants could last for 39 days on little food, surely we could live on delicious soup! This was a family favorite.

—DEBRA KEIL OWASSO, OKLAHOMA

Hearty Split Pea Soup

PREP: 30 MIN. **COOK:** 7 HOURS
MAKES: 6 SERVINGS (2¼ QUARTS)

- 1 large onion, chopped
- 1 cup chopped celery
- 1 cup chopped fresh carrots
- 2 tablespoons olive oil
- 1 teaspoon dried thyme
- 1 package (16 ounces) dried green split peas, rinsed
- 4 cups vegetable broth
- 2 cups water
- 6 ounces Canadian bacon, chopped
- ¼ teaspoon pepper

1. In a large skillet, saute the onion, celery and carrots in oil until tender. Add thyme; cook 1 minute longer.

2. Transfer to a 5-qt. slow cooker. Add the peas, broth and water. Cover and cook on low for 7-8 hours or until peas are tender.

3. Cool slightly. In a blender, process half of the soup until smooth. Return all to the slow cooker. Add bacon and pepper; heat through.

I love this chicken soup because it combines some of my favorite ingredients, like savory herbs, kidney beans and fresh spinach. To create a hearty meal, serve it with crusty bread slathered in butter. —**TANYA MACDONALD** ANTIGONISH COUNTY, NOVA SCOTIA

HERBED CHICKEN & SPINACH SOUP

Herbed Chicken & Spinach Soup

PREP: 20 MIN. **COOK:** 4½ HOURS
MAKES: 4 SERVINGS

- 1 **pound boneless skinless chicken thighs, cut into ½-inch pieces**
- 1 **can (16 ounces) kidney beans, rinsed and drained**
- 1 **can (14½ ounces) chicken broth**
- 1 **medium onion, chopped**
- 1 **medium sweet red pepper, chopped**
- 1 **celery rib, chopped**
- 2 **tablespoons tomato paste**
- 3 **garlic cloves, minced**
- ½ **teaspoon minced fresh rosemary or ¼ teaspoon dried rosemary, crushed**
- ½ **teaspoon minced fresh thyme or ¼ teaspoon dried thyme**
- ½ **teaspoon dried oregano**
- ¼ **teaspoon salt**
- ¼ **teaspoon pepper**
- 3 **cups fresh baby spinach**
- ¼ **cup shredded Parmesan cheese**

In a 3-qt. slow cooker, combine the first 13 ingredients. Cover and cook on low for 4-5 hours or until chicken is tender. Stir in spinach; cook 30 minutes longer or until spinach is wilted. Top with cheese.

Ham and Lentil Soup

Here's a delicious way to use up leftover ham. The hearty broth makes it perfect for a cold day. Just serve with fresh bread and butter.

—CONNIE JONES PIXLEY
ROXBORO, NORTH CAROLINA

PREP: 10 MIN. **COOK:** 4 HOURS
MAKES: 11 SERVINGS

- 1 **cup chopped celery**
- 1 **cup chopped carrots**
- ½ **cup chopped onion**
- 1 **tablespoon butter**
- 8 **cups water**
- 2 **cups dried lentils, rinsed**
- 1 **cup cubed fully cooked ham**
- 2 **teaspoons salt**
- 1 **teaspoon dried marjoram**
- ½ **teaspoon pepper**

In a large skillet, saute the celery, carrots and onion in butter for 3-4

SLOW-COOKED PORK BARBEQUE

> I need only five ingredients to make sweet and tender pulled pork for sandwiches. You can easily adjust or add seasonings to suit your family's tastes.
>
> **—CONNIE JOHNSON** SPRINGFIELD, MISSOURI

minutes or until crisp-tender. In a 5-qt. slow cooker, combine the water, lentils, ham, salt, marjoram and pepper. Stir in the celery mixture. Cover and cook on low for 4-5 hours or until lentils are tender.

Slow-Cooked Pork Barbecue

PREP: 15 MIN. **COOK:** 5 HOURS
MAKES: 10 SERVINGS

- 1 **boneless pork loin roast (3 to 4 pounds)**
- 1½ **teaspoons seasoned salt**
- 1 **teaspoon garlic powder**
- 1 **cup cola, divided**
- 1 **cup barbecue sauce**
- 10 **sandwich buns, split**

1. Cut the roast in half; place in a 5-qt. slow cooker. Sprinkle with seasoned salt and garlic powder. Pour ¼ cup cola over roast. Cover and cook on low for 4-5 hours or until meat is tender.

2. Remove roast; cool slightly. Shred meat with two forks and return to slow cooker. Combine barbecue sauce and remaining cola; pour over meat. Cover and cook on high for 1-2 hours or until sauce is thickened. Serve on buns.

VEGGIE POTATO SOUP

> Chock-full of potatoes, my vegetarian soup is as filling as it is flavorful. Serve it on cool spring nights or take a thermos of it to work.
>
> —**HANNAH THOMPSON** SCOTTS VALLEY, CALIFORNIA

Veggie Potato Soup

PREP: 20 MIN. **COOK:** 5½ HOURS
MAKES: 11 SERVINGS (2¾ QUARTS)

- 3 cans (14½ ounces each) vegetable broth
- 6 medium potatoes, cubed
- 1 medium carrot, thinly sliced
- 1 large leek (white portion only), chopped
- ¼ cup butter, cubed
- 1 garlic clove, minced
- 1 teaspoon dried thyme
- ¾ teaspoon salt
- ¼ teaspoon dried marjoram
- ¼ teaspoon pepper
- ¼ cup all-purpose flour
- 1½ cups half-and-half cream
- 1 cup frozen peas, thawed

1. In a 5-qt. slow cooker, combine the first 10 ingredients. Cover and cook on low for 5-6 hours or until vegetables are tender.

2. In a small bowl, combine flour and cream until smooth; add to slow cooker. Stir in peas. Cover and cook on high for 30 minutes or until slightly thickened.

Red Bean Vegetable Soup

Cajun seasoning boosts the flavor of my nutritious soup that's loaded with fresh vegetables.

—**RONNIE LAPPE** BROWNWOOD, TEXAS

PREP: 15 MIN. **COOK:** 6 HOURS
MAKES: 12 SERVINGS (3 QUARTS)

- 3 large sweet red peppers, chopped
- 3 celery ribs, chopped
- 2 medium onions, chopped
- 4 cans (16 ounces each) red kidney beans, rinsed and drained
- 4 cups chicken broth
- 2 bay leaves
- ½ to 1 teaspoon salt
- ½ to 1 teaspoon Cajun seasoning
- ½ teaspoon pepper
- ¼ to ½ teaspoon hot pepper sauce

In a 5-qt. slow cooker, combine the peppers, celery, onions and beans. Stir in the remaining ingredients. Cover and cook on low for 6 hours or until vegetables are tender. Discard bay leaves before serving.

Potluck Candied Sweet Potatoes

PREP: 20 MIN. **COOK:** 5 HOURS
MAKES: 12 SERVINGS (¾ CUP EACH)

- 1 cup packed brown sugar
- 1 cup sugar
- 8 medium sweet potatoes, peeled and cut into ½-inch slices
- ¼ cup butter, melted
- 2 teaspoons vanilla extract
- ¼ teaspoon salt
- 2 tablespoons cornstarch
- 2 tablespoons cold water
  Minced fresh parsley, optional

1. In a bowl, combine sugars. In a greased 5-qt. slow cooker, layer a third of the sweet potatoes; sprinkle with a third of the sugar mixture. Repeat layers twice. In a small bowl, combine the butter, vanilla and salt; drizzle over potatoes. Cover and cook on low for 5-6 hours or until sweet potatoes are tender.

2. Using a slotted spoon, transfer potatoes to a serving dish; keep warm. Pour cooking juices into a small saucepan; bring to a boil. In a small bowl, combine cornstarch and water until smooth; stir into pan. Return to a boil, stirring constantly; cook and stir for 1-2 minutes or until thickened. Spoon over the sweet potatoes.

3. Sprinkle with parsley if desired.

To make it easier to bring this traditional Southern staple to a potluck or gathering, I updated it so that it can be cooked in a slow cooker. It's hard to go wrong with candied sweet potatoes when it comes to pleasing a crowd.
—**DEIRDRE DEE COX** KANSAS CITY, KANSAS

POTLUCK CANDIED SWEET POTATOES

You can add virtually any extras you might have, such as chopped bell peppers or sliced fresh mushrooms, to this easy chili. Create your own specialty!
—**GINNY PUCKETT** LUTZ, FLORIDA

SLOW 'N' EASY CHILI

Slow 'n' Easy Chili

PREP: 15 MIN. **COOK:** 6 HOURS
MAKES: 6-8 SERVINGS

- ½ pound ground beef, cooked and drained
- ½ pound bulk pork sausage, cooked and drained
- 1 can (28 ounces) crushed tomatoes
- 1 can (16 ounces) chili beans, undrained
- 1 can (10¾ ounces) condensed tomato soup, undiluted
- 1 large onion, chopped
- 2 envelopes chili seasoning
  Shredded cheddar cheese, optional

In a 3-qt. slow cooker, combine the first seven ingredients. Cover and cook on low for 6-8 hours or until thickened and heated through, stirring occasionally. Garnish with cheese if desired.

Tomato Hamburger Soup

As a full-time teacher, I only have time to cook from scratch a few nights each week. This recipe makes a big enough batch to feed my family for two nights.
—JULIE KRUGER ST. CLOUD, MINNESOTA

PREP: 10 MIN. **COOK:** 4 HOURS
MAKES: 12 SERVINGS (3 QUARTS)

- 1 can (46 ounces) V8 juice
- 2 packages (16 ounces each) frozen mixed vegetables
- 1 pound ground beef, cooked and drained
- 1 can (10¾ ounces) condensed cream of mushroom soup, undiluted
- 2 teaspoons dried minced onion
  Salt and pepper to taste

1. In a 5-qt. slow cooker, combine the first five ingredients.
2. Cover and cook on high for 4-5 hours or until heated through. Season with salt and pepper.

CORN AND BROCCOLI IN CHEESE SAUCE

This popular dish is a standby at our house. My daughter likes to add leftover ham to it. No one will guess it's lightened up! —JOYCE JOHNSON UNIONTOWN, OHIO

EAT SMART
Corn and Broccoli in Cheese Sauce

PREP: 10 MIN. **COOK:** 3 HOURS
MAKES: 8 SERVINGS

- 1 package (16 ounces) frozen corn, thawed
- 1 package (16 ounces) frozen broccoli florets, thawed
- 4 ounces reduced-fat process cheese (Velveeta), cubed
- ½ cup shredded cheddar cheese
- 1 can (10¼ ounces) reduced-fat reduced-sodium condensed cream of chicken soup, undiluted
- ¼ cup fat-free milk

1. In a 4-qt. slow cooker, combine the corn, broccoli and cheeses. In a small bowl, combine soup and milk; pour over vegetable mixture.
2. Cover and cook on low for 3-4 hours or until heated through. Stir before serving.
PER SERVING 148 cal., 5 g fat (3 g sat. fat), 16 mg chol., 409 mg sodium, 21 g carb., 3 g fiber, 8 g pro. *Diabetic Exchanges: 1 starch, 1 medium-fat meat.*

> This creamy oven favorite slow-cooks in the kitchen while I'm away. It's ready to serve when I get home, making it a real winner in my book!
>
> —**JONI HILTON** ROCKLIN, CALIFORNIA

Scalloped Potatoes & Ham

PREP: 25 MIN. **COOK:** 8 HOURS
MAKES: 16 SERVINGS (¾ CUP EACH)

- 1 can (10¾ ounces) condensed cheddar cheese soup, undiluted
- 1 can (10¾ ounces) condensed cream of mushroom soup, undiluted
- 1 cup 2% milk
- 10 medium potatoes, peeled and thinly sliced
- 3 cups cubed fully cooked ham
- 2 medium onions, chopped
- 1 teaspoon paprika
- 1 teaspoon pepper

1. In a small bowl, combine the soups and milk. In a greased 5-qt. slow cooker, layer half of the potatoes, ham, onions and soup mixture. Repeat layers. Sprinkle with paprika and pepper.
2. Cover and cook on low for 8-10 hours or until potatoes are tender.

Rich & Creamy Potato Soup

I make this thick soup every year for St. Patrick's Day, and we always look forward to it.

—**MARY JO O'BRIEN**
HASTINGS, MINNESOTA

PREP: 30 MIN. **COOK:** 5 HOURS
MAKES: 2 SERVINGS

- 2¾ cups cubed peeled potatoes, divided
- 1⅓ cups water
- 2 tablespoons butter, cubed
- ⅔ cup cubed fully cooked ham
- 1 celery rib, chopped
- ⅓ cup chopped onion
- ¼ teaspoon garlic powder
- ¼ teaspoon paprika
  Dash pepper
- ¼ pound process cheese (Velveeta), cubed
- ⅓ cup sour cream
  Milk, optional

1. Place 2 cups potatoes in a saucepan; add water. Bring to a boil. Reduce heat; cover and cook for 10-15 minutes or until tender. Remove from the heat (do not drain). Mash potatoes; stir in butter.
2. In a 1½-qt. slow cooker, combine the ham, celery, onion, garlic powder, paprika, pepper and remaining cubed potatoes. Stir in mashed potatoes; top with cheese.
3. Cover and cook on low for 5-6 hours or until vegetables are tender. Stir in the sour cream until blended. Thin soup with milk if desired.

Tex-Mex Shredded Beef Sandwiches

PREP: 5 MIN. **COOK:** 8 HOURS
MAKES: 8 SERVINGS

- 1 boneless beef chuck roast (3 pounds)
- 1 envelope chili seasoning
- ½ cup barbecue sauce
- 8 onion rolls, split
- 8 slices cheddar cheese

1. Cut roast in half; place in a 3-qt. slow cooker. Sprinkle with chili seasoning. Pour barbecue sauce over top. Cover and cook on low for 8-10 hours or until meat is tender.
2. Remove roast; cool slightly. Shred meat with two forks. Skim fat from cooking juices. Return meat to slow cooker; heat through. Using a slotted spoon, place ½ cup meat mixture on each roll bottom; top with cheese. Replace tops.

Slow-cooker meals, like this shredded beef sandwich, are my favorite kind because after I combine a few ingredients and let them cook, there's time for me to do my own thing. Plus, I have a hearty and enticing meal waiting when I come home!

—KATHERINE WHITE CLEMMONS, NORTH CAROLINA

TEX-MEX SHREDDED BEEF SANDWICHES

Snacks & Sweets

91

85

94

You'll have time to enjoy the party when you **create irresistible meatballs, dips and snacks** in the slow cooker. Also cook up **sweet, yummy desserts and memorable drinks** that are sure to be **the talk of the table!**

PEPPERONI PIZZA DIP

Wassail Bowl Punch

All ages will enjoy this warming punch. The blend of spice, fruit and hot tea is scrumptious. You can assemble it before heading out for a winter activity and sip away the chill when you return. It's ready whenever you are.

—MARGARET HARMS
JENKINS, KENTUCKY

PREP: 10 MIN. **COOK:** 1 HOUR
MAKES: 3½ QUARTS

- 4 **cups hot brewed tea**
- 4 **cups cranberry juice**
- 4 **cups unsweetened apple juice**
- 2 **cups orange juice**
- 1 **cup sugar**
- ¾ **cup lemon juice**
- 3 **cinnamon sticks (3 inches)**
- 12 **whole cloves**

1. In a 5-qt. slow cooker, combine the first six ingredients. Place the cinnamon sticks and cloves on a double thickness of cheesecloth; bring up corners of cloth and tie with string to form a bag. Add spice bag to slow cooker.
2. Cover and cook on high for 1 hour or until punch begins to boil. Discard spice bag. Serve warm.

> Everybody loves this simple pizza-flavored dip. If you have any left over, spoon it over a toasted English muffin for a great open-faced sandwich.
>
> **—SARA NOWACKI** FRANKLIN, WISCONSIN

Pepperoni Pizza Dip

PREP: 10 MIN. **COOK:** 1½ HOURS
MAKES: 5½ CUPS

- 2 **packages (8 ounces each) cream cheese, cubed**
- 1 **can (15 ounces) pizza sauce**
- 1 **package (8 ounces) sliced pepperoni, chopped**
- 1 **can (3.8 ounces) chopped ripe olives, drained**
- 2 **cups (8 ounces) shredded part-skim mozzarella cheese**
  Bagel chips or garlic toast

1. Place cream cheese in a 3-qt. slow cooker. Combine the pizza sauce, pepperoni and olives; pour over the cream cheese. Top with mozzarella cheese.
2. Cover and cook on low for 1-2 hours or until cheese is melted. Stir; serve warm with bagel chips or garlic toast.

SLOW-COOKED CRAB DIP

> I love slow-cooked dips for the holidays because they free up the oven for my turkey. Plus, leftovers are great served over a baked potato the next day.
>
> **—SUSAN D'AMORE** WEST CHESTER, PENNSYLVANIA

Slow-Cooked Crab Dip

PREP: 20 MIN. **COOK:** 2 HOURS
MAKES: 2⅓ CUPS

- 1 **package (8 ounces) cream cheese, softened**
- 2 **green onions, chopped**
- ¼ **cup chopped sweet red pepper**
- 2 **tablespoons minced fresh parsley**
- 2 **tablespoons mayonnaise**
- 1 **tablespoon Dijon mustard**
- 1 **teaspoon Worcestershire sauce**
- ¼ **teaspoon salt**
- ¼ **teaspoon pepper**
- 2 **cans (6 ounces each) lump crabmeat, drained**
- 2 **tablespoons capers, drained**
     Dash hot pepper sauce
     Assorted crackers

1. In a 1½-qt. slow cooker, combine the first nine ingredients; stir in crab.
2. Cover and cook on low for 1-2 hours. Stir in capers and pepper sauce; cook 30 minutes longer to allow flavors to blend. Serve the dip with crackers.

Slow Cooker Chocolate Lava Cake

Everyone who tries this dessert falls in love with it. I recommend using a slow-cooker liner. It makes cleanup a breeze.

—LATONA DWYER
PALM BEACH GARDENS, FLORIDA

PREP: 15 MIN. **COOK:** 3 HOURS
MAKES: 12 SERVINGS

- 1 **package devil's food cake mix (regular size)**
- 1⅔ **cups water**
- 3 **eggs**
- ⅓ **cup canola oil**
- 2 **cups cold 2% milk**
- 1 **package (3.9 ounces) instant chocolate pudding mix**
- 2 **cups (12 ounces) semisweet chocolate chips**

1. In a large bowl, combine the cake mix, water, eggs and oil; beat on low speed for 30 seconds. Beat on medium for 2 minutes. Transfer to a greased 4-qt. slow cooker.
2. In another bowl, whisk milk and pudding mix for 2 minutes. Let stand for 2 minutes or until soft-set. Spoon over cake batter; sprinkle with chocolate chips. Cover and cook on high for 3-4 hours or until a toothpick inserted in cake portion comes out with moist crumbs. Serve warm.

Jalapeno Spinach Dip

Everyone loves spinach dip, and my version is as easy as it is delicious. Just mix the ingredients together in the slow cooker for a savory and creamy appetizer.
—MICHAELA DEBELIUS
WADDELL, ARIZONA

PREP: 10 MIN. **COOK:** 2 HOURS
MAKES: 16 SERVINGS (¼ CUP EACH)

- 2 **packages (10 ounces each) frozen chopped spinach, thawed and squeezed dry**
- 2 **packages (8 ounces each) cream cheese, softened**
- 1 **cup grated Parmesan cheese**
- 1 **cup half-and-half cream**
- ½ **cup finely chopped onion**
- ¼ **cup chopped seeded jalapeno peppers**
- 2 **teaspoons Worcestershire sauce**
- 2 **teaspoons hot pepper sauce**
- 1 **teaspoon garlic powder**
- 1 **teaspoon dill weed**
  Tortilla chips

In a 1½-qt. slow cooker, combine the first 10 ingredients. Cover and cook on low for 2-3 hours or until heated through. Serve with chips.
NOTE *Wear disposable gloves when cutting hot peppers; the oils can burn skin. Avoid touching your face.*

For a slightly milder dip, substitute a small can of **chopped green chilies** for the jalapenos. Or stir in some finely chopped **red or yellow pepper** for a **sweet crunch.**

PARTY MEATBALLS

Tangy Barbecue Wings

When I took these savory chicken wings to work, they were gone before I even got a bite! Spicy ketchup, vinegar, molasses and honey create a tangy sauce that's lip-smacking good.
—**SHERRY PITZER** TROY, MISSOURI

PREP: 1½ HOURS **COOK:** 3 HOURS
MAKES: ABOUT 4 DOZEN

    5 pounds chicken wings
    2½ cups hot and spicy ketchup
    ⅔ cup white vinegar
    ½ cup plus 2 tablespoons honey
    ½ cup molasses
    1 teaspoon salt
    1 teaspoon Worcestershire sauce
    ½ teaspoon onion powder
    ½ teaspoon chili powder
    ½ to 1 teaspoon liquid smoke, optional

1. Cut chicken wings into three sections; discard wing tip sections. Place chicken wings in two greased 15-in. x 10-in. x 1-in. baking pans. Bake, uncovered, at 375° for 30 minutes; drain. Turn wings; bake 20-25 minutes longer or until juices run clear.
2. Meanwhile, in a large saucepan, combine the ketchup, vinegar, honey, molasses, salt, Worcestershire sauce, onion powder and chili powder. Add liquid smoke if desired. Bring to a boil. Reduce heat; simmer, uncovered, for 25-30 minutes.
3. Drain wings; place a third of them in a 5-qt. slow cooker. Top with about 1 cup sauce. Repeat layers twice. Cover and cook on low for 3-4 hours. Stir before serving.
NOTE *Uncooked chicken wing sections (wingettes) may be substituted for whole chicken wings.*

> **Meatballs are always great for parties. This is an easy twist on the usual recipe, and it's very fast to make.**
> —**DEBBIE PAULSEN** APOLLO BEACH, FLORIDA

Party Meatballs

PREP: 10 MIN. **COOK:** 3 HOURS
MAKES: ABOUT 5 DOZEN

    1 package (32 ounces) frozen fully
       cooked homestyle meatballs,
       thawed
    1 bottle (14 ounces) ketchup
    ¼ cup A.1. steak sauce
    1 tablespoon minced garlic
    1 teaspoon Dijon mustard

Place meatballs in a 3-qt. slow cooker. In a small bowl, combine the ketchup, steak sauce, garlic and mustard. Pour over meatballs. Cover and cook on low for 3-4 hours or until meatballs are heated through.

Crispy Snack Mix

This recipe proves that you can make just about anything in the slow cooker, even a delightfully crispy snack mix.

—JANE PAIR SIMS DE LEON, TEXAS

PREP: 10 MIN. **COOK:** 2½ HOURS
MAKES: ABOUT 2½ QUARTS

- 4½ cups crispy chow mein noodles
- 4 cups Rice Chex
- 1 can (9¾ ounces) salted cashews
- 1 cup flaked coconut, toasted
- ½ cup butter, melted
- 2 tablespoons reduced-sodium soy sauce
- 2¼ teaspoons curry powder
- ¾ teaspoon ground ginger

1. In a 5-qt. slow cooker, combine the noodles, cereal, cashews and coconut. In a small bowl, whisk the butter, soy sauce, curry powder and ginger; drizzle over cereal mixture and mix well.
2. Cover and cook on low for 2½ hours, stirring every 30 minutes. Serve warm or at room temperature.

Butterscotch Apple Crisp

Here's a cozy way to warm up winter nights. Apple crisp gets a sweet surprise with the addition of creamy butterscotch. Your house will smell marvelous as this dessert cooks!

—JOLANTHE ERB
HARRISONBURG, VIRGINIA

PREP: 10 MIN. **COOK:** 5 HOURS
MAKES: 6 SERVINGS

- 6 cups sliced peeled tart apples (about 5 large)
- ¾ cup packed brown sugar
- ½ cup all-purpose flour
- ½ cup quick-cooking oats
- 1 package (3½ ounces) cook-and-serve butterscotch pudding mix
- 1 teaspoon ground cinnamon
- ½ cup cold butter, cubed
  Vanilla ice cream, optional

1. Place apples in a 3-qt. slow cooker. In a large bowl, combine the brown sugar, flour, oats, pudding mix and cinnamon. Cut in butter until mixture resembles coarse crumbs. Sprinkle over apples.
2. Cover and cook on low for 5-6 hours or until apples are tender. Serve with ice cream if desired.

CRISPY SNACK MIX

This tempting and tangy appetizer pairs pineapple chunks with barbecue sauce and three kinds of sausage. It'll tide over even the biggest appetites until dinner.
—**REBEKAH RANDOLPH** GREER, SOUTH CAROLINA

BARBECUE SAUSAGE BITES

Barbecue Sausage Bites

PREP: 10 MIN. **COOK:** 2½ HOURS
MAKES: 12-14 SERVINGS

- 1 **package (16 ounces) miniature smoked sausages**
- ¾ **pound fully cooked bratwurst links, cut into ½-inch slices**
- ¾ **pound smoked kielbasa or Polish sausage, cut into ½-inch slices**
- 1 **bottle (18 ounces) barbecue sauce**
- ⅔ **cup orange marmalade**
- ½ **teaspoon ground mustard**
- ⅛ **teaspoon ground allspice**
- 1 **can (20 ounces) pineapple chunks, drained**

1. In a 3-qt. slow cooker, combine the sausages. In a small bowl, whisk the barbecue sauce, marmalade, mustard and allspice. Pour over sausage mixture; stir to coat.
2. Cover and cook on high for 2½ to 3 hours or until heated through. Stir in pineapple. Serve with toothpicks.

Hearty Broccoli Dip

You'll need just five ingredients to stir up my no-fuss appetizer. People often ask me to bring the creamy dip to potlucks and parties. I never leave with leftovers.
—SUE CALL BEECH GROVE, INDIANA

PREP: 15 MIN. **COOK:** 2 HOURS
MAKES: 5½ CUPS

- 1 **pound ground beef**
- 1 **pound process cheese (Velveeta), cubed**
- 1 **can (10¾ ounces) condensed cream of mushroom soup, undiluted**
- 3 **cups frozen chopped broccoli, thawed**
- 2 **tablespoons salsa**
  Tortilla chips

1. In a large skillet, cook beef over medium heat until no longer pink; drain. Transfer to a 3-qt. slow cooker. Add cheese, soup, broccoli and salsa; mix well.
2. Cover and cook on low for 2-3 hours or until heated through, stirring after 1 hour. Serve with chips.

WARM CHRISTMAS PUNCH

Warm Christmas Punch

Red-hot candies add rich color and spiciness to festive punch, and cranberry juice gives it a little tang.
—JULIE STERCHI JACKSON, MISSOURI

PREP: 5 MIN. **COOK:** 2 HOURS
MAKES: 8 SERVINGS (2 QUARTS)

- 1 **bottle (32 ounces) cranberry juice**
- 5 **cans (6 ounces each) unsweetened pineapple juice**
- ⅓ **cup red-hot candies**
- 1 **cinnamon stick (3½ inches)**
  Additional cinnamon sticks, optional

1. In a 3-qt. slow cooker, combine juices, red-hots and cinnamon stick. Cover and cook on low for 2-4 hours or until heated through and candies are dissolved.
2. Discard cinnamon stick before serving. Use additional cinnamon sticks as stirrers if desired.

Cocktail Franks

Don't want any leftovers from your party? Serve these tempting sausages in a sweet and savory sauce. I've never had even one piece go uneaten.

—JO ANN RENNER XENIA, OHIO

PREP: 15 MIN. **COOK:** 1 HOUR
MAKES: 16 SERVINGS

- 2 pounds smoked sausage links
- 1 bottle (8 ounces) Catalina salad dressing
- 1 bottle (8 ounces) Russian salad dressing
- ½ cup packed brown sugar
- ½ cup pineapple juice

1. Cut sausages diagonally into ½-in. slices; cook in a skillet over medium heat until lightly browned. Transfer sausages to a 3-qt. slow cooker; discard drippings.

2. Add dressings, brown sugar and juice to skillet; cook and stir over medium-low heat until sugar is dissolved. Pour over sausages. Cover and cook on low for 1-2 hours or until heated through.

NOTE *French salad dressing may be substituted for one or both dressings.*

Hot Spiced Cherry Cider

This heartwarming cider is great to have in the slow cooker after being out in the cold.

—MARLENE WICZEK

LITTLE FALLS, MINNESOTA

PREP: 5 MIN. **COOK:** 4 HOURS
MAKES: 4 QUARTS

- 1 gallon apple cider or juice
- 2 cinnamon sticks (3 inches)
- 2 packages (3 ounces each) cherry gelatin

Place cider in a 6-qt. slow cooker; add cinnamon sticks. Cover and cook on high for 3 hours. Stir in gelatin; cook 1 hour longer. Discard cinnamon sticks before serving.

BREAD PUDDING WITH BOURBON SAUCE

There's nothing I like better than this comforting bread pudding recipe on a cold, wintry day. The bourbon sauce makes the dessert taste special, but you wouldn't believe how easy it is to prepare—the slow cooker does the bulk of it!

—HOPE JOHNSON YOUNGWOOD, PENNSYLVANIA

Bread Pudding with Bourbon Sauce

PREP: 20 MIN. **COOK:** 3 HOURS
MAKES: 6 SERVINGS

- 3 eggs
- 1¼ cups 2% milk
- ½ cup sugar
- 3 teaspoons vanilla extract
- ½ teaspoon ground cinnamon
- ¼ teaspoon ground nutmeg
- ⅛ teaspoon salt
- 4½ cups cubed day-old brioche or egg bread
- 1¼ cups raisins

BOURBON SAUCE
- ¼ cup butter, cubed
- ½ cup sugar
- ¼ cup light corn syrup
- 3 tablespoons bourbon

1. In a large bowl, whisk the first seven ingredients; stir in bread and raisins. Transfer to a greased 4-qt. slow cooker. Cover and cook on low for 3 hours.

2. In a small saucepan, heat butter. Stir in sugar and corn syrup; bring to a boil. Reduce heat; cook and stir until sugar is dissolved. Remove from the heat; stir in bourbon. Serve warm with bread pudding.

Mulled Merlot

Our delightful recipe is sure to warm up your holiday guests! Keeping it ready to serve in the slow cooker means that you can enjoy the party.

—TASTE OF HOME TEST KITCHEN

PREP: 10 MIN. **COOK:** 1 HOUR
MAKES: 9 SERVINGS

- 4 cinnamon sticks (3 inches)
- 4 whole cloves
- 2 bottles (750 milliliters each) merlot
- ½ cup sugar
- ½ cup orange juice
- ½ cup brandy
- 1 medium orange, thinly sliced

1. Place cinnamon sticks and cloves on a double thickness of cheesecloth; bring up corners of cloth and tie with string to form a bag.
2. In a 3-qt. slow cooker, combine the wine, sugar, orange juice, brandy and orange slices. Add spice bag. Cover and cook on high for 1 hour or until heated through. Discard spice bag and orange slices. Serve warm.

Viennese Coffee

This isn't your regular cup of joe! I dress it up with chocolate, whipped cream and more, making it a drink to savor.

—SHARON DELANEY-CHRONIS
SOUTH MILWAUKEE, WISCONSIN

PREP: 10 MIN. **COOK:** 3 HOURS
MAKES: 4 SERVINGS

- 3 cups strong brewed coffee
- 3 tablespoons chocolate syrup
- 1 teaspoon sugar
- ⅓ cup heavy whipping cream
- ¼ cup creme de cacao or Irish cream liqueur
  Whipped cream and chocolate curls, optional

1. In a 1½-qt. slow cooker, combine the coffee, chocolate syrup and sugar. Cover and cook on low for 2½ hours.
2. Stir in heavy cream and creme de cacao. Cover and cook 30 minutes longer or until heated through.
3. Ladle coffee into mugs. Garnish with whipped cream and chocolate curls if desired.

Elvis' Pudding Cake

I love the flavors of peanut butter and banana together, and this slow-cooker pudding cake is just like eating an Elvis sandwich...only sweeter! Banana chips add a surprisingly crunchy texture—find them near the dried fruit in your local grocery store.

—LISA RENSHAW KANSAS CITY, MISSOURI

PREP: 10 MIN. **COOK:** 3 HOURS +
STANDING **MAKES:** 12 SERVINGS

- 3 cups cold 2% milk
- 1 package (3.4 ounces) instant banana cream pudding mix
- 1 package banana cake mix (regular size)
- ½ cup creamy peanut butter
- 2 cups peanut butter chips
- 1 cup chopped dried banana chips

1. In a small bowl, whisk milk and pudding mix for 2 minutes. Let stand for 2 minutes or until soft-set. Transfer to a greased 5-qt. slow cooker.
2. Prepare cake mix batter according to package directions, adding peanut butter before mixing. Pour over pudding. Cover and cook on low for 3 to 3½ hours or until a toothpick inserted near the center comes out with moist crumbs.
3. Sprinkle with peanut butter chips; cover and let stand for 15-20 minutes or until partially melted. Top with banana chips.

ELVIS' PUDDING CAKE

EAT SMART Chili Cheese Dip

After trying to create a Mexican soup, I ended up with this outstanding dip that eats like a meal. My husband and two young children love it! Now it's popular for football game days or family gatherings.

—**SANDRA FICK** LINCOLN, NEBRASKA

PREP: 20 MIN. **COOK:** 4½ HOURS
MAKES: 8 CUPS

- 1 **pound lean ground beef (90% lean)**
- 1 **cup chopped onion**
- 1 **can (16 ounces) kidney beans, rinsed and drained**
- 1 **can (15 ounces) black beans, rinsed and drained**
- 1 **can (14½ ounces) diced tomatoes in sauce**
- 1 **cup frozen corn**
- ¾ **cup water**
- 1 **can (2¼ ounces) sliced ripe olives, drained**
- 3 **teaspoons chili powder**
- ½ **teaspoon dried oregano**
- ½ **teaspoon chipotle hot pepper sauce**
- ¼ **teaspoon garlic powder**
- ¼ **teaspoon ground cumin**
- 1 **package (16 ounces) reduced-fat process cheese (Velveeta), cubed**
  Corn chips

1. In a large skillet, cook beef and onion over medium heat until no longer pink; drain. Transfer to a 5-qt. slow cooker. Stir in the beans, tomatoes, corn, water, olives, chili powder, oregano, pepper sauce, garlic powder and cumin.

2. Cover and cook on low for 4-5 hours or until heated through; stir in cheese. Cover and cook for 30 minutes or until cheese is melted. Serve with corn chips.

PER (¼-CUP) SERVING *87 cal., 3 g fat (1 g sat. fat), 12 mg chol., 330 mg sodium, 9 g carb., 2 g fiber, 7 g pro.* **Diabetic Exchanges:** *1 lean meat, ½ starch.*

EAT SMART Italian Appetizer Meatballs

Store-bought spaghetti sauce speeds up the preparation of tender homemade meatballs. Leftovers make terrific sub sandwiches.

—**RENE MCCRORY**
INDIANAPOLIS, INDIANA

PREP: 40 MIN. **COOK:** 2 HOURS
MAKES: 4 DOZEN

- 2 **eggs, lightly beaten**
- ½ **cup dry bread crumbs**
- ¼ **cup 2% milk**
- 2 **teaspoons grated Parmesan cheese**
- 1 **teaspoon salt**
- ¼ **teaspoon pepper**
- ⅛ **teaspoon garlic powder**
- 1 **pound ground beef**
- 1 **pound bulk Italian sausage**
- 2 **jars (24 ounces each) spaghetti sauce**

1. In a large bowl, combine the first seven ingredients. Crumble beef and sausage over mixture and mix well. Shape into 1-in. balls.

2. Place meatballs on a greased rack in a shallow baking pan. Bake at 400° for 15-20 minutes or until no longer pink.

3. Transfer meatballs to a 4-qt. slow cooker; add spaghetti sauce. Cover and cook on high for 2-3 hours or until heated through.

PER SERVING *67 cal., 4 g fat (1 g sat. fat), 20 mg chol., 264 mg sodium, 4 g carb., 1 g fiber, 4 g pro.* **Diabetic Exchanges:** *1 lean meat, ½ fat.*

You can **prepare meatballs in bulk** to save time. **Bake several batches,** then freeze until needed. Thaw in the refrigerator and **you'll be ready to go.**

CHILI CHEESE DIP

CHERRY & SPICE RICE PUDDING

Pumpkin Pie Pudding

My husband loves anything pumpkin, and this creamy, comforting dessert is one of his favorites. Although we make the super-easy pudding all year long, it's especially lovely in the fall.
—ANDREA SCHAAK
BLOOMINGTON, MINNESOTA

PREP: 10 MIN. **COOK:** 6 HOURS
MAKES: 6 SERVINGS

- 1 **can (15 ounces) solid-pack pumpkin**
- 1 **can (12 ounces) evaporated milk**
- ¾ **cup sugar**
- ½ **cup biscuit/baking mix**
- 2 **eggs, beaten**
- 2 **tablespoons butter, melted**
- 2½ **teaspoons pumpkin pie spice**
- 2 **teaspoons vanilla extract**
  Whipped topping, optional

1. In a large bowl, combine the first eight ingredients. Transfer mixture to a 3-qt. slow cooker coated with cooking spray.
2. Cover and cook on low for 6-7 hours or until a thermometer reads 160°. Serve in bowls with whipped topping if desired.

Slow-Cooked Reuben Spread

I love Reuben anything, and this appetizer is a favorite. It's a warm and yummy crowd-pleaser, perfect for rallying your game-day crowd!
—JUNE HERKE WATERTOWN, SOUTH DAKOTA

PREP: 10 MIN. **COOK:** 4 HOURS
MAKES: 3¾ CUPS

- 2 **packages (8 ounces each) cream cheese, cubed**
- 4 **cups (16 ounces) shredded Swiss cheese**
- 1 **can (14 ounces) sauerkraut, rinsed and well drained**
- 4 **packages (2 ounces each) thinly sliced deli corned beef, chopped**
- ½ **cup Thousand Island salad dressing**
  Snack rye bread

In a 1½-qt. slow cooker, combine the first five ingredients. Cover and cook on low for 4 hours; stir to blend. Serve with snack rye bread.

EAT SMART Cherry & Spice Rice Pudding

I live in Traverse City, the Cherry Capital of the World, and what better way to celebrate our wonderful orchards than by using plump dried cherries in my favorite desserts? Slow-cooked rice pudding is always rich and wonderful.
—DEB PERRY TRAVERSE CITY, MICHIGAN

PREP: 10 MIN. **COOK:** 2 HOURS
MAKES: 12 SERVINGS

- 4 **cups cooked long grain rice**
- 1 **can (12 ounces) evaporated milk**
- 1 **cup 2% milk**
- ⅓ **cup sugar**
- ¼ **cup water**
- ¾ **cup dried cherries**
- 3 **tablespoons butter, softened**
- 2 **teaspoons vanilla extract**
- ½ **teaspoon ground cinnamon**
- ¼ **teaspoon ground nutmeg**

1. In a large bowl, combine the rice, evaporated milk, milk, sugar and water. Stir in the remaining ingredients. Transfer to a 3-qt. slow cooker coated with cooking spray.
2. Cover and cook on low for 2-3 hours or until thickened. Stir lightly before serving. Serve warm or cold. Refrigerate leftovers.
PER SERVING *193 cal., 5 g fat (4 g sat. fat), 19 mg chol., 61 mg sodium, 31 g carb., trace fiber, 4 g pro.*
Diabetic Exchanges: *2 starch, 1 fat.*

HOT WING DIP

> Since I usually have the ingredients on hand, this is a great go-to recipe that I serve often.
>
> —COLEEN CORNER GROVE CITY, PENNSYLVANIA

Hot Wing Dip

PREP: 10 MIN. **COOK:** 1 HOUR
MAKES: 4½ CUPS

- 2 **cups shredded cooked chicken**
- 1 **package (8 ounces) cream cheese, cubed**
- 2 **cups (8 ounces) shredded cheddar cheese**
- 1 **cup ranch salad dressing**
- ½ **cup Louisiana-style hot sauce**
  Tortilla chips and/or celery sticks
  Minced fresh parsley, optional

In a 3-qt. slow cooker, combine the chicken, cream cheese, cheddar cheese, salad dressing and hot sauce. Cover and cook on low for 1-2 hours or until cheese is melted. Serve with chips and/or celery. Sprinkle with parsley if desired.

Butterscotch Dip

If you like the sweetness of butterscotch chips, you'll enjoy my warm rum-flavored fruit dip. I serve it with apple and pear wedges. It holds nicely for up to 2 hours in the slow cooker.

—JEAUNE HADL VAN METER
LEXINGTON, KENTUCKY

PREP: 5 MIN. **COOK:** 45 MIN.
MAKES: ABOUT 3 CUPS

- 2 **packages (10 to 11 ounces each) butterscotch chips**
- ⅔ **cup evaporated milk**
- ⅔ **cup chopped pecans**
- 1 **tablespoon rum extract**
  Apple and pear wedges

In a 1½-qt. slow cooker, combine butterscotch chips and milk. Cover and cook on low for 45-50 minutes or until chips are softened; stir until smooth. Stir in pecans and extract. Serve warm with fruit.

Chocolate Peanut Drops

PREP: 20 MIN. **COOK:** 1½ HOURS + STANDING
MAKES: ABOUT 11 DOZEN

- 4 **ounces German sweet chocolate, chopped**
- 1 **package (12 ounces) semisweet chocolate chips**
- 4 **packages (10 to 12 ounces each) white baking chips**
- 2 **jars (16 ounces each) lightly salted dry roasted peanuts**

1. In a 6-qt. slow cooker, layer ingredients in order listed (do not stir). Cover and cook on low for 1½ hours. Stir to combine. (If chocolate is not melted, cover and cook 15 minutes longer; stir. Repeat in 15-minute increments until chocolate is melted.)

2. Drop mixture by rounded tablespoonfuls onto waxed paper. Let stand until set. Store in an airtight container at room temperature.

CHOCOLATE PEANUT BARK *Cook chocolate mixture as directed; spread into two 15-in. x 10-in. x 1-in. waxed paper-lined baking pans. Refrigerate 30 minutes or until firm. Cut into bite-sized pieces.*

When **serving appetizers instead of a meal,** offer your guests a variety of hearty and lighter choices. Count on **8 to 9 servings per guest,** or more for a longer event.

CHOCOLATE PEANUT DROPS

BROCCOLI SHRIMP ALFREDO, PAGE 151

> **"**After tasting fettuccine Alfredo at a restaurant, I tried to duplicate the recipe at home. You can't imagine how pleased I was when I came up with this delicious version. Not only does my family love the creamy dish, but my husband prefers it to the one at the restaurant.**"**

—**RAE NATOLI** KINGSTON, NEW YORK
about her recipe, Broccoli Shrimp Alfredo, on page 151

Stovetop Suppers

Beef & Ground Beef

107   101   104

From **pot roast and sloppy joes** to **stir-fries and tacos**, there's no shortage of **convenient one-dish beef meals** that are ready in an instant on your stovetop. What will you **whip up** tonight?

Tortellini Beef Salad

My original pasta salad recipe is loaded with flavors that family and friends love to eat. I usually serve it warm for dinner and chilled for potlucks.

—KELLY SCHMITZ MAPES
FORT COLLINS, COLORADO

PREP/TOTAL TIME: 30 MIN.
MAKES: 6 SERVINGS

- 1 **pound ground beef**
- 1 **envelope Italian salad dressing mix**
- ¼ **cup water**
- 1 **package (19 ounces) frozen cheese tortellini, cooked and drained**
- 3 **to 4 plum tomatoes, chopped**
- 1 **medium zucchini, chopped**
- 1 **cup (4 ounces) shredded mozzarella cheese**
- 2 **tablespoons olive oil**
- 2 **tablespoons red wine vinegar**

1. In a large skillet, cook beef over medium heat until no longer pink; drain. Add salad dressing mix and water. Bring to a boil. Reduce heat; simmer, uncovered, for 3 minutes.
2. In a large bowl, combine the tortellini, tomatoes, zucchini, cheese and beef mixture. Combine oil and vinegar; pour over salad and toss to coat. Chill if desired.

The **tortellini salad** is a great way to use up an **abundance of garden tomatoes** and zucchini. You could **double up on the veggies** if desired; just make a little more dressing so the salad is still well-coated.

This stovetop favorite is tasty and filling. It's easy to prepare, even after a long day at work.
—CARMEN EDWARDS MIDLAND, TEXAS

EAT SMART Beef Macaroni Skillet

PREP: 15 MIN. **COOK:** 30 MIN.
MAKES: 2 SERVINGS

- ½ **pound lean ground beef (90% lean)**
- ⅓ **cup chopped onion**
- ¼ **cup chopped green pepper**
- 1½ **cups spicy hot V8 juice**
- ½ **cup uncooked elbow macaroni**
- 1 **teaspoon Worcestershire sauce**
- ¼ **teaspoon pepper**

In a large skillet, cook the beef, onion and green pepper over medium heat until meat is no longer pink; drain. Stir in the remaining ingredients. Bring to a boil. Reduce heat; cover and simmer for 18-20 minutes or until macaroni is tender.
PER SERVING *291 cal., 9 g fat (4 g sat. fat), 56 mg chol., 689 mg sodium, 25 g carb., 2 g fiber, 26 g pro.* **Diabetic Exchanges:** *3 lean meat, 2 vegetable, 1 starch.*

Here's a traditional main dish that's tried and true. It's been a favorite in my family for many years. —VERA BURKE WEST PITTSTON, PENNSYLVANIA

YANKEE POT ROAST

Yankee Pot Roast

PREP: 20 MIN. **COOK:** 2½ HOURS
MAKES: 12-14 SERVINGS

- 1 boneless beef chuck roast (4 to 5 pounds)
- 1 tablespoon canola oil
- 2 large onions, coarsely chopped
- 2 cups sliced carrots
- 2 celery ribs, sliced
- 2 cans (14½ ounces each) Italian stewed tomatoes
- 1¾ cups water
- 1 teaspoon salt
- ½ teaspoon dried thyme
- ¼ teaspoon pepper
- 4 medium potatoes, peeled and cut into eighths

1. In a Dutch oven, brown roast on all sides over medium-high heat in oil. Remove roast and set aside.
2. Add the onions, carrots, celery, tomatoes, water, salt, thyme and pepper to the pan. Bring to a boil. Return roast to pan. Reduce heat; cover and simmer for 2 hours.
3. Add potatoes. Cover; cook 30-40 minutes longer or until meat and vegetables are tender.

Roast Beef Pasta Skillet

Leftover beef is the star in a skillet dinner that's perfect for two. Chopped tomato adds a burst of fresh flavor.
—BILL HILBRICH ST. CLOUD, MINNESOTA

PREP/TOTAL TIME: 20 MIN.
MAKES: 2 SERVINGS

- 1 cup uncooked spiral pasta
- ½ cup chopped onion
- 1 teaspoon olive oil
- 1 teaspoon butter
- 1 cup cubed cooked roast beef
- 1 teaspoon pepper
- ½ cup chopped tomato
- ½ cup grated Parmesan cheese

Cook pasta according to package directions. Meanwhile, in a large skillet, saute onion in oil and butter until tender. Add roast beef and pepper; heat through. Drain pasta; add to beef mixture. Stir in tomato and cheese.

ASIAN BEEF NOODLES

> We've raised beef for most of our lives, so I like to try new dishes that feature it. This simple recipe is absolutely delicious. **—MARGERY BRYAN** MOSES LAKE, WASHINGTON

Asian Beef Noodles

PREP/TOTAL TIME: 30 MIN.
MAKES: 4 SERVINGS

- 1 package (3 ounces) beef-flavored ramen noodles
- 1 pound beef top sirloin steak
- 1 jalapeno pepper, seeded and finely chopped
- 1 tablespoon canola oil
- 2 tablespoons water
- 1 tablespoon steak sauce
- 1 medium carrot, shredded
- 2 tablespoons sliced green onion
- ¼ cup salted peanuts

1. Set aside seasoning packet from noodles. Prepare noodles according to package directions; drain and set aside.

2. Cut steak into thin strips. In a large skillet, stir-fry the beef and jalapeno in oil for 1-2 minutes or until meat is no longer pink. Remove and keep warm.
3. In the same skillet, combine the noodles, water, steak sauce, carrot, onion and contents of seasoning packet. Cook and stir until heated through. Return beef to the pan. Sprinkle with peanuts. Serve immediately.
NOTE *Wear disposable gloves when cutting hot peppers; the oils can burn skin. Avoid touching your face.*

Red River Beef Stroganoff

Years ago, I spent several weeks at a beautiful mountain lodge in Red River, New Mexico. When we arrived, the aroma of this dish greeted us. It was delicious, so I asked for the recipe. It quickly became a family favorite.

—MARY ALICE COX
CLINTON, TENNESSEE

PREP/TOTAL TIME: 25 MIN.
MAKES: 8 SERVINGS

- ¼ cup all-purpose flour
- 2 pounds beef top sirloin steak, cut into thin strips
- ½ cup butter, divided
- 2 large onions, chopped
- 1 can (10½ ounces) beef broth
- 1 jar (4½ ounces) sliced mushrooms, drained
- 1 tablespoon Worcestershire sauce
- 1 teaspoon dried basil
  Salt and pepper to taste
- 1 cup (8 ounces) sour cream
  Cooked rice or noodles

1. Place flour in a shallow bowl. Dip beef in flour to coat. In a large skillet, brown beef in ¼ cup butter in batches. Remove from pan and set aside.

2. In the same skillet, saute onions in remaining butter until crisp-tender. Return beef to pan. Add the broth, mushrooms, Worcestershire sauce, basil, salt and pepper. Cook and stir until mixture is thickened, about 5 minutes.

3. Just before serving, stir in sour cream; heat through (do not boil). Serve with rice.

Short Ribs With Dumplings

I've heard that these tender ribs and cornmeal dumplings were typical chuck-wagon fare for cowboys on the trail. I like making them for my husband and me on cold, rainy days. Our house smells so inviting when these ribs are simmering.

—EVELYN HYND GRAVETTE, ARKANSAS

PREP: 40 MIN. **COOK:** 1¾ HOURS
MAKES: 6-8 SERVINGS

- 3 pounds boneless beef short ribs
- 2 tablespoons canola oil
- 1 medium onion, cut into wedges
- 1 garlic clove, minced
- 1 can (28 ounces) diced tomatoes, undrained
- 1 cup beef broth, divided
- 2 tablespoons soy sauce
- 1 tablespoon sugar
- ½ teaspoon salt
- ¼ teaspoon pepper
- ¼ teaspoon crushed red pepper flakes
- ⅛ teaspoon ground nutmeg
- 2 to 3 tablespoons cornstarch

CORNMEAL DUMPLINGS
- ¾ cup water
- ½ cup cornmeal
- ½ teaspoon salt
- 1 egg, beaten
- ½ cup all-purpose flour
- 1 teaspoon baking powder
  Dash pepper
- 1 can (7 ounces) whole kernel corn, drained

1. Cut ribs into 1-in. pieces. In a Dutch oven over medium heat, brown beef in oil on all sides. Add onion and garlic; cook until onion is tender, stirring occasionally. Stir in tomatoes, ½ cup broth, soy sauce and seasonings; bring to a boil. Reduce heat; cover and simmer for 1½ to 2 hours or until meat is tender.

2. Combine cornstarch and remaining broth until smooth; stir into beef mixture. Bring mixture to a boil; cook and stir for 2 minutes or until thickened.

3. For dumplings, combine the water, cornmeal and salt in a saucepan; bring to a boil. Cook and stir for 1-2 minutes or until thickened; remove from the heat. Stir a small amount into egg; return all to pan, stirring constantly. Combine flour, baking powder and pepper; stir into cornmeal mixture. Stir in corn.

4. Drop by rounded tablespoonfuls into simmering stew. Cover and simmer for 10-12 minutes (do not lift lid) or until a toothpick inserted in a dumpling comes out clean.

SHORT RIBS WITH DUMPLINGS

Chili-ghetti

I came up with this recipe when unexpected guests stopped by and I didn't have enough chili. The spur-of-the-moment main dish is now a favorite in our house.

—CINDY CUYKENDALL
SKANEATELES, NEW YORK

PREP/TOTAL TIME: 30 MIN.
MAKES: 5 SERVINGS

- 1 package (7 ounces) spaghetti
- 1 pound ground beef
- 1 small onion, chopped
- 1 can (16 ounces) kidney beans, rinsed and drained
- 1 can (14½ ounces) diced tomatoes, undrained
- 1 can (4 ounces) mushroom stems and pieces, drained
- ⅓ cup water
- 1 envelope chili seasoning
- 2 tablespoons grated Parmesan cheese
- ¼ cup shredded part-skim mozzarella cheese

1. Cook spaghetti according to package directions. Meanwhile, in a large skillet, cook beef and onion over medium heat until meat is no longer pink; drain.

2. Drain spaghetti; add to beef mixture. Stir in the beans, tomatoes, mushrooms, water, chili seasoning and Parmesan cheese. Cover and simmer for 10 minutes. Sprinkle with mozzarella cheese.

ALL-AMERICAN BEEF STEW

My mother was born and raised in Japan and wasn't familiar with many American dishes when she married my father and moved to the States. My paternal grandmother gave her this mouthwatering recipe. **—FRANCES ALDAL** ANTELOPE, CALIFORNIA

EAT SMART All-American Beef Stew

PREP: 40 MIN. **COOK:** 1¾ HOURS
MAKES: 8 SERVINGS (2½ QUARTS)

- ¾ cup all-purpose flour, divided
- ½ teaspoon seasoned salt
- ½ teaspoon pepper, divided
- 2 pounds beef stew meat, cut into 1-inch cubes
- 1 tablespoon olive oil
- 4½ cups water, divided
- 1 large onion, halved and sliced
- 2 tablespoons Worcestershire sauce
- 1 tablespoon lemon juice
- 2 garlic cloves, minced
- 1 teaspoon sugar
- ½ teaspoon salt
- ½ teaspoon paprika
- ⅛ teaspoon ground allspice
- 1 bay leaf
- 4 medium potatoes, cubed
- 6 medium carrots, sliced

1. Place ½ cup flour, seasoned salt and ¼ teaspoon pepper in a large resealable plastic bag. Add beef, a few pieces at a time, and shake to coat.

2. In a Dutch oven, brown meat in oil in batches. Remove and set aside. Add 4 cups water to the pan, stirring to loosen browned bits. Add the onion, Worcestershire sauce, lemon juice, garlic, sugar, salt, paprika, allspice, bay leaf and remaining pepper. Return beef to the pan. Bring to a boil. Reduce heat; cover and simmer for 1 hour.

3. Stir in potatoes and carrots. Bring to a boil. Reduce heat; cover and simmer for 30-35 minutes or until meat and vegetables are tender.

4. Combine remaining flour and water until smooth; stir into the pan. Bring to a boil; cook and stir for 2 minutes or until thickened. Discard bay leaf.

PER SERVING *324 cal., 10 g fat (3 g sat. fat), 70 mg chol., 322 mg sodium, 33 g carb., 4 g fiber, 25 g pro.* **Diabetic Exchanges:** *3 lean meat, 2 starch, 1 vegetable.*

SLOPPY JOES

Everybody in the family will love the zesty flavor of this yummy comfort food. Try it spooned over warmed corn bread if you don't have buns.
—**KAREN ANDERSON** CUYAHOGA FALLS, OHIO

Sloppy Joes

PREP/TOTAL TIME: 30 MIN.
MAKES: 6 SERVINGS

- 1½ pounds ground beef
- 1 can (10 ounces) diced tomatoes and green chilies, undrained
- 1 can (6 ounces) tomato paste
- ¼ cup ketchup
- 2 tablespoons brown sugar
- 1 tablespoon spicy brown mustard
- ¼ teaspoon salt
- 6 sandwich buns, split

In a large skillet, cook beef over medium heat until no longer pink; drain. Stir in the tomatoes, tomato paste, ketchup, brown sugar, mustard and salt. Bring to a boil. Reduce heat; simmer, uncovered, for 5 minutes. Serve on buns.

Tomatoes, brown sugar and a hint of spicy brown mustard give **sloppy joes** a **classic flavor combination** that's both sweet and tangy. If you like, try topping each sandwich with **dill pickles and cheddar cheese.**

Sombrero Pasta Salad

I take this slightly spicy salad to almost every party or picnic I attend. Every time, I come home with lots of compliments, but never any leftovers!
—**PATTY EHLEN**
BURLINGTON, WISCONSIN

PREP: 30 MIN. + CHILLING
MAKES: 10 SERVINGS

- 1 package (16 ounces) spiral pasta
- 1 pound ground beef
- ¾ cup water
- 1 envelope taco seasoning
- 2 cups (8 ounces) shredded cheddar cheese
- 1 large green pepper, chopped
- 1 medium onion, chopped
- 1 medium tomato, chopped
- 2 cans (2¼ ounces each) sliced ripe olives, drained
- 1 bottle (16 ounces) Catalina or Western salad dressing

1. Cook pasta according to package directions. Meanwhile, in a skillet, cook beef over medium heat until no longer pink; drain. Add water and taco seasoning; simmer, uncovered, for 15 minutes.
2. Rinse pasta in cold water and drain; place in a large bowl. Add beef mixture, cheese, green pepper, onion, tomato and olives; mix well. Add the dressing and toss to coat.
3. Cover and refrigerate for at least 1 hour.
NOTE *If you'll be refrigerating Sombrero Pasta Salad for more than 1 hour, reserve ½ cup dressing to stir into the salad just before serving.*

Dinner's in the Bag

I get a head start on this family-pleasing dinner by assembling a "pantry kit." I measure dry macaroni and the spice mixture into separate plastic bags, then store them in a paper bag with canned tomatoes.

—**DARLENE BRENDEN** SALEM, OREGON

PREP: 5 MIN. **COOK:** 25 MIN.
MAKES: 4 SERVINGS

- 1 **pound ground beef**
- 2 **cans (14½ ounces each) stewed tomatoes**
- ¼ **cup dried minced onion**
- 1 **teaspoon salt**
- 1 **teaspoon chili powder**
- ¼ to ½ **teaspoon pepper**
- ¼ **teaspoon sugar**
- 1 **cup uncooked elbow macaroni**

1. In a large skillet, cook beef over medium heat until no longer pink; drain. Add the tomatoes, seasonings and sugar; bring to a boil. Reduce heat and simmer for 5 minutes. Stir in macaroni; cover and simmer for 15 minutes. Uncover; simmer until macaroni is tender and sauce is thickened.

Classic Cashew Beef

My family loves stir-fries, and I love them even more because they are healthy and easy to prepare. I've been making this recipe for years.

—**SHERRI MELOTIK**
OAK CREEK, WISCONSIN

PREP/TOTAL TIME: 30 MIN.
MAKES: 4 SERVINGS

- 4 **teaspoons cornstarch**
- 4 **teaspoons soy sauce**
- 1 **teaspoon sesame oil**
- 1 **teaspoon oyster sauce**
- ¼ **teaspoon ground ginger**
- **Dash cayenne pepper**
- ½ **cup cold water**
- 1 **pound beef top sirloin steak, cut into ½-inch pieces**
- 2 **tablespoons canola oil, divided**
- 8 **green onions, cut into 1-inch lengths**
- ⅔ **cup lightly salted cashews**
- 2 **garlic cloves, minced**
  Hot cooked rice

1. In a bowl, combine the first seven ingredients until smooth; set aside.
2. In a large skillet or wok, stir-fry beef in 1 tablespoon oil until no longer pink. Remove and keep warm. Stir-fry onions, cashews and garlic in remaining oil for 1 minute.
3. Stir cornstarch mixture and add to the pan. Bring to a boil; cook and stir for 2 minutes or until thickened. Add beef; heat through. Serve with rice.

My husband loves my simple stovetop lasagna. It's easy and is loaded with beef and cheeses. It makes a super supper...in one dish! —**LUCINDA WALKER** SOMERSET, PENNSYLVANIA

SKILLET LASAGNA

Skillet Lasagna

PREP: 25 MIN. **COOK:** 40 MIN. + STANDING
MAKES: 6-8 SERVINGS

- 1½ pounds lean ground beef (90% lean)
- 1 small onion, chopped
- 1 medium green pepper, chopped
- 1 jar (24 ounces) spaghetti sauce with mushrooms
- 1 teaspoon dried oregano
- 1 teaspoon dried basil
- 6 lasagna noodles, cooked and rinsed
- 3 cups (12 ounces) shredded mozzarella cheese
- ½ cup grated Parmesan cheese

1. In a Dutch oven, brown beef, onion and pepper; drain if necessary. Stir in spaghetti sauce, oregano and basil. Simmer, uncovered, for 10-15 minutes.
2. In a 10-in. skillet, spread ¼ cup of the meat sauce. Top with three noodles, cutting to fit as needed. Layer with half of the remaining sauce and half of the mozzarella and Parmesan cheeses. Top with remaining noodles, meat sauce and Parmesan.
3. Cover and heat on medium for 3 minutes. Reduce heat to low; cook for 35 minutes. Sprinkle with remaining mozzarella and let stand for 10 minutes with cover ajar.

To **boost the flavor** of the lasagna, substitute two turkey or pork Italian sausage links for ½ pound of the ground beef.

HEARTY MAC & CHEESE

> Whether a cold winter night or rainy summer day, this is quick and easy comfort food at its very best!
> —CAROL WOHLGEMUTH RIDING MOUNTAIN, MANITOBA

Hearty Mac & Cheese

PREP: 15 MIN. **COOK:** 25 MIN.
MAKES: 6 SERVINGS

- 1 package (7¼ ounces) macaroni and cheese dinner mix
- 1 pound ground beef
- 3 tablespoons chopped onion
- 2 tablespoons chopped green pepper
- 1 can (10¾ ounces) condensed tomato soup, undiluted
- 2 tablespoons water
- 2 tablespoons ketchup
- 2 teaspoons prepared mustard
- 1 teaspoon seasoned salt
- 1 teaspoon chili powder
- ½ teaspoon dried oregano
- ¼ teaspoon ground cumin
- ¼ teaspoon pepper
- 1 cup frozen corn, thawed
- 1 cup (4 ounces) shredded cheddar cheese
- ¼ cup butter, cubed
- ¼ cup 2% milk

1. Cook macaroni according to package directions; set cheese packet aside. Meanwhile, in a large skillet, cook the beef, onion and green pepper over medium heat until meat is no longer pink and vegetables are tender; drain.
2. Add the soup, water, ketchup, mustard and seasonings. Bring to a boil. Reduce heat; simmer, uncovered, for 4 minutes.
3. Drain macaroni; add to beef mixture. Add the corn, cheese, contents of reserved cheese packet, butter and milk. Cook and stir until cheese and butter are melted.

SOUP-BOWL CABBAGE ROLLS

> This fabulous alternative to traditional stuffed cabbage rolls is simple to prepare, so it's perfect for busy weeknights. It's nutritious and filling.
>
> **—TERRI PEARCE** HOUSTON, TEXAS

Soup-Bowl Cabbage Rolls

PREP: 15 MIN. **COOK:** 35 MIN.
MAKES: 4 SERVINGS

- 1 **pound lean ground beef (90% lean)**
- 1 **garlic clove, minced**
- 1 **small head cabbage, chopped**
- 2½ **cups water**
- ⅔ **cup uncooked long grain rice**
- 1 **tablespoon Worcestershire sauce**
- 1 **teaspoon onion powder**
- 1 **teaspoon dried basil**
- ¼ **teaspoon cayenne pepper**
- ¼ **teaspoon pepper**
- 1 **can (28 ounces) crushed tomatoes**
- ½ **teaspoon salt**
  Grated Parmesan cheese, optional

1. In a nonstick Dutch oven, cook beef and garlic over medium heat until meat is no longer pink; drain. Stir in the cabbage, water, rice, Worcestershire sauce, onion powder, basil, cayenne and pepper; bring to a boil. Reduce heat; cover and simmer for 25-30 minutes or until rice is tender.
2. Stir in tomatoes and salt; heat through. Sprinkle with cheese if desired.

Crispy Fried Tacos

My mother has been making these for as long as I can remember. Frying the tacos makes them extra crispy and delicious. Our five grown sons request these whenever they visit.

—CATHERINE GIBBS
GAMBRILLS, MARYLAND

PREP: 10 MIN. **COOK:** 25 MIN.
MAKES: 12 TACOS

SALSA
- 1 **can (28 ounces) diced tomatoes, undrained**
- 1 **can (8 ounces) tomato sauce**
- 1 **can (4 ounces) sliced jalapeno peppers**
- 1 **small onion, quartered**
- 1 **teaspoon garlic salt**

TACOS
- 1 **pound ground beef**
- ½ **teaspoon salt**
- 12 **corn tortillas (6 inches)**
- ½ **cup canola oil**
- 1 **cup (4 ounces) shredded cheddar cheese**
- 4 **cups shredded lettuce**

1. In a blender, combine the salsa ingredients; cover and pulse until salsa reaches desired consistency. Transfer to a large bowl; cover and refrigerate.
2. In a large skillet, cook beef over medium heat until no longer pink; drain. Sprinkle with salt. Meanwhile, in another large skillet, fry tortillas in oil in batches just until crisp; drain on paper towels.
3. Fill tortillas with beef; sprinkle with cheese. Fold in half. Serve with lettuce and salsa.
NOTE *Wear disposable gloves when cutting hot peppers; the oils can burn skin. Avoid touching your face.*

Spaghetti Bolognese

Travel to Italy with this hearty pasta that's a breeze to prepare. We jazzed up store-bought spaghetti sauce, infusing it with fresh-from-the-garden flavor. You'll swear it's homemade!

—TASTE OF HOME TEST KITCHEN

PREP: 20 MIN. **COOK:** 20 MIN.
MAKES: 2 SERVINGS

- ½ **pound lean ground beef (90% lean)**
- 1 **medium carrot, shredded**
- 1 **celery rib, thinly sliced**
- ¼ **cup chopped onion**
- 1 **garlic clove, minced**
- 1 **jar (14 ounces) spaghetti sauce**
- ½ **teaspoon Italian seasoning**
- 1 **tablespoon heavy whipping cream or milk**
- 1 **tablespoon minced fresh parsley**
- 4 **ounces uncooked spaghetti**

1. In a large skillet, cook the beef, carrot, celery, onion and garlic over medium heat until meat is no longer pink. Stir in spaghetti sauce and Italian seasoning; bring to a boil. Stir in cream and parsley. Reduce heat; simmer, uncovered, for 10 minutes.
2. Meanwhile, cook spaghetti according to package directions; drain. Add to sauce and toss. Cook for 1-2 minutes or until heated through. Serve immediately.

Indiana Swiss Steak

I won first place in the Indiana State Beef Contest with this recipe. A mixture of picante sauce, ketchup, cider vinegar and veggies enhances the tender slow-simmered steak. I like to serve it with bow tie pasta.

—ANN DIXON NORTH VERNON, INDIANA

PREP: 20 MIN. **COOK:** 1¼ HOURS
MAKES: 6 SERVINGS

- ¼ **cup all-purpose flour**
- 1 **teaspoon salt**
- ½ **teaspoon pepper**
- 1½ **pounds boneless beef top round steak, cut into serving-size pieces**
- 1 **tablespoon canola oil**
- 1 **medium onion, chopped**
- ¾ **cup grated carrot**
- ¾ **cup water**
- ½ **cup chopped celery**
- ½ **cup chopped green pepper**
- ½ **cup ketchup**
- ¼ **cup picante sauce**
- 1 **tablespoon cider vinegar**
  Hot cooked pasta

1. In a large resealable plastic bag, combine the flour, salt and pepper. Add beef, a few pieces at a time, and shake to coat. In a large skillet, brown beef in oil.
2. Combine the onion, carrot, water, celery, green pepper, ketchup, picante sauce and vinegar; pour over beef. Bring to a boil. Reduce heat; cover and simmer for 60-75 minutes or until beef is tender. Serve with pasta.

WESTERN RANGE SANDWICHES

I found these easy open-faced sandwiches in a cookbook that my mother left me more than 20 years ago. Using English muffins instead of hamburger buns is a nice change.

—**MAUVEREEN CANNADY** PORTAGE, WISCONSIN

Western Range Sandwiches

PREP: 15 MIN. **COOK:** 20 MIN.
MAKES: 6 SERVINGS

- **4 bacon strips, diced**
- **1 pound lean ground beef (90% lean)**
- **1 medium onion, chopped**
- **½ cup chopped green pepper**
- **2 cans (16 ounces each) kidney beans, rinsed and drained**
- **1 can (8 ounces) tomato sauce**
- **2 tablespoons chili powder**
- **½ teaspoon salt**
- **⅛ teaspoon pepper**
- **2 cups (8 ounces) shredded cheddar cheese**
- **6 English muffins, split and toasted**

1. In a large skillet, cook bacon until crisp. Remove to paper towels. Drain, reserving 2 tablespoons of drippings. Cook beef, onion and green pepper in drippings until meat is no longer pink. Add beans, tomato sauce, chili powder, salt, pepper and bacon.

2. Bring to a boil. Reduce heat; add cheese. Cook and stir over low heat until cheese is melted. Spoon onto English muffin halves.

EAT SMART St. Paddy's Irish Beef Dinner

PREP: 25 MIN. **COOK:** 35 MIN.
MAKES: 4 SERVINGS

- **2 medium Yukon Gold potatoes**
- **2 small parsnips**
- **¾ pound lean ground beef (90% lean)**
- **1 medium onion, chopped**
- **2 cups finely shredded cabbage**
- **2 medium carrots, halved and sliced**
- **1 teaspoon dried thyme**
- **1 teaspoon Worcestershire sauce**
- **1 tablespoon all-purpose flour**
- **¼ cup tomato paste**
- **1 can (14½ ounces) reduced-sodium chicken or beef broth**
- **½ cup frozen peas**
- **¾ teaspoon salt, divided**
- **½ teaspoon pepper, divided**
- **¼ cup 2% milk**
- **1 tablespoon butter**

1. Peel potatoes and parsnips and cut into large pieces; place in a large saucepan and cover with water. Bring to a boil. Reduce heat; cover and cook for 10-15 minutes or until tender. Drain.

2. Meanwhile, in a large skillet, cook beef and onion over medium heat until meat is no longer pink; drain. Stir in the cabbage, carrots, thyme and Worcestershire sauce.

3. In a small bowl, combine the flour, tomato paste and broth until smooth. Gradually stir into meat mixture. Bring to a boil. Reduce heat; cover and simmer for 15-20 minutes or until vegetables are tender. Stir in the peas, ¼ teaspoon salt and ¼ teaspoon pepper.

4. Drain potatoes and parsnips; mash with milk, butter and the remaining salt and pepper. Serve with meat mixture.

PER SERVING *369 cal., 11 g fat (5 g sat. fat), 62 mg chol., 849 mg sodium, 46 g carb., 8 g fiber, 24 g pro.* **Diabetic Exchanges:** *3 lean meat, 2 starch, 2 vegetable.*

A variation on shepherd's pie, this hearty dish brings together saucy beef with mashed potatoes, parsnips and other vegetables. It's always the star of our March 17 meal. —**LORRAINE CALAND** SHUNIAH, ONTARIO

ST. PADDY'S IRISH BEEF DINNER

Greek-Style Ribeyes

Because our children are grown, I often cook for just my husband and me. When I want to serve something special, this is the entree I usually reach for.

—RUBY WILLIAMS BOGALUSA, LOUISIANA

PREP/TOTAL TIME: 25 MIN.
MAKES: 2 SERVINGS

- 1½ teaspoons garlic powder
- 1½ teaspoons dried oregano
- 1½ teaspoons dried basil
- ½ teaspoon salt
- ⅛ teaspoon pepper
- 2 beef ribeye steaks (1½ inches thick and 16 ounces each)
- 1 tablespoon olive oil
- 1 tablespoon lemon juice
- 2 tablespoons crumbled feta cheese
- 1 tablespoon sliced ripe olives

Combine the first five ingredients; rub onto both sides of steaks. In a large skillet, cook steaks in oil for 7-9 minutes on each side or until meat reaches desired doneness (for medium-rare a thermometer should read 145°; medium, 160°; well-done, 170°). Sprinkle with lemon juice, cheese and olives.

Simple Meatball Stroganoff

Here's an easy way to make comfort food for your family. To save time, you can defrost the meatballs in the microwave.

—SARITA POWERS MADISON, VIRGINIA

PREP/TOTAL TIME: 20 MIN.
MAKES: 4 SERVINGS

- 1 package (12 ounces) frozen fully cooked homestyle meatballs, thawed
- 1 jar (12 ounces) home-style beef gravy
- ½ cup sour cream
  Hot cooked egg noodles

Prepare meatballs according to package directions for the microwave. Meanwhile, in a large saucepan, bring gravy and sour cream just to a boil. Stir in the meatballs. Reduce heat; cook, stirring occasionally, until heated through. Serve over noodles.

MUSHROOM BEEF TIPS WITH RICE

Here's a quick and simple version of the beef tips my husband loves. Even though the recipe calls for premade tips, the finished dish tastes delightfully homemade. Think: savory Stroganoff flavor with only five ingredients! **—PAMELA SHANK** PARKERSBURG, WEST VIRGINIA

Mushroom Beef Tips With Rice

PREP/TOTAL TIME: 10 MIN.
MAKES: 3 SERVINGS

- 1 cup sliced fresh mushrooms
- 2 tablespoons butter
- 1 package (17 ounces) refrigerated beef tips with gravy
- 1 package (8.8 ounces) ready-to-serve long grain rice
- ½ cup sour cream

1. In a skillet, saute mushrooms in butter for 2 minutes. Add beef to pan; cook for 4-6 minutes or until heated through, stirring occasionally.
2. Meanwhile, cook rice according to package directions. Remove beef mixture from the heat; stir in sour cream. Serve with rice.

EAT SMART Gingered Beef Stir-Fry

A friend who owns a bed and breakfast in Maryland shared this recipe with me. It's a delicious and different way to cook asparagus.

—**SONJA BLOW** NIXA, MISSOURI

PREP: 20 MIN. + MARINATING
COOK: 20 MIN. **MAKES:** 4 SERVINGS

- 3 tablespoons reduced-sodium soy sauce, divided
- 1 tablespoon sherry
- ¼ teaspoon minced fresh gingerroot or dash ground ginger
- ½ pound beef flank steak, cut into thin strips
- 1 teaspoon cornstarch
- ½ cup beef broth
- 1½ teaspoons hoisin sauce
- ⅛ teaspoon sugar
- 2 tablespoons canola oil, divided
- 2 pounds fresh asparagus, cut into 1-inch lengths
- 1 garlic clove, minced
- 3 cups hot cooked rice

1. In a large resealable plastic bag, combine 2 tablespoons soy sauce, sherry and ginger; add the beef. Seal bag and turn to coat; refrigerate for 30 minutes.

2. In a small bowl, combine the cornstarch, broth, hoisin sauce, sugar and remaining soy sauce until smooth; set aside.

3. In a large skillet or wok, stir-fry beef in 1 tablespoon oil until no longer pink. Remove and set aside. Stir-fry asparagus in remaining oil until crisp-tender. Add garlic; cook 1 minute longer.

4. Stir cornstarch mixture and add to the pan. Bring to a boil; cook and stir for 2 minutes or until thickened. Return beef to the pan; heat through. Serve with rice.

PER SERVING *347 cal., 12 g fat (2 g sat. fat), 27 mg chol., 645 mg sodium, 41 g carb., 2 g fiber, 18 g pro.* **Diabetic Exchanges:** *2 starch, 2 fat, 1 lean meat, 1 vegetable.*

Lone Star Pot Roast

Pot roast is made especially flavorful with the addition of chopped green chilies and taco seasoning.

—**HELEN CARPENTER**
ALBUQUERQUE, NEW MEXICO

PREP: 20 MIN. **COOK:** 2 HOURS
MAKES: 6-8 SERVINGS

- 1 boneless beef chuck roast (3 to 3½ pounds)
- 2 tablespoons canola oil
- 1 can (14½ ounces) diced tomatoes, undrained
- 1 can (4 ounces) chopped green chilies
- 2 tablespoons taco seasoning
- 2 teaspoons beef bouillon granules
- 1 teaspoon sugar
- ¼ cup cold water
- 3 tablespoons all-purpose flour

1. In a Dutch oven, brown roast in oil. Combine tomatoes, chilies, taco seasoning, bouillon and sugar; pour over the roast. Cover and simmer 2 to 2½ hours or until meat is tender.

2. Remove roast to a platter and keep warm. For gravy, pour 2 cups pan juices into a saucepan. Combine cold water and flour; stir into pan juices over high heat until thickened and bubbly, about 3 minutes. Serve with roast.

GINGERED BEEF STIR-FRY

Poultry

119   125   122

Savor **rich classics** such as dumpling stew and saucy drumsticks; **lightened-up versions** of burgers and chili mac; and fresh-tasting **crispy chicken salads**. No matter what the season, you'll find a flock of foolproof recipes right here.

TURKEY PICCATA

Strawberry Chicken Salad

Salads are the meal of choice when our Texas temperatures hover in the 90s. In this one, I use locally grown strawberries, fresh greens and chicken strips. It makes a light, refreshing lunch on a summer day.
—LORNA DRESSLER UNIVERSAL CITY, TEXAS

PREP/TOTAL TIME: 30 MIN.
MAKES: 4 SERVINGS

DRESSING
- ½ cup honey
- ½ cup red wine vinegar
- 4 teaspoons soy sauce
- 1 garlic clove, minced
- ½ teaspoon ground ginger
- ¼ teaspoon salt
  Dash pepper

SALAD
- 1 pound boneless skinless chicken breasts, cut into strips
- 1 tablespoon canola oil
- 1 teaspoon butter
- 8 cups torn mixed salad greens
- 1 pint fresh strawberries, sliced
- ¼ cup chopped walnuts
  Additional whole strawberries, optional

1. In a small bowl, combine the dressing ingredients. In a large skillet, cook and stir chicken in oil and butter until no longer pink. Add ½ cup salad dressing; cook 1 minute longer.

2. Place the salad greens in a serving bowl. Top with chicken, sliced strawberries and walnuts. Garnish with whole strawberries if desired. Serving immediately with remaining dressing.

Quick, flavorful and special, this lightened-up take on a classic has the same buttery lemon-caper sauce that people love. **—LESLIE RODRIGUEZ** EL CAJON, CALIFORNIA

Turkey Piccata

PREP/TOTAL TIME: 25 MIN.
MAKES: 4 SERVINGS

- ¼ cup all-purpose flour
- ½ teaspoon salt
- ¼ teaspoon pepper
- 1 package (17.6 ounces) turkey breast cutlets
- 2 tablespoons olive oil
- ½ cup chicken broth
- 3 tablespoons butter
- 1 tablespoon lemon juice
- 1 tablespoon minced fresh parsley
- 1 tablespoon capers, drained

1. In a shallow bowl, combine the flour, salt and pepper. Add the turkey slices, one at a time, and turn to coat.

2. In a large skillet, cook turkey in oil in batches for 2-3 minutes on each side or until no longer pink. Remove to a serving platter and keep warm.

3. Add broth to the pan, stirring to loosen browned bits. Bring to a boil; cook until liquid is reduced by half. Stir in the remaining ingredients until butter is melted. Pour sauce over turkey.

My chicken dish is excellent for Sunday dinner because it's so simple to prepare. It's inexpensive besides...and loaded with lots of vegetables.

—**BARBARA ROBERTS** COURTENAY, BRITISH COLUMBIA

CHICKEN CACCIATORE

Chicken Cacciatore

PREP: 15 MIN. **COOK:** 1½ HOURS
MAKES: 6 SERVINGS

- 1 broiler/fryer chicken (3½ to 4 pounds), cut up
- ¼ cup all-purpose flour
  Salt and pepper to taste
- 2 tablespoons olive oil
- 2 tablespoons butter
- 1 large onion, chopped
- 2 celery ribs, sliced
- 1 large green pepper, cut into strips
- ½ pound sliced fresh mushrooms
- 1 can (28 ounces) tomatoes, cut up and juice reserved
- 1 can (8 ounces) tomato sauce
- 1 can (6 ounces) tomato paste
- 1 cup dry red wine or water
- 1 teaspoon dried thyme
- 1 teaspoon dried rosemary, crushed
- 1 teaspoon dried oregano
- 1 teaspoon dried basil
- 3 garlic cloves, minced
- 1 tablespoon sugar
  Hot cooked pasta
  Grated Parmesan cheese

1. Dust chicken with flour. Season with salt and pepper. In a large skillet, brown chicken on all sides in oil and butter over medium-high heat. Remove chicken to platter.
2. In the same skillet, cook and stir the onion, celery, pepper and mushrooms for 5 minutes. Stir in the tomatoes, tomato sauce, tomato paste, wine, herbs, garlic and sugar. Bring to a boil. Reduce heat; cover and simmer for 30 minutes.
3. Return chicken to skillet. Cover and simmer for 45-60 minutes or until chicken is tender. Serve over pasta and sprinkle with Parmesan cheese.

SAUSAGE ZUCCHINI SKILLET

I began serving a version of this easy recipe as a side dish with my grilled salmon. I later added sausage and rice to make it a complete meal on its own.
—**DEBBY ABEL** FLAT ROCK, NORTH CAROLINA

EAT SMART Sausage Zucchini Skillet

PREP/TOTAL TIME: 25 MIN.
MAKES: 4 SERVINGS

- 1 pound Italian turkey sausage links, casings removed
- 2 large zucchini, chopped
- 1 large sweet onion, chopped
- 2 garlic cloves, minced
- 1 can (14½ ounces) no-salt-added diced tomatoes, undrained
- ¼ teaspoon pepper
- 2 cups hot cooked rice

1. Crumble sausage into a large nonstick skillet coated with cooking spray. Add zucchini and onion; cook and stir over medium heat until meat is no longer pink. Add garlic; cook 1 minute longer. Drain.
2. Stir in tomatoes and pepper; bring to a boil. Reduce heat; simmer, uncovered, for 4-5 minutes or until liquid is evaporated. Serve with rice.
PER SERVING *329 cal., 11 g fat (2 g sat. fat), 68 mg chol., 724 mg sodium, 36 g carb., 5 g fiber, 23 g pro.* **Diabetic Exchanges:** *3 lean meat, 2 vegetable, 1½ starch.*

Chicken Cacciatore is a classic blend of tomatoes, mushrooms and herbs. Serve it with your favorite pasta to soak up all of the delicious sauce.

BLACKENED CHICKEN AND BEANS

My husband loves any spicy food, and this is one quick-fix and low-fat recipe we can both agree on. As the chicken cooks, whip up salads of lettuce, tomato, avocado and shredded cheddar cheese. Dinner's done! —CHRISTINE ZONGKER SPRING HILL, KANSAS

EAT SMART Blackened Chicken and Beans

PREP/TOTAL TIME: 20 MIN.
MAKES: 4 SERVINGS

- 2 teaspoons chili powder
- ¼ teaspoon salt
- ¼ teaspoon pepper
- 4 boneless skinless chicken breast halves (4 ounces each)
- 1 tablespoon canola oil
- 1 can (15 ounces) black beans, rinsed and drained
- 1 cup frozen corn
- 1 cup chunky salsa

1. Combine the chili powder, salt and pepper; rub over both sides of chicken. In a large nonstick skillet, cook chicken in oil over medium heat for 4-5 minutes on each side or until a thermometer reads 170°. Remove and keep warm.
2. Add the beans, corn and salsa to the pan; heat through. Serve with chicken.
PER SERVING *297 cal., 7 g fat (1 g sat. fat), 63 mg chol., 697 mg sodium, 26 g carb., 8 g fiber, 29 g pro.* **Diabetic Exchanges:** *3 lean meat, 1½ starch, 1 fat.*

EAT SMART Kielbasa Cabbage Stew

If you like German potato salad, you'll love my sweet-and-sour stew. Caraway, smoky kielbasa, tender potatoes and shredded cabbage make it delicious.
—**VALRIE BURROWS** SHELBY, MICHIGAN

PREP: 10 MIN. **COOK:** 35 MIN.
MAKES: 4 SERVINGS

- ½ pound smoked turkey kielbasa or Polish sausage, sliced
- 1 pound potatoes, peeled and cubed
- 2 cups shredded cabbage
- 1 large onion, chopped
- 1 can (14½ ounces) reduced-sodium chicken broth
- ¾ cup water, divided
- 2 tablespoons sugar
- 1 teaspoon caraway seeds
- ¼ teaspoon pepper
- 1 can (16 ounces) kidney beans, rinsed and drained
- 3 tablespoons cider vinegar
- 2 tablespoons all-purpose flour

1. In a large saucepan or nonstick skillet, brown sausage over medium heat. Add the potatoes, cabbage, onion, broth, ½ cup water, sugar, caraway and pepper. Bring to a boil. Reduce heat; cover and simmer for 15-18 minutes or until potatoes are tender, stirring occasionally.
2. Add the beans and vinegar; cover and simmer 5-10 minutes longer. Combine flour and remaining water until smooth; stir into stew. Bring to a boil; cook and stir for 2 minutes or until thickened.
PER SERVING *322 cal., 3 g fat (1 g sat. fat), 25 mg chol., 1,143 mg sodium, 57 g carb., 7 g fiber, 17 g pro.* **Diabetic Exchanges:** *3 starch, 2 lean meat, 1 vegetable.*

SAUSAGE AND PUMPKIN PASTA

EAT SMART Sausage and Pumpkin Pasta

My family really enjoys this meal. Cubed leftover turkey may be substituted for sausage. Just add to the skillet with the cooked pasta for a quick dinner that's special enough for company.

—KATIE WOLLGAST FLORISSANT, MISSOURI

PREP: 20 MIN. **COOK:** 15 MIN.
MAKES: 4 SERVINGS

- 2 cups uncooked multigrain bow tie pasta
- ½ pound Italian turkey sausage links, casings removed
- ½ pound sliced fresh mushrooms
- 1 medium onion, chopped
- 4 garlic cloves, minced
- 1 cup reduced-sodium chicken broth
- 1 cup canned pumpkin
- ½ cup white wine or additional reduced-sodium chicken broth
- ½ teaspoon rubbed sage
- ¼ teaspoon salt
- ¼ teaspoon garlic powder
- ¼ teaspoon pepper
- ¼ cup grated Parmesan cheese
- 1 tablespoon dried parsley flakes

1. Cook the pasta according to package directions.
2. Meanwhile, in a large nonstick skillet coated with cooking spray, cook the sausage, mushrooms and onion over medium heat until meat is no longer pink. Add garlic; cook 1 minute longer. Stir in the broth, pumpkin, wine, sage, salt, garlic powder and pepper. Bring to a boil. Reduce heat; simmer, uncovered, for 5-6 minutes or until sauce is slightly thickened.
3. Drain pasta; add to the skillet and heat through. Just before serving, sprinkle with cheese and parsley.
PER SERVING *348 cal., 9 g fat (2 g sat. fat), 38 mg chol., 733 mg sodium, 42 g carb., 7 g fiber, 23 g pro. Diabetic Exchanges: 2½ starch, 2 lean meat, 1 vegetable, ½ fat.*

Multigrain pasta can be a great compromise between regular (white) pasta and whole wheat. It **tastes like white** pasta but typically has **more fiber and nutrients.**

GROUND TURKEY AND HOMINY

Hominy is a real favorite of mine, so when I saw this fast-to-fix recipe, I had to try it. With its flavorful combination of spices, it makes a warming meal on a cool night. —ESTHER HOFF-SHERROW DENVER, COLORADO

Ground Turkey and Hominy

PREP/TOTAL TIME: 20 MIN.
MAKES: 8 SERVINGS

- 1½ pounds ground turkey
- 1 large onion, chopped
- 2 tablespoons olive oil
- 1 teaspoon minced garlic
- 2 cans (14½ ounces each) diced tomatoes, undrained
- 1 tablespoon chili powder
- 1½ teaspoons ground cumin
- 1 teaspoon salt
- ½ teaspoon ground mustard
- ½ teaspoon dried thyme
- ¼ teaspoon ground cinnamon
- ¼ teaspoon ground allspice
- ¼ teaspoon pepper
- 2 cans (15½ ounces each) hominy, rinsed and drained

In a large skillet, cook turkey and onion in oil over medium heat until meat is no longer pink. Add garlic; cook 1 minute longer. Drain. Stir in tomatoes and seasonings; heat through. Add hominy and heat through.

Breaded Chicken Tenders With Noodles

My daughter, Chelsea, and her friend Becca created and cooked this dish for my husband and me. It was an impressive surprise and a real treat. What a delightfully garlicky lunch or dinner.
—JODI HARRE NASHVILLE, ILLINOIS

PREP/TOTAL TIME: 25 MIN.
MAKES: 4 SERVINGS

- 5 cups uncooked egg noodles
- 1 tablespoon lemon juice
- 1 tablespoon lime juice
- ½ cup seasoned bread crumbs
- 8 chicken tenderloins
- 1 teaspoon minced garlic
- 6 tablespoons butter, divided
- ⅛ teaspoon garlic salt
- ⅛ teaspoon garlic powder

1. Cook noodles according to package directions. Meanwhile, combine lemon and lime juices; set aside. Place the bread crumbs in a large resealable plastic bag; add chicken, one piece at a time, and shake to coat.

2. In a large skillet over medium heat, cook chicken and garlic in 2 tablespoons butter until chicken is no longer pink, turning and sprinkling occasionally with the juice mixture.

3. Drain noodles; toss with garlic salt, garlic powder and remaining butter until butter is melted. Serve with chicken tenders.

Sausage Chicken Jambalaya

PREP: 20 MIN. **COOK:** 30 MIN.
MAKES: 9 SERVINGS

- 6 fully cooked spicy chicken sausage links (3 ounces each), cut into ½-inch slices
- ½ pound chicken tenderloins, cut into ½-inch slices
- 1 tablespoon olive oil
- 3 celery ribs, chopped
- 1 large onion, chopped
- 2¾ cups chicken broth
- 1 can (14½ ounces) diced tomatoes, undrained
- 1½ cups uncooked long grain rice
- 1 teaspoon dried thyme
- 1 teaspoon Cajun seasoning

1. In a large saucepan, saute sausage and chicken in oil for 5 minutes. Add celery and onion; saute 6-8 minutes longer or until vegetables are tender. Stir in the broth, tomatoes, rice, thyme and Cajun seasoning.

2. Bring to a boil. Reduce heat; cover and simmer for 15-20 minutes or until rice is tender. Let stand for 5 minutes.

> For anyone who enjoys entertaining, this jambalaya is the perfect one-pot meal to feed a group. It's a fun crowd-pleaser that's easy to make.
> —**BETTY BENTHIN** GRASS VALLEY, CALIFORNIA

SAUSAGE CHICKEN JAMBALAYA

WEST AFRICAN CHICKEN STEW

> I really love African flavors, but you don't really encounter them much in America. Here the combination of native African ingredients, all of which are readily accessible to Americans, transports you to a new culinary place.
>
> —**MICHAEL COHEN** LOS ANGELES, CALIFORNIA

EAT SMART West African Chicken Stew

PREP: 20 MIN. **COOK:** 30 MIN.
MAKES: 8 SERVINGS (2½ QUARTS)

- 1 pound boneless skinless chicken breasts, cut into 1-inch cubes
- ½ teaspoon salt
- ¼ teaspoon pepper
- 3 teaspoons canola oil, divided
- 1 medium onion, thinly sliced
- 6 garlic cloves, minced
- 2 tablespoons minced fresh gingerroot
- 2 cans (15½ ounces each) black-eyed peas, rinsed and drained
- 1 can (28 ounces) crushed tomatoes
- 1 large sweet potato, peeled and cut into 1-inch cubes
- 1 cup reduced-sodium chicken broth
- ¼ cup creamy peanut butter
- 1½ teaspoons minced fresh thyme or ½ teaspoon dried thyme, divided
- ¼ teaspoon cayenne pepper
  Hot cooked brown rice, optional

1. Sprinkle chicken with salt and pepper. In a Dutch oven, cook chicken over medium heat in 2 teaspoons oil for 4-6 minutes or until no longer pink; remove and set aside.
2. In the same pan, saute onion in remaining oil until tender. Add garlic and ginger; cook 1 minute longer.
3. Stir in peas, tomatoes, sweet potato, broth, peanut butter, 1¼ teaspoons thyme and cayenne. Bring to a boil. Reduce heat; cover and simmer 15-20 minutes or until sweet potato is tender. Add chicken and heat through.
4. Serve with rice if desired. Sprinkle with remaining thyme.
PER SERVING *275 cal., 7 g fat (1 g sat. fat), 31 mg chol., 636 mg sodium, 32 g carb., 6 g fiber, 22 g pro.* **Diabetic Exchanges:** *3 lean meat, 2 vegetable, 1 starch, 1 fat.*

EAT SMART Quick Turkey Spaghetti

My family never tires of this versatile entree. We can have it once a week, and it's different each time! I sometimes omit the turkey for a meatless meal, change up the veggies or use my own tomato sauce.
—**MARY LOU MOELLER** WOOSTER, OHIO

PREP: 15 MIN. **COOK:** 25 MIN.
MAKES: 4 SERVINGS

- 1 pound lean ground turkey
- 1 small green pepper, chopped
- ½ cup sliced fresh mushrooms
- ¼ cup chopped onion
- 1 can (15 ounces) tomato sauce
- 6 ounces uncooked multigrain spaghetti, broken into 2-inch pieces
- ¾ cup water
- ¼ teaspoon garlic salt
  Grated Parmesan cheese, optional

1. In a large nonstick skillet coated with cooking spray, cook the turkey, pepper, mushrooms and onion over medium heat until meat is no longer pink and vegetables are crisp-tender.
2. Stir in the tomato sauce, spaghetti, water and garlic salt. Bring to a boil. Reduce heat; cover and simmer for 15-20 minutes or until spaghetti and vegetables are tender. Garnish with cheese if desired.
PER SERVING *357 cal., 10 g fat (3 g sat. fat), 90 mg chol., 728 mg sodium, 36 g carb., 4 g fiber, 30 g pro.* **Diabetic Exchanges:** *3 lean meat, 2 starch, 1 vegetable.*

EAT SMART

Pepperoni Penne Carbonara

Sun-dried tomatoes and turkey pepperoni lend fantastic flavor to creamy, hearty pasta. It's a great change of pace from everyday spaghetti.

—TASTE OF HOME TEST KITCHEN

PREP/TOTAL TIME: 30 MIN.
MAKES: 6 SERVINGS

- 3 cups uncooked penne pasta
- 2 cups chopped sun-dried tomatoes (not packed in oil)
- 3 cups boiling water
- ¼ cup butter
- ½ teaspoon minced garlic
- 1 cup chopped turkey pepperoni
- 1 cup shredded Parmesan cheese
- 1 cup heavy whipping cream
- 3 tablespoons minced fresh basil
- ½ teaspoon salt
- ¼ teaspoon pepper

1. Cook pasta according to package directions. Meanwhile, soak tomatoes in boiling water for 10 minutes; drain well.

2. In a large skillet, saute tomatoes in butter for 3 minutes. Add garlic; cook 1 minute longer.

3. Stir in the pepperoni, cheese, cream, basil, salt and pepper. Cook over low heat until heated through. Drain pasta; toss with sauce.

Carbonara is a traditional Italian pasta sauce of **heavy cream**, Parmesan **cheese** and **bacon**. Our version uses turkey pepperoni instead of bacon.

Ever since I discovered this chicken in an old church cookbook, it's been a favorite for both family dinners and gatherings with friends. Everyone asks for seconds.
—**CRYSTAL GARZA** SHAMROCK, TEXAS

HUNGARIAN CHICKEN

Hungarian Chicken

PREP: 10 MIN. **COOK:** 1 HOUR
MAKES: 4-6 SERVINGS

- 6 **tablespoons all-purpose flour**
  Salt and pepper to taste
- 1 **broiler/fryer chicken (about 3½ pounds), cut up**
- ¼ **cup butter, divided**
- 1 **large onion, chopped**
- ⅔ **cup tomato juice**
- 1 **to 2 tablespoons paprika**
- 1 **teaspoon sugar**
- 1 **teaspoon salt**
- 1 **bay leaf**
- ⅔ **cup chicken broth**
- ⅔ **cup sour cream**
  Hot cooked egg noodles

1. Combine flour, salt and pepper in a large resealable plastic bag. Add chicken, a few pieces at a time, and shake to coat.

2. Melt 1 tablespoon butter in a large skillet. Add onion and cook until tender. Remove from pan and set aside. In the same skillet, melt remaining butter and brown chicken on all sides.

3. Combine tomato juice, paprika, sugar and salt; add to chicken. Add bay leaf, broth and onion. Cover and simmer 45-60 minutes or until chicken is tender.

4. Remove chicken to a platter; keep warm. Reduce heat to low, remove bay leaf and stir in sour cream. Heat through (do not boil). Pour sauce over chicken. Serve with noodles.

EAT SMART Buffalo Turkey Burgers

PREP/TOTAL TIME: 25 MIN.
MAKES: 4 SERVINGS

- 2 **tablespoons Louisiana-style hot sauce, divided**
- 2 **teaspoons ground cumin**
- 2 **teaspoons chili powder**
- 2 **garlic cloves, minced**
- ½ **teaspoon salt**
- ⅛ **teaspoon pepper**
- 1 **pound lean ground turkey**
- 4 **whole wheat hamburger buns, split**
- 1 **cup shredded lettuce**
- 2 **celery ribs, chopped**

BUFFALO TURKEY BURGERS

> Celery and blue cheese dressing help tame the hot sauce. For a skinnier, crunchier version, skip the bun and add lettuce leaves, sliced onion and tomato.
> —**MARY PAX-SHIPLEY** BEND, OREGON

- 2 **tablespoons fat-free blue cheese salad dressing**

1. In a large bowl, combine 1 tablespoon hot sauce, cumin, chili powder, garlic, salt and pepper. Crumble turkey over mixture and mix well. Shape into four patties.

2. In a large nonstick skillet coated with cooking spray, cook patties over medium heat for 4-5 minutes on each side or until a thermometer reads 165° and juices run clear.

3. Serve on buns with lettuce, celery, blue cheese dressing and remaining hot sauce.

PER SERVING *312 cal., 12 g fat (3 g sat. fat), 90 mg chol., 734 mg sodium, 28 g carb., 5 g fiber, 24 g pro.* **Diabetic Exchanges:** *3 lean meat, 2 starch, ½ fat.*

EAT SMART Chicken Rice Salad

I start this salad by poaching chicken breasts in a mixture of white wine, garlic and lemon juice. It gives them great flavor and helps keep them moist. What a deliciously versatile salad.

—JANNE ROWE WICHITA, KANSAS

PREP: 15 MIN. **COOK:** 25 MIN.
MAKES: 7 SERVINGS

- 1 cup white wine or chicken broth
- 1 tablespoon lemon juice
- 1 garlic clove, minced
- ¾ teaspoon ground ginger, divided
- 1¼ pounds boneless skinless chicken breasts
- 3 cups chicken broth
- 1½ cups uncooked long grain rice
- 1 package (10 ounces) frozen peas, thawed
- ½ cup sliced green onions
- ½ cup diced celery
- 2 tablespoons diced sweet red pepper
- 2 tablespoons diced green pepper

DRESSING

- ¼ cup cider vinegar
- 2 tablespoons Dijon mustard
- 1 tablespoon reduced-sodium soy sauce
- 1 tablespoon olive oil
- 1 tablespoon sesame oil
- 2 teaspoons honey
- 1 garlic clove, minced
  Dash ground ginger

1. In a large nonstick skillet, combine the wine, lemon juice, garlic and ¼ teaspoon ginger. Bring to a boil; reduce heat. Add chicken; poach, uncovered, over medium-low heat for 15 minutes or until a thermometer reads 170°. Remove chicken from cooking liquid; cool.

2. In a large saucepan, bring broth and remaining ginger to a boil. Stir in rice. Reduce heat; cover and simmer for 15-20 minutes or until liquid is absorbed and rice is tender. Fluff with a fork.

3. Transfer to a large bowl; cool. Add the peas, onions, celery and peppers. Cut chicken into bite-size pieces; add to rice mixture and toss.

4. Whisk the dressing ingredients; drizzle over salad and toss to coat.

MONTEREY BARBECUED CHICKEN

It's easy to turn regular chicken into a dish to savor with barbecue sauce, crisp bacon and melted cheese. It gets even better with a sprinkling of fresh tomato and green onion. **—LINDA COLEMAN** CEDAR RAPIDS, IOWA

PER SERVING *350 cal., 6 g fat (1 g sat. fat), 47 mg chol., 704 mg sodium, 43 g carb., 3 g fiber, 25 g pro.* **Diabetic Exchanges:** *2½ starch, 2 lean meat, 1 fat.*

Monterey Barbecued Chicken

PREP/TOTAL TIME: 25 MIN.
MAKES: 4 SERVINGS

- 4 bacon strips
- 4 boneless skinless chicken breast halves (4 ounces each)
- 1 tablespoon butter
- ½ cup barbecue sauce
- 3 green onions, chopped
- 1 medium tomato, chopped
- 1 cup (4 ounces) shredded cheddar cheese

1. Cut bacon strips in half widthwise. In a large skillet, cook bacon over medium heat until cooked but not crisp. Remove to paper towels to drain.

2. Drain drippings from skillet; cook chicken in butter over medium heat for 5-6 minutes on each side or until a thermometer reads 170°.

3. Top each chicken breast with the barbecue sauce, green onions, tomato and two reserved bacon pieces; sprinkle with cheese. Cover and cook for 5 minutes or until cheese is melted.

Turkey Dumpling Stew

My mom made this stew when I was young, and it was always a hit. Since it's not too time-consuming, I often make it on weekends for our children, who love the tender dumplings.

—**BECKY MOHR** APPLETON, WISCONSIN

PREP: 20 MIN. **COOK:** 50 MIN.
MAKES: 6 SERVINGS

- 4 **bacon strips, diced**
- 1½ **pounds turkey breast tenderloins, cut into 1-inch pieces**
- 4 **medium carrots, sliced**
- 2 **cups water, divided**
- 1 **can (14½ ounces) reduced-sodium chicken broth**
- 2 **small onions, quartered**
- 2 **celery ribs, sliced**
- ¼ **teaspoon dried rosemary, crushed**
- 1 **bay leaf**
- 3 **tablespoons all-purpose flour**
- ½ **teaspoon salt**
- ⅛ **to ¼ teaspoon pepper**
- 1 **cup reduced-fat biscuit/baking mix**
- ⅓ **cup plus 1 tablespoon fat-free milk**

1. In a Dutch oven, cook bacon over medium heat until crisp. Remove to paper towels; drain, reserving 2 teaspoons drippings.

2. Cook turkey in the drippings until no longer pink. Add the carrots, 1¾ cups of water, broth, onions, celery, rosemary and bay leaf. Bring to a boil. Reduce heat; cover and simmer for 20-30 minutes or until vegetables are tender.

3. Combine flour and remaining water until smooth; stir into turkey mixture. Bring to a boil; cook and stir for 2 minutes or until thickened. Discard bay leaf. Stir in the salt, pepper and reserved bacon.

4. In a small bowl, combine biscuit mix and milk. Drop batter in six mounds onto simmering stew. Cover and simmer for 15 minutes or until a toothpick inserted in a dumpling comes out clean (do not lift the cover while simmering).

New Orleans-Style Chicken

This hearty one-dish meal is loaded with tender chunks of chicken, veggies, beans and rice. It's a favorite of mine. You can also make it with cooked sausages and bacon instead of chicken.

—**JASON BAGLEY**

KENNEWICK, WASHINGTON

PREP: 25 MIN. **COOK:** 50 MIN.
MAKES: 6 SERVINGS

- 1¼ **pounds boneless skinless chicken breasts, cubed**
- 3 **teaspoons canola oil, divided**
- 2 **medium carrots, chopped**
- 2 **large portobello mushrooms, stems removed, chopped**
- 1 **large onion, chopped**
- 1 **medium green pepper, chopped**
- 1 **medium sweet red pepper, chopped**
- 3 **garlic cloves, minced**
- 2¾ **cups water**
- 1 **can (15 ounces) black beans, rinsed and drained**
- 1 **package (8 ounces) red beans and rice mix**
- 1 **can (14½ ounces) diced tomatoes, drained**
- ⅓ **cup shredded Asiago cheese**

1. In a large nonstick skillet over medium-high heat, brown chicken in 1 teaspoon oil; remove and set aside. In the same skillet, saute the carrots, mushrooms, onion and peppers in remaining oil for 5 minutes. Add garlic; cook 1 minute longer.

2. Add water; bring to a boil. Stir in the beans, rice mix and chicken; return to a boil. Reduce heat; cover and simmer for 30-35 minutes or until liquid is absorbed and the rice is tender.

3. Stir in the tomatoes and heat through. Just before serving, sprinkle with cheese.

NOTE *This recipe was prepared with Zatarain's New Orleans-style red beans and rice.*

TURKEY DUMPLING STEW

Chicken & Dumplings For Two

Here's a tasty one-pot meal that's sized right for a pair. The whole dinner comes together on the stovetop, so you can enjoy a great meal and still get out of the kitchen in a jiffy.

—**CLAIRE BRUNO** TUCSON, ARIZONA

PREP: 10 MIN. **COOK:** 30 MIN.
MAKES: 2 SERVINGS

- ½ pound boneless skinless chicken breast, cubed
- 1½ cups chicken broth
- 1 medium carrot, sliced
- 1 small potato, peeled and cubed
- ¼ cup chopped onion
- 2 tablespoons chopped celery
- 1 bay leaf
- ¼ teaspoon salt
- ⅛ teaspoon pepper

DUMPLINGS

- ¼ cup all-purpose flour
- 1 teaspoon dried parsley flakes
- ½ teaspoon baking powder
  Pinch ground cloves
  Pinch salt
- 3 tablespoons milk

1. In a small saucepan, combine the first nine ingredients; bring to a boil. Reduce heat; cover and simmer for 15 minutes or until vegetables are tender. Discard bay leaf.
2. For dumplings, in a small bowl, combine the flour, parsley, baking powder, cloves and salt. Stir in milk just until moistened. Drop by heaping teaspoonfuls onto simmering chicken mixture. Cover and simmer for 15 minutes or until a toothpick inserted in a dumpling comes out clean (do not lift the cover while simmering).

CHILI MAC

Family and friends love this recipe. I use three power foods: tomatoes, black beans and olive oil, plus whole wheat pasta. It's comfort food to feel good about!

—**KRISSY BLACK** MT. VERNON, OHIO

EAT SMART Chili Mac

PREP/TOTAL TIME: 30 MIN.
MAKES: 6 SERVINGS

- 2 cups uncooked whole wheat elbow macaroni
- 1 pound lean ground turkey
- 1 small onion, chopped
- 2 to 3 jalapeno peppers, seeded and chopped
- 2 teaspoons olive oil
- 2 garlic cloves, minced
- 1 can (15 ounces) black beans, rinsed and drained
- 1 can (14½ ounces) diced tomatoes, undrained
- 1 can (8 ounces) tomato sauce
- 1 to 2 tablespoons hot pepper sauce
- 2 to 3 teaspoons chili powder
- 1 teaspoon ground cumin
- ¼ teaspoon cayenne pepper
- ¼ teaspoon pepper
- ¾ cup shredded reduced-fat cheddar cheese

1. Cook macaroni according to package directions. Meanwhile, in a large nonstick skillet coated with cooking spray, cook the turkey, onion and jalapenos in oil over medium heat until meat is no longer pink. Add garlic; cook 1 minute longer. Drain.
2. Add the beans, tomatoes, tomato sauce, pepper sauce and seasonings. Drain macaroni; stir into turkey mixture. Cook over medium-low heat for 5 minutes or until heated through.
3. Sprinkle with cheese. Remove from the heat; cover and let stand until cheese is melted.
NOTE *Wear disposable gloves when cutting hot peppers; the oils can burn skin. Avoid touching your face.*
PER SERVING *396 cal., 12 g fat (4 g sat. fat), 70 mg chol., 581 mg sodium, 45 g carb., 9 g fiber, 28 g pro.* **Diabetic Exchanges:** *3 lean meat, 2½ starch, 1 vegetable, 1 fat.*

Sweet & Sour Chicken Thighs

Bamboo shoots, sweet red pepper and sugar snap peas give this homemade weeknight wonder a lovely look and pleasant crunch.

—**LORRAINE CALAND** SHUNIAH, ONTARIO

PREP: 15 MIN. **COOK:** 25 MIN.
MAKES: 6 SERVINGS

- 6 bone-in chicken thighs (about 2¼ pounds)
- 1 teaspoon olive oil
- ½ cup chicken broth
- 2 jars (4½ ounces each) sliced mushrooms, drained
- 1½ cups frozen sugar snap peas, thawed
- 1 medium sweet red pepper, cut into strips
- ½ cup canned bamboo shoots
- ⅓ cup thinly sliced green onions
- 1 can (20 ounces) pineapple tidbits
- 7½ teaspoons cornstarch
- ¼ cup cider vinegar
- 3 tablespoons soy sauce
- 2 tablespoons sugar
  Hot cooked rice noodles

1. In a large skillet, brown chicken in oil; drain. Add broth. Bring to a boil. Reduce heat; cover and cook for 10 minutes.

2. Add the mushrooms, peas, red pepper, bamboo shoots and onions. Cover and cook 5-10 minutes longer or until a thermometer reads 180° and vegetables are tender.

3. Meanwhile, drain pineapple, reserving juice; set pineapple aside. In a small bowl, combine the cornstarch, reserved juice, vinegar, soy sauce and sugar. Pour into the skillet. Bring to a boil; cook and stir for 2 minutes or until thickened.

4. Stir in pineapple; heat through. Serve with noodles.

Curried Turkey

With a freshly tossed salad, this dish makes an easy meal! You'll like the flavor accents of apple and curry. Another bonus? It's a good way to use leftover turkey from a holiday dinner.

—**EVELYN GUNN** ANDREWS, TEXAS

PREP/TOTAL TIME: 25 MIN.
MAKES: 6 SERVINGS

- 2 cups milk
- 2 chicken bouillon cubes
- 2 cups diced peeled apples
- 1 cup chopped onion
- ¼ cup canola oil
- 2 tablespoons all-purpose flour
- 2 teaspoons curry powder
- ½ teaspoon salt
- ¼ teaspoon pepper
- 1 tablespoon lemon juice
- 4 cups diced cooked turkey
  Hot cooked rice

1. In a small saucepan, heat the milk and bouillon, stirring until bouillon is dissolved. Set aside.

2. In a large saucepan, saute apples and onion in oil until tender. Stir in the flour, curry powder, salt and pepper until blended. Gradually add milk mixture and lemon juice. Bring to a boil; cook and stir for 2 minutes or until thickened. Add turkey and heat through. Serve over rice.

SWEET & SOUR CHICKEN THIGHS

This scrumptious recipe is a meal in itself. It uses a convenient Rice-A-Roni mix and only one pan...so cleanup is as short as the prep time.
—**TERRI CHRISTENSEN** MONTAGUE, MICHIGAN

ASIAN CHICKEN SKILLET

Asian Chicken Skillet

PREP/TOTAL TIME: 30 MIN.
MAKES: 4 SERVINGS

- 1 package (5.9 ounces) chicken and garlic-flavored rice and vermicelli mix
- 2 tablespoons butter
- 1 pound boneless skinless chicken breasts, cut into strips
- 2¼ cups water
- ¼ cup reduced-sodium teriyaki sauce
- ½ teaspoon ground ginger
- 1 package (16 ounces) frozen stir-fry vegetable blend, thawed

1. In a large skillet, saute rice mix in butter until golden brown. Stir in the chicken, water, teriyaki sauce, ginger and contents of rice seasoning packet. Bring to a boil. Reduce heat; cover and simmer for 10 minutes.
2. Stir in the vegetable blend. Cover and cook 5-8 minutes longer or until the rice is tender and chicken is no longer pink.

Chicken Coleslaw Wraps

Serve these wraps with veggie chips and iced tea for a delicious meal.
—TASTE OF HOME TEST KITCHEN

PREP/TOTAL TIME: 20 MIN.
MAKES: 4 SERVINGS

- 1 pound boneless skinless chicken breasts, cut into 1-inch strips
- ¼ teaspoon salt
- ⅛ teaspoon pepper
- 1 tablespoon canola oil
- 1½ cups deli coleslaw
- ½ cup pineapple tidbits
- 4 sun-dried tomato tortillas (10 inches), warmed
- 1 medium tomato, sliced
- 1 cup (4 ounces) shredded cheddar cheese

1. Sprinkle chicken with salt and pepper. In a skillet, cook chicken in oil over medium heat for 10-15 minutes or until no longer pink.
2. Combine coleslaw and pineapple; spread over tortillas. Layer with tomato, cheese and chicken; roll up tightly.

> This easy chicken dish is best made with sweet corn fresh from the field. Just add your favorite picnic sides. **—SUSAN BICE** LITCHFIELD, NEBRASKA

Midwest Chicken Drumsticks

PREP: 15 MIN. **COOK:** 35 MIN.
MAKES: 2 SERVINGS

- ¼ cup all-purpose flour
- ¼ teaspoon salt
- ¼ teaspoon garlic powder
  Dash cayenne pepper
- 4 chicken drumsticks, skin removed
- 2 tablespoons canola oil
- 4 green onions, sliced
- 1 cup fresh or frozen corn
- ½ cup barbecue sauce

1. In a large resealable plastic bag, combine the flour, salt, garlic powder and cayenne. Add drumsticks; seal bag and shake to coat. In a large skillet, brown chicken in oil on all sides. Remove and keep warm.
2. In the same skillet, saute onions until tender. Add corn; cook for 5 minutes. Stir in barbecue sauce. Return chicken to the pan and coat with sauce. Cover and cook for 25-30 minutes or until a thermometer reads 180°.

Pork

136 135 140

Serve up **satisfying pasta, your new favorite pork chops** and **company-perfect tenderloin** with the recipes in this colorful chapter. It will be hard to choose which hearty **protein-packed** entree to cook up first!

> I had a pork tenderloin and ripe peaches that begged to be put together. The results couldn't have been more irresistible! Here's a fresh entree that tastes like summer. —JULIA GOSLIGA ADDISON, VERMONT

EAT SMART Just Peachy Pork Tenderloin

PREP/TOTAL TIME: 20 MIN.
MAKES: 4 SERVINGS

- 1 pork tenderloin (1 pound), cut into 12 slices
- ½ teaspoon salt
- ¼ teaspoon pepper
- 2 teaspoons olive oil
- 4 medium peaches, peeled and sliced
- 1 tablespoon lemon juice
- ¼ cup peach preserves

1. Flatten each tenderloin slice to ¼-in. thickness. Sprinkle with salt and pepper. In a large nonstick skillet over medium heat, cook pork in oil until juices run clear. Remove and keep warm.

2. Add peaches and lemon juice, stirring to loosen browned bits. Cook and stir over medium heat for 3-4 minutes or until peaches are tender. Stir in the pork and preserves; heat through.

PER SERVING *241 cal., 6 g fat (2 g sat. fat), 63 mg chol., 340 mg sodium, 23 g carb., 2 g fiber, 23 g pro.* **Diabetic Exchanges:** *3 lean meat, 1 starch, ½ fruit, ½ fat.*

Swiss-Stuffed Chops

These delectable stuffed chops are easy, yet they taste full of love. Add your favorite veggie and dinner's ready.
—JOAN HALLFORD
NORTH RICHLAND HILLS, TEXAS

PREP: 25 MIN. **COOK:** 45 MIN.
MAKES: 4 SERVINGS

- 1 cup (4 ounces) shredded Swiss cheese
- 1 jar (4½ ounces) sliced mushrooms, drained
- ¼ cup minced fresh parsley
- 4 bone-in pork loin chops (7 ounces each)
- 1 egg
- 6 tablespoons dry bread crumbs
  Dash pepper
- 2 tablespoons canola oil
- ⅓ cup water
- 1 tablespoon all-purpose flour
- ¼ cup cold water

1. In a bowl, combine the cheese, mushrooms and parsley. Cut a pocket in each pork chop by slicing almost to the bone. Stuff chops with cheese mixture; secure with toothpicks.

2. In a shallow bowl, beat the egg. In another shallow bowl, combine bread crumbs and pepper. Dip chops in egg, then coat with crumbs.

3. In a large skillet, brown chops in oil on both sides. Add water. Cover and simmer for 35-40 minutes or until juices run clear. Remove chops and keep warm; discard toothpicks.

4. Combine flour and cold water until smooth; stir into pan juices. Cook and stir for 2 minutes or until thickened. Spoon over pork chops.

I adapted this elegant main dish from a recipe my mother-in-law cooked for our family. Cayenne lends a bit of heat to its rich, creamy sauce.

—JUDY ARMSTRONG PRAIRIEVILLE, LOUISIANA

PORK MEDALLIONS WITH BRANDY CREAM SAUCE

Pork Medallions With Brandy Cream Sauce

PREP: 25 MIN. **COOK:** 25 MIN.
MAKES: 4 SERVINGS

- 12 ounces uncooked linguine
- 1 pound pork tenderloin, cut into 1-inch slices
- ¼ cup all-purpose flour
- 2 tablespoons olive oil
- 3 tablespoons butter, divided
- 1¾ cups sliced baby portobello mushrooms
- 5 green onions, thinly sliced
- 2 garlic cloves, minced
- 1½ cups heavy whipping cream
- ¼ cup brandy
- 2 tablespoons minced fresh thyme
- 1 tablespoon Dijon mustard
- ½ teaspoon salt
- ½ teaspoon pepper
- ¼ teaspoon cayenne pepper
- 2 plum tomatoes, seeded and chopped
- 2 tablespoons shredded Parmesan cheese

1. Cook linguine according to package directions. Meanwhile, flatten pork slices to ¼-in. thickness. Place flour in a large resealable plastic bag. Add pork, a few pieces at a time, and shake to coat.

2. In a large skillet over medium-high heat, cook pork in oil and 2 tablespoons butter in batches for 3-4 minutes on each side or until juices run clear. Set aside and keep warm.

3. In the same skillet, saute mushrooms and onions in remaining butter until tender. Add garlic; cook 1 minute longer. Add the cream, brandy, thyme, mustard, salt, pepper and cayenne. Bring to a boil; cook until liquid is reduced by half, about 8 minutes.

4. Drain linguine. Stir tomatoes into sauce mixture; add pork and heat through. Serve with linguine and sprinkle with cheese.

I've always been fascinated by Fire Island, and thought the name was fitting for this slightly spicy pasta dish. —**CANDACE REED** DESOTO, TEXAS

Fire Island Ziti

PREP: 30 MIN. **COOK:** 20 MIN.
MAKES: 5 SERVINGS

- 2 pounds plum tomatoes, halved lengthwise
- 3 tablespoons olive oil, divided
- 2 garlic cloves, minced
- 1 teaspoon salt
- 8 ounces ziti or small tube pasta
- 2 cups fresh broccoli florets
- 1 pound Italian sausage links, cut into ½-inch slices
- ½ teaspoon crushed red pepper flakes
- ⅓ cup grated Romano cheese

1. Toss the tomatoes with 2 tablespoons oil, garlic and salt. Place cut side down in a 15-in. x 10-in. x 1-in. baking pan. Bake at 450° for 20-25 minutes or until tender. Chop when cool enough to handle.

2. Cook ziti according to package directions, adding broccoli during the last 4 minutes. Meanwhile, in a large skillet over medium heat, cook sausage in remaining oil until no longer pink. Add pepper flakes; cook 1 minute longer. Stir in tomatoes and heat through.

3. Drain ziti mixture; toss with sausage mixture. Sprinkle with cheese.

PORK CHOPS WITH PARMESAN SAUCE

Moist and tender chops make a speedy weeknight meal. They're dressed with a creamy and flavorful Parmesan sauce. Here's a new family favorite!

—TASTE OF HOME TEST KITCHEN

EAT SMART Pork Chops With Parmesan Sauce

PREP/TOTAL TIME: 20 MIN.
MAKES: 4 SERVINGS

- 4 **boneless pork loin chops (4 ounces each)**
- ½ **teaspoon salt**
- ¼ **teaspoon pepper**
- 1 **tablespoon butter**
- 2 **tablespoons all-purpose flour**
- 1 **cup fat-free milk**
- ⅓ **cup grated Parmesan cheese**
- 2 **tablespoons grated onion**
- 3 **teaspoons minced fresh parsley**
- ¼ **teaspoon dried thyme**
- ¼ **teaspoon ground nutmeg**

1. Sprinkle pork chops with salt and pepper. In a large nonstick skillet coated with cooking spray, cook chops in butter over medium heat until juices run clear; remove and keep warm.

2. Combine flour and milk until smooth; stir into pan. Bring to a boil; cook and stir for 2 minutes or until thickened. Stir in the remaining ingredients; heat through. Serve with chops.

PER SERVING *244 cal., 11 g fat (5 g sat. fat), 69 mg chol., 475 mg sodium, 7 g carb., trace fiber, 27 g pro.* **Diabetic Exchanges:** *4 lean meat, ½ starch, ½ fat.*

Polynesian Sausage Supper

When my sister first served us this unusual medley, I couldn't believe how good it was because she had thrown it together so quickly. Sweet pineapple really adds to the taste.

—**LAURA MCCARTHY** BUTTE, MONTANA

PREP/TOTAL TIME: 30 MIN.
MAKES: 6 SERVINGS

- 1 **pound smoked sausage, cut into ½-inch slices**
- 1 **medium onion, chopped**
- 1 **medium green pepper, cut into 1-inch chunks**
- 1 **can (14½ ounces) diced tomatoes, undrained**
- ½ **cup beef broth**
- 1 **tablespoon brown sugar**
- ¼ **teaspoon garlic powder**
- ¼ **teaspoon pepper**
- 1 **can (20 ounces) unsweetened pineapple chunks**
- 2 **tablespoons cornstarch**
   Hot cooked rice

1. In a large skillet, cook the sausage, onion and green pepper until the vegetables are tender.

2. Add the tomatoes, broth, brown sugar, garlic powder and pepper. Drain pineapple, reserving juice. Stir pineapple into sausage mixture. Bring to a boil; cook, uncovered, for 5 minutes.

3. Combine the cornstarch and reserved pineapple juice until smooth; gradually add to sausage mixture. Bring to a boil; cook and stir for 2 minutes or until thickened. Serve with rice.

Braised Pork With Red Chili Sauce

My mom shared the quick recipe for tender, flavorful pork. It's great with rice and salad or scooped into tortillas.

—KARA DE LA VEGA

SANTA ROSA, CALIFORNIA

PREP: 20 MIN. **COOK:** 20 MIN.
MAKES: 2 SERVINGS

- ¾ pound pork chop suey meat
- 1 teaspoon canola oil
- 1 medium onion, chopped
- 1 garlic clove, minced
- 1½ to 2 teaspoons chili powder
- ½ teaspoon dried oregano
- ½ teaspoon ground cumin
- ⅔ cup water
- 1 tablespoon tomato paste
- ½ teaspoon sugar
- ¼ teaspoon salt
- ¼ cup heavy whipping cream

1. In a large skillet, brown pork in oil. Remove and keep warm. In the same skillet, saute the onion, garlic, chili powder, oregano and cumin for 2-3 minutes or until onion is tender.
2. Stir in the pork, water, tomato paste, sugar and salt. Bring to a boil. Reduce heat; cover and simmer for 18-20 minutes or until pork is tender. Stir in cream and bring to a boil, stirring constantly.

Ham and Blue Cheese Pasta Salad

When I first saw this recipe, it piqued my interest. I made some adjustments each time I made it, and now the salad is a real winner at our house.

—CARAL KIRBY CLAYTON, MISSOURI

PREP/TOTAL TIME: 30 MIN.
MAKES: 6 SERVINGS

- 6 cups uncooked bow tie pasta
- 2 cups julienned fully cooked ham
- ⅓ cup crumbled blue or feta cheese
- ⅓ cup minced fresh parsley
- 1 garlic clove, minced
- 1½ teaspoons minced fresh rosemary or ½ teaspoon dried rosemary, crushed
- ¼ teaspoon pepper
- ⅓ cup olive oil
- 1 cup coarsely chopped pecans, toasted
  Grated Parmesan cheese

1. Cook pasta according to package directions; drain and rinse in cold water. Transfer to a large bowl.
2. Stir in the ham, blue cheese, parsley, garlic, rosemary and pepper. Add oil and pecans; mix well. Sprinkle with Parmesan cheese. Serve immediately.

SKEWERLESS STOVETOP KABOBS

> My family loves this quick and easy recipe so much, we never have any leftovers. It's also great on the grill. —JENNIFER MITCHELL ALTOONA, PENNSYLVANIA

EAT SMART Skewerless Stovetop Kabobs

PREP/TOTAL TIME: 30 MIN.
MAKES: 4 SERVINGS

- 1 pound pork tenderloin, cut into ¾-inch cubes
- ¾ cup fat-free Italian salad dressing, divided
- 2 large green peppers, cut into ¾-inch pieces
- 2 small zucchini, cut into ½-inch slices
- ½ pound medium fresh mushrooms, halved
- 1 large sweet onion, cut into wedges
- 1 cup cherry tomatoes
- ¼ teaspoon pepper
- ⅛ teaspoon seasoned salt

1. In a large nonstick skillet, saute pork in ¼ cup salad dressing until no longer pink. Remove and keep warm.

2. In the same pan, cook the peppers, zucchini, mushrooms, onion, tomatoes, pepper and seasoned salt in remaining salad dressing until vegetables are tender. Return pork to skillet; heat through.

PER SERVING *236 cal., 5 g fat (2 g sat. fat), 65 mg chol., 757 mg sodium, 22 g carb., 4 g fiber, 27 g pro.* **Diabetic Exchanges:** *3 lean meat, 2 starch.*

EAT SMART Italian Pork Stew

PREP: 30 MIN. **COOK:** 2¼ HOURS
MAKES: 8 SERVINGS (2 QUARTS)

- ⅔ cup all-purpose flour
- 2 pounds boneless pork loin, cut into 1-inch pieces
- 4 tablespoons olive oil, divided
- 1 large onion, chopped
- 5 garlic cloves, crushed
- 1 can (28 ounces) diced tomatoes, undrained
- 1 cup dry red wine or beef broth
- 3 bay leaves
- 1 cinnamon stick (3 inches)
- 1 tablespoon tomato paste
- 1 tablespoon red wine vinegar
- 1 teaspoon anchovy paste
- 1 teaspoon each dried oregano, basil and sage leaves
- ½ teaspoon salt
- ½ teaspoon crushed red pepper flakes
- ¼ teaspoon pepper
- ¼ cup minced fresh parsley
  Hot cooked bow tie pasta
  Grated Parmesan cheese

1. Place flour in a large resealable plastic bag. Add pork, a few pieces at a time, and shake to coat. In a Dutch oven, brown pork in 3 tablespoons oil in batches. Remove and set aside.

2. In the same pan, saute onion in remaining oil until tender. Add garlic; cook 1 minute longer. Stir in the tomatoes, wine, bay leaves, cinnamon, tomato paste, vinegar, anchovy paste, herbs, salt, pepper flakes, pepper and pork; bring to a boil.

3. Reduce heat; cover and simmer for 1½ hours, stirring occasionally. Stir in parsley. Cover and cook 30-40 minutes longer or until meat is tender. Skim fat; discard bay leaves and cinnamon.

4. Serve stew with pasta; sprinkle with cheese.

PER SERVING *256 cal., 12 g fat (3 g sat. fat), 59 mg chol., 349 mg sodium, 12 g carb., 2 g fiber, 24 g pro.* **Diabetic Exchanges:** *3 lean meat, 1 vegetable, 1 fat.*

Don't skip the anchovy paste in this stew! It gives a savory, salty flavor, but doesn't taste fishy at all. Add a salad and artisan bread for an incredible meal.

—LYNNE GERMAN CUMMING, GEORGIA

ITALIAN PORK STEW

BACON & TOMATO SPAGHETTI

Our summer-perfect pasta features baby spinach, cherry tomatoes and crisp bacon tossed with a tangy balsamic vinaigrette. —TASTE OF HOME TEST KITCHEN

Bacon & Tomato Spaghetti

PREP/TOTAL TIME: 25 MIN.
MAKES: 4 SERVINGS

- 8 ounces uncooked spaghetti
- ½ pound thick-sliced bacon strips, chopped
- 2 cups cherry tomatoes, halved
- 3 cups fresh baby spinach
- ¼ cup balsamic vinaigrette
- ½ teaspoon salt
- ¼ teaspoon pepper
  Grated Parmesan cheese

1. Cook the spaghetti according to package directions.
2. Meanwhile, in a large skillet, cook bacon over medium heat until crisp. Remove to paper towels with a slotted spoon; drain, reserving 2 tablespoons drippings. Saute tomatoes in drippings until tender.
3. Drain spaghetti; stir into skillet. Add the spinach, bacon, vinaigrette, salt and pepper; heat through. Sprinkle with cheese.

Baby spinach is convenient for using in recipes because the **young, tender leaves** don't need to be trimmed. **The entire leaf**—stem and all—is edible, unlike older spinach.

EAT SMART Mediterranean Pork and Orzo

All of the food groups are represented in this fresh and fabulous meal. It's one of my family's favorites.
—**MARY RELYEA** CANASTOTA, NEW YORK

PREP/TOTAL TIME: 30 MIN.
MAKES: 6 SERVINGS

- 2 pork tenderloins (¾ pound each)
- 1 teaspoon coarsely ground pepper
- 2 tablespoons olive oil
- 3 quarts water
- 1¼ cups uncooked orzo pasta
- ¼ teaspoon salt
- 1 package (6 ounces) fresh baby spinach
- 1 cup grape tomatoes, halved
- ¾ cup crumbled feta cheese

1. Rub pork with pepper; cut into 1-in. cubes. In a large nonstick skillet, cook pork in oil over medium heat for 8-10 minutes or until no longer pink.
2. Meanwhile, in a large saucepan, bring water to a boil. Stir in orzo and salt; cook, uncovered, for 8 minutes. Stir in spinach; cook 45-60 seconds longer or until orzo is tender and spinach is wilted.
3. Add tomatoes to the pork; cook and stir for 1 minute or until heated through. Drain orzo mixture; toss with pork mixture and cheese.
PER SERVING *372 cal., 11 g fat (4 g sat. fat), 71 mg chol., 306 mg sodium, 34 g carb., 3 g fiber, 31 g pro.* **Diabetic Exchanges:** *3 lean meat, 2 starch, 1 vegetable, 1 fat.*

Sausage Macaroni

Kids of all ages really go for hearty, creamy skillet meals. Your family will adore this macaroni.

—**PHYLLIS SCHMALZ** KANSAS CITY, KANSAS

PREP/TOTAL TIME: 30 MIN.
MAKES: 5 SERVINGS

- 1 **pound bulk Italian sausage**
- ¼ **cup chopped onion**
- 2 **tablespoons chopped green pepper**
- 2 **tablespoons chopped sweet red pepper**
- 2 **cups uncooked elbow macaroni**
- 2 **cups water**
- 1 **cup chili sauce**
- 1 **can (5 ounces) evaporated milk**
- ½ **cup shredded cheddar cheese**

1. In a large skillet, cook the sausage, onion and peppers over medium heat until meat is no longer pink; drain.

2. Add macaroni and water. Bring to a boil. Reduce heat; cover and simmer for 7-8 minutes or until macaroni is tender. Stir in chili sauce and milk; heat through.

3. Remove from the heat. Sprinkle with cheese. Cover and let stand for 5 minutes or until cheese is melted.

Au Gratin Sausage Skillet

By using frozen vegetables and packaged au gratin potatoes, I can get this satisfying dinner on the table in no time. It's an excellent way of getting kids to eat their vegetables. Even our oldest daughter, who can be a picky eater, loves it.

—**PENNY GREENE** LANCASTER, OHIO

PREP: 15 MIN.   **COOK:** 30 MIN.
MAKES: 4 SERVINGS

- 1 **pound smoked kielbasa or Polish sausage, halved and sliced**
- 2 **tablespoons canola oil**
- 1 **package (4.9 ounces) au gratin potatoes**
- 2½ **cups water**
- 1 **package (8 ounces) frozen California-blend vegetables**
- 1 **to 2 cups (4 to 8 ounces) shredded cheddar cheese**

1. In a large skillet, cook sausage in oil until lightly browned; drain. Add potatoes with contents of sauce mix and water. Cover and cook over medium heat for 18-20 minutes or until the potatoes are almost tender, stirring occasionally.

2. Add vegetables; cover and cook for 8-10 minutes or until potatoes and vegetables are tender. Sprinkle with cheese. Remove from the heat; cover and let stand for 2 minutes or until the cheese is melted.

NOTE *The milk and butter listed on the potato package are not used in this recipe.*

My husband, Ronald, works long hours and frequently won't arrive home until past 7 p.m. But these creamy noodles are still tasty after warming in the microwave.
—**BARB MARSHALL** PICKERINGTON, OHIO

BROCCOLI-HAM NOODLES

Broccoli-Ham Noodles

PREP/TOTAL TIME: 25 MIN.
MAKES: 8 SERVINGS

- 1 package (12 ounces) egg noodles
- 1 package (16 ounces) frozen broccoli cuts
- 3 cups cubed fully cooked ham
- 1 cup (4 ounces) shredded part-skim mozzarella cheese
- 1 cup (4 ounces) shredded Parmesan cheese
- ⅓ cup butter, cubed
- ½ cup half-and-half cream
- ¼ teaspoon each garlic powder, salt and pepper

1. In a Dutch oven, cook noodles in boiling water for 5 minutes.
2. Add the broccoli and ham; cook 5-10 minutes longer or until noodles are tender.
3. Drain; return to pan. Stir in the remaining ingredients. Cook and stir over low heat until butter is melted and mixture is heated through.

Lasagna Sandwiches

These cheesy grilled sandwiches really do taste like lasagna. They're perfect for a quick evening meal. Our children loved them with vegetable soup and crunchy potato sticks.

—GAIL ROTHEISER HIGHLAND PARK, ILLINOIS

PREP/TOTAL TIME: 15 MIN.
MAKES: 4 SERVINGS

- ¼ cup sour cream
- 2 tablespoons chopped onion
- ½ teaspoon dried oregano
- ¼ teaspoon seasoned salt
- 8 slices Italian or other white bread
- 8 bacon strips, halved and cooked
- 8 slices tomato
- 4 slices part-skim mozzarella cheese
- 2 to 3 tablespoons butter

1. In a small bowl, combine the first four ingredients; spread on four slices of bread. Layer with bacon, tomato and cheese; top with remaining bread.
2. In a large skillet or griddle, melt 2 tablespoons butter. Toast sandwiches until lightly browned on both sides and cheese is melted, adding butter if necessary.

Pork tenderloin gets delightful Italian flavor from prosciutto, tomatoes and herbs. The aroma is divine as the rich and creamy sauce cooks.

—LORRAINE CALAND SHUNIAH, ONTARIO

Tuscan Pork Medallions

PREP/TOTAL TIME: 30 MIN.
MAKES: 2 SERVINGS

- ¾ pound pork tenderloin, cut into 1-inch slices
- ¼ teaspoon salt
- ⅛ teaspoon pepper
- 1 tablespoon butter
- 2 thin slices prosciutto or deli ham, chopped
- 2 garlic cloves, minced
- 1½ teaspoons minced fresh sage or ½ teaspoon dried sage leaves
- 2 tablespoons balsamic vinegar
- ½ cup heavy whipping cream
- ¾ cup chopped plum tomatoes
- 4 fresh basil leaves, thinly sliced
- 1 teaspoon grated Parmesan cheese

1. Sprinkle pork with salt and pepper. In a large skillet over medium heat, cook pork in butter until a thermometer reads 145°. Remove and set aside.
2. Meanwhile, in the same skillet, saute prosciutto in the drippings until browned. Add garlic and sage; cook 1 minute longer. Add vinegar, stirring to loosen browned bits from pan.
3. Stir in cream; bring to a boil. Reduce heat; cook and stir for 1-2 minutes or until slightly thickened. Add tomatoes and pork; heat through. Sprinkle each serving with basil and cheese.

Barbecue Ham Sandwiches

My mother would buy the ham and make a batch of sauce on Saturday. Then after church on Sunday, our hungry family would be able to quickly sit down and enjoy a hearty, delicious meal.

—MOLLIE FRY

RALEIGH, NORTH CAROLINA

PREP/TOTAL TIME: 25 MIN.
MAKES: 6 SERVINGS

- 1 cup plus 2 tablespoons chili sauce
- ¾ cup packed brown sugar
- ½ cup plus 1 tablespoon water
- ¾ teaspoon prepared mustard
- ¼ to ½ teaspoon chili powder
- ⅛ teaspoon ground cloves
- 1½ pounds shaved fully cooked ham
- 6 hamburger buns, split and toasted

In a large saucepan, combine the first six ingredients. Cook, uncovered, over low heat for 15 minutes. Stir in ham; heat through. Using a slotted spoon, serve on buns.

Pork Chops Over Rice

If you asked my husband to name his favorite foods, he'd likely mention these chops. I've also served this appealing skillet supper to company.

—NANCY CHRISTENBERRY

ORTONVILLE, MICHIGAN

PREP: 10 MIN. **COOK:** 30 MIN.
MAKES: 8 SERVINGS

- 8 boneless pork loin chops
  (4 ounces each)
- 1 tablespoon canola oil
- 1 cup uncooked long grain rice
- 1 can (14½ ounces) chicken broth
- ½ cup water
- 1 small onion, chopped
- 1 package (10 ounces) frozen peas
- ½ teaspoon salt
- ½ teaspoon dried thyme

1. In a large skillet over medium heat, brown pork chops in oil; remove. Add the remaining ingredients to the skillet; top with pork chops.
2. Bring to a boil. Reduce heat; cover and simmer for 20-25 minutes or until rice is tender.

SPRINGTIME PENNE

With ham and asparagus in a creamy sauce, this simple pasta is tasty enough for even your pickiest guests. It's wonderful for Easter or to use up leftover ham. **—CHERYL NEWENDORP** PELLA, IOWA

Springtime Penne

PREP/TOTAL TIME: 20 MIN.
MAKES: 5 SERVINGS

- 3 cups uncooked penne pasta
- 1 pound fresh asparagus, cut into 1-inch pieces
- 1 large onion, chopped
- ¼ cup butter
- ½ pound cubed fully cooked ham
- ½ cup heavy whipping cream
- ¼ teaspoon pepper
- ⅛ teaspoon salt

Cook pasta according to package directions. Meanwhile, in a large skillet, saute asparagus and onion in butter for 5-8 minutes or until asparagus is crisp-tender. Add the ham, cream, pepper and salt; bring to a boil. Reduce heat; cook over low heat for 1 minute. Drain pasta. Add to the asparagus mixture; toss to coat.

Warm Pork and Raspberry Salad

For a light and refreshing salad that is fancy enough for company, try this recipe. Pork tenderloin tastes lovely with fresh salad greens, savory herbs and a tangy raspberry sauce.

—TASTE OF HOME COOKING SCHOOL

PREP/TOTAL TIME: 20 MIN.
MAKES: 4 SERVINGS

- 1 to 1¼ pounds pork tenderloin
  Salt and pepper to taste
- 2 tablespoons olive oil, divided
- ¼ cup sliced red onion
- 1 garlic clove, minced
- ½ cup chicken broth
- ½ cup seedless raspberry preserves
- ⅓ cup raspberry vinegar
- ½ teaspoon dried rosemary, crushed
- ½ teaspoon rubbed sage
- 4 cups spring mix salad greens
- ½ cup crumbled Gorgonzola cheese
- ½ cup chopped pecans, toasted
- ½ cup grape tomatoes

1. Slice the pork tenderloin into 16 slices. Season with salt and pepper.
2. In a large skillet over medium-high heat, cook pork in 1 tablespoon oil until no longer pink. Remove and keep warm.
3. In the same skillet, saute onion in remaining oil for 2 minutes. Add garlic; cook and stir for 30 seconds.
4. Stir in the chicken broth, preserves, vinegar, rosemary and sage. Cook and stir for 2-3 minutes or until sauce is thickened. Season with salt and pepper.
5. Place the greens in a salad bowl and toss with a third of the raspberry sauce. Sprinkle with cheese, pecans and tomatoes. Top with the warm pork slices. Serve immediately with remaining sauce.

WARM PORK AND RASPBERRY SALAD

Tortellini Carbonara

Here's a rich and wonderful pasta that comes together with just five ingredients.

—CATHY CROYLE DAVIDSVILLE, PENNSYLVANIA

PREP/TOTAL TIME: 20 MIN.
MAKES: 4 SERVINGS

- 1 package (9 ounces) refrigerated cheese tortellini
- 8 bacon strips, cooked and crumbled
- 1 cup heavy whipping cream
- ½ cup minced fresh parsley
- ½ cup grated Parmesan cheese

1. Cook tortellini according to package directions. Meanwhile, in a large saucepan, combine the bacon, cream, parsley and cheese; cook over medium heat until heated through.
2. Drain tortellini; toss with cream sauce. Serve immediately.

Jiffy Pork & Penne

Some people call it dinnertime, but many of us call it rush hour. Slow down with this super-easy meal. The only thing you'll have left over is time to share with your family at the table.

—BRIGITTE SCHALLER
FLEMINGTON, MISSOURI

PREP/TOTAL TIME: 30 MIN.
MAKES: 5 SERVINGS

- 1½ cups uncooked penne pasta
- 1 pound ground pork
- ½ cup chopped onion
- 1 can (14½ ounces) stewed tomatoes, undrained
- 1 can (8 ounces) tomato sauce
- 1 teaspoon Italian seasoning
- 1 medium zucchini, cut into ¼-inch slices

1. Cook pasta according to package directions. Meanwhile, in a large skillet, cook pork and onion over medium heat until meat is no longer pink; drain. Add the tomatoes, tomato sauce and Italian seasoning. Bring to a boil. Reduce heat; cover and cook for 5 minutes to allow flavors to blend.
2. Drain pasta; add to skillet. Stir in zucchini. Cover and cook for 3-5 minutes or until zucchini is tender.

My husband and I live on a small farm with our two young sons. We're always blessed with plenty of zucchini from our garden in summer, so I try lots of different zucchini recipes. This is one of my family's favorites.

—DIANE BANASZAK WEST BEND, WISCONSIN

SKILLET PORK CHOPS WITH ZUCCHINI

Skillet Pork Chops With Zucchini

PREP: 15 MIN. **COOK:** 40 MIN.
MAKES: 6 SERVINGS

- 3 tablespoons all-purpose flour
- 2 tablespoons plus ¼ cup grated Parmesan cheese, divided
- 1½ teaspoons salt
- ½ teaspoon dill weed
- ¼ teaspoon pepper
- 6 boneless pork loin chops (4 ounces each)
- 1 tablespoon canola oil
- 2 medium onions, sliced
- ⅓ cup warm water
- 3 medium zucchini (about 1 pound), sliced
- ½ teaspoon paprika

1. In a shallow dish, combine the flour, 2 tablespoons cheese, salt, dill and pepper. Dip the pork chops in flour mixture to coat both sides; shake off excess.

2. In a large skillet, brown the chops on both sides in oil. Top with onions; add water. Bring to a boil. Reduce heat; cover and simmer for 15 minutes.

3. Place zucchini over the onions. Sprinkle remaining cheese over zucchini. Sprinkle with paprika. Cover and simmer for 10-15 minutes or until vegetables are tender and a thermometer inserted in pork reads 145°. Let stand 5 minutes.

To quickly peel garlic, gently smash the cloves with the side of a large **kitchen knife** or the end of a heavy can. The peel **quickly separates** from the crushed cloves.

BLT SALAD

It's hard to find a vegetable or salad that everyone in my family of six will eat, but they all raved about this one. With garden-fresh basil and tomatoes, the salad is simply amazing.

—**SUSIE CLAYTON** SOUTH ST. PAUL, MINNESOTA

BLT Salad

PREP/TOTAL TIME: 25 MIN.
MAKES: 6 SERVINGS

- 1 pound sliced bacon, cut into 1-inch pieces
- ¼ cup butter, cubed
- 4 slices white bread, crusts removed and cut into 1-inch cubes
- ½ cup mayonnaise
- 3 to 5 tablespoons minced fresh basil
- 2 tablespoons red wine vinegar
- ½ teaspoon pepper
- ½ teaspoon minced garlic
- 6 cups torn romaine
- 1½ cups grape tomatoes

1. In a large skillet, cook bacon over medium heat until crisp. Using a slotted spoon, remove to paper towels; drain, reserving 2 tablespoons drippings. Set bacon and drippings aside.

2. In another large skillet, melt butter. Add bread cubes; cook over medium heat for 4-5 minutes or until golden brown, stirring frequently. Remove to paper towels; cool.

3. For dressing, in a small bowl, whisk the mayonnaise, basil, vinegar, pepper, garlic and reserved drippings. In a large bowl, combine the romaine, tomatoes and bacon. Drizzle with dressing and toss to coat. Top with croutons.

Fish & Seafood

154   159   153

Eating fresh and healthy has never **tasted so good** as with these **delightful choices** from home cooks across the country. Indulge in **buttery scallops**, family-pleasing fish tacos, **heart-healthy salmon** and more. Here's to your good appetite!

EASY SALMON FETTUCCINE

I found a recipe for quick and nutritious salmon pasta in our local newspaper, but I adapted it to suit our tastes. The dish has become a standby dinner that I serve often. —**DOROTHY WRAY** SWEETWATER, TEXAS

EAT SMART **Tilapia With Jasmine Rice**

This zesty tilapia is to die for. Fragrant jasmine rice brings a special touch to the meal. And it gets even better—each serving has only 5 grams of fat!
—**SHIRL PARSONS**

CAPE CARTERET, NORTH CAROLINA

PREP/TOTAL TIME: 30 MIN.
MAKES: 2 SERVINGS

- ¾ cup water
- ½ cup uncooked jasmine rice
- 1½ teaspoons butter
- ¼ teaspoon ground cumin
- ¼ teaspoon seafood seasoning
- ¼ teaspoon pepper
- ⅛ teaspoon salt
- 2 tilapia fillets (6 ounces each)
- ¼ cup fat-free Italian salad dressing

1. In a large saucepan, bring the water, rice and butter to a boil. Reduce heat; cover and simmer for 15-20 minutes or until liquid is absorbed and rice is tender.
2. Combine the seasonings; sprinkle over fillets. Place salad dressing in a large skillet; cook over medium heat until heated through. Add fish; cook for 3-4 minutes on each side or until fish flakes easily with a fork. Serve with rice.
PER SERVING *356 cal., 5 g fat (3 g sat. fat), 91 mg chol., 743 mg sodium, 41 g carb., 1 g fiber, 35 g pro.* **Diabetic Exchanges:** *4 lean meat, 3 starch, ½ fat.*

Easy Salmon Fettuccine

PREP/TOTAL TIME: 25 MIN.
MAKES: 2 SERVINGS

- 4 ounces uncooked fettuccine
- 2 tablespoons chopped onion
- 3 tablespoons butter
- 1 plum tomato, seeded and cut into strips
- 3 tablespoons lemon juice
- 1 teaspoon dried parsley flakes
- ½ teaspoon grated lemon peel
- ¼ teaspoon salt
- 1 pouch (7.1 ounces) boneless skinless pink salmon
- 2 tablespoons pine nuts

1. Cook fettuccine according to package directions.
2. Meanwhile, in a large skillet, saute onion in butter until tender. Add the tomato, lemon juice, parsley, lemon peel and salt; cook and stir until heated through.
3. Drain fettuccine; add to skillet. Stir in salmon and heat through. Sprinkle with pine nuts.

After tasting fettuccine Alfredo at a restaurant, I tried to duplicate the recipe at home. You can't imagine how pleased I was when I came up with this delicious version. Not only does my family love the creamy dish, but my husband prefers it to the one at the restaurant. —**RAE NATOLI** KINGSTON, NEW YORK

BROCCOLI SHRIMP ALFREDO

Broccoli Shrimp Alfredo

PREP/TOTAL TIME: 30 MIN.
MAKES: 4 SERVINGS

- 8 ounces uncooked fettuccine
- 1 pound uncooked medium shrimp, peeled and deveined
- 3 garlic cloves, minced
- ½ cup butter, cubed
- 1 package (8 ounces) cream cheese, cubed
- 1 cup milk
- ½ cup shredded Parmesan cheese
- 4 cups frozen broccoli florets
- ½ teaspoon salt
  Dash pepper

1. Cook fettuccine according to package directions. Meanwhile, in a large skillet, saute shrimp and garlic in butter until shrimp turn pink. Remove and set aside.

2. In the same skillet, combine the cream cheese, milk and Parmesan cheese; cook and stir until cheeses are melted and mixture is smooth.

3. Place 1 in. of water in a saucepan; add broccoli. Bring to a boil. Reduce heat; cover and simmer for 6-8 minutes or until tender. Drain. Stir the broccoli, shrimp, salt and pepper into cheese sauce; heat through. Drain fettuccine and top with the shrimp mixture.

EAT SMART Tuna Delight

A handful of ingredients is all it takes to put a meal on the table. This makes a speedy dinner on busy weeknights or a tasty lunch when unexpected guests drop by.
—MARIE GREEN
BELLE FOURCHE, SOUTH DAKOTA

PREP/TOTAL TIME: 10 MIN.
MAKES: 3 SERVINGS

- 1¾ cups frozen mixed vegetables
- 1 can (12 ounces) light tuna in water, drained and flaked
- 1 can (10¾ ounces) condensed cream of chicken or celery soup, undiluted
  Hot cooked rice or noodles

In a large saucepan, combine the vegetables, tuna and soup. Cook and stir until heated through. Serve over rice or noodles.

PER SERVING *260 cal., 4 g fat (1 g sat. fat), 42 mg chol., 1,116 mg sodium, 21 g carb., 5 g fiber, 34 g pro.* **Diabetic Exchanges:** *3 lean meat, 1 starch, 1 vegetable.*

EAT SMART Southwest-Style Cod

PREP/TOTAL TIME: 30 MIN.
MAKES: 4 SERVINGS

- 1 small onion, chopped
- 1 small green pepper, chopped
- 2 teaspoons olive oil
- 2 garlic cloves, minced
- 1 can (15 ounces) tomato sauce
- 2 medium tomatoes, chopped
- 1 can (2¼ ounces) sliced ripe olives, drained
- ½ teaspoon ground cumin
- ¼ teaspoon hot pepper sauce
- ⅛ teaspoon pepper
- 4 cod fillets (6 ounces each)

1. In a large skillet, saute onion and green pepper in oil until tender. Add garlic; saute 1 minute longer. Stir in the tomato sauce, tomatoes, olives, cumin, pepper sauce and pepper. Bring to a boil. Reduce heat; simmer, uncovered, for 5 minutes.

2. Add fillets. Cover and cook over medium heat for 10-14 minutes or until fish flakes easily with a fork, turning once.

PER SERVING *226 cal., 6 g fat (1 g sat. fat), 65 mg chol., 734 mg sodium, 12 g carb., 3 g fiber, 30 g pro.* **Diabetic Exchanges:** *4 lean meat, 2 vegetable, 1 fat.*

Make tonight Fish Night! This festive recipe with a little zip will guarantee the night is anything but boring. **—TASTE OF HOME TEST KITCHEN**

SALMON QUESADILLAS

I like recipes that get me out of the kitchen fast so I can spend more time with my family. These super-quick quesadillas are a tasty change of pace from salmon patties. —HEIDI MAIN ANCHORAGE, ALASKA

Salmon Quesadillas

PREP/TOTAL TIME: 15 MIN.
MAKES: 4 SERVINGS

- 2 garlic cloves, minced
- 1 teaspoon canola oil
- 1 can (14¾ ounces) salmon, drained, bones and skin removed
- 1 to 2 teaspoons dried basil
- ½ teaspoon pepper
- 1 tablespoon butter, softened
- 4 flour tortillas (8 inches), warmed
- 2 cups (8 ounces) part-skim shredded mozzarella cheese
  Guacamole or salsa

1. In a skillet, saute garlic in oil until fragrant. Stir in the salmon, basil and pepper; heat through.
2. Meanwhile, spread butter over one side of each tortilla. Place tortillas on a griddle, buttered side down. Sprinkle one half of each tortilla with ¼ cup cheese and a fourth of the salmon; top each with ¼ cup cheese. Fold other half over filling.
3. Cook over medium heat 1-2 minutes on each side or until golden brown and cheese is melted. Cut each into wedges; serve with guacamole or salsa.

EAT SMART Egg Foo Yong

Forget the Chinese takeout! You'll have fun making a colorful, crunchy and delicious version of the classic dish at home in just 30 minutes.
—**SHERRI MELOTIK** OAK CREEK, WISCONSIN

PREP/TOTAL TIME: 30 MIN.
MAKES: 4 SERVINGS

- 1 can (14 ounces) chop suey vegetables, drained
- ½ pound peeled and deveined cooked small shrimp, coarsely chopped
- 4 green onions, thinly sliced
- 4 eggs, beaten
- 2 tablespoons canola oil

GREEN PEA SAUCE

- 2 tablespoons cornstarch
- 1 teaspoon chicken bouillon granules
- 2 cups water
- 1½ teaspoons reduced-sodium soy sauce
- ½ cup frozen peas, thawed

1. In a large bowl, combine the chop suey vegetables, shrimp and green onions. Stir in eggs. In a large nonstick skillet, heat 1 teaspoon oil. Drop vegetable mixture by ¼ cupfuls into skillet. Cook in batches until browned on both sides, using remaining oil as needed.
2. In a small saucepan, combine cornstarch and bouillon. Gradually stir in water and soy sauce. Bring to a boil; cook and stir for 2 minutes or until thickened. Stir in peas; heat through. Serve with egg foo yong.
PER SERVING *242 cal., 13 g fat (2 g sat. fat), 298 mg chol., 497 mg sodium, 10 g carb., 2 g fiber, 20 g pro.* **Diabetic Exchanges:** *3 lean meat, 1½ fat, ½ starch.*

SHRIMP PAD THAI

Shrimp Pad Thai

You can make this yummy Thai classic in no time. Find fish sauce and chili garlic sauce in the Asian foods aisle of your grocery store.

—ELISE RAY SHAWNEE, KANSAS

PREP/TOTAL TIME: 30 MIN.
MAKES: 4 SERVINGS

- 4 ounces uncooked thick rice noodles
- ½ pound uncooked small shrimp, peeled and deveined
- 2 teaspoons canola oil
- 1 large onion, chopped
- 1 garlic clove, minced
- 1 egg, lightly beaten
- 3 cups coleslaw mix
- 4 green onions, thinly sliced
- ⅓ cup rice vinegar
- ¼ cup sugar
- 3 tablespoons reduced-sodium soy sauce
- 2 tablespoons fish sauce or additional reduced-sodium soy sauce
- 2 to 3 teaspoons chili garlic sauce
- 2 tablespoons chopped salted peanuts
  Chopped fresh cilantro leaves

1. Cook noodles according to package directions.
2. In a large nonstick skillet or wok, stir-fry shrimp in oil until shrimp turn pink; remove and set aside. Add onion and garlic to the pan. Make a well in the center of the onion mixture; add egg. Stir-fry for 2-3 minutes or until egg is completely set. Add the coleslaw mix, green onions, vinegar, sugar, soy sauce, fish sauce, chili garlic sauce and peanuts; heat through.
3. Return shrimp to the pan and heat through. Drain noodles; toss with the shrimp mixture. Garnish with cilantro.

Rice vinegar has a **sweet and mild** taste. Try using it instead of white wine vinegar or champagne vinegar for an easy switch. It's a **versatile** ingredient.

SHRIMP RISOTTO

EAT SMART Scallops with Chipotle-Orange Sauce

PREP/TOTAL TIME: 15 MIN.
MAKES: 2 SERVINGS

- ¾ pound sea scallops, halved
- ¼ teaspoon paprika
- ¼ teaspoon salt, divided
- 2 teaspoons butter
- ¼ cup orange juice
- ¼ teaspoon ground chipotle pepper
  Hot cooked linguine, optional
- 2 tablespoons thinly sliced green onion

1. Sprinkle scallops with paprika and ⅛ teaspoon salt. In a nonstick skillet coated with cooking spray, melt butter over medium heat. Add scallops; cook for 3-4 minutes on each side or until firm and opaque.
2. Add orange juice and remaining salt to the pan; bring to a boil. Remove from the heat; stir in chipotle pepper.
3. Serve over linguine if desired. Garnish with green onion.
PER SERVING *200 cal., 5 g fat (3 g sat. fat), 66 mg chol., 608 mg sodium, 8 g carb., trace fiber, 29 g pro.* **Diabetic Exchanges:** *4 lean meat, ½ fat.*

This delightful main dish will add elegance to family meals. Instant rice makes it come together quickly for a special dinner any day of the week.
—TASTE OF HOME TEST KITCHEN

If your sea scallops are very large, you may wish to **split them in half** horizontally prior to cooking. **Decrease the cook time** to ensure they are **tender and buttery,** not overcooked.

Shrimp Risotto

PREP/TOTAL TIME: 30 MIN.
MAKES: 4 SERVINGS

- 1 small onion, chopped
- 2 tablespoons butter
- 1¾ cups uncooked instant rice
- 2 garlic cloves, minced
- ½ teaspoon dried basil
- ¼ teaspoon pepper
- 2 cans (14½ ounces each) chicken broth
- 1 pound peeled and deveined cooked medium shrimp
- 2 cups fresh baby spinach, coarsely chopped
- 1 cup frozen corn, thawed
- 1 plum tomato, chopped
- ¼ cup grated Parmesan cheese
- 2 tablespoons 2% milk

1. In a large skillet, saute onion in butter until tender. Add the rice, garlic, basil and pepper; cook 2 minutes longer. Stir in one can of broth. Cook and stir until most of the liquid is absorbed.
2. Add the remaining broth, ½ cup at a time, stirring constantly. Allow the liquid to absorb between additions. Cook until risotto is creamy and rice is tender.
3. Add the remaining ingredients; cook and stir until spinach is wilted and shrimp are heated through.

Tender scallops with a sprinkle of paprika and ground chipotle make this recipe a surefire way to warm up dinnertime. —JAN JUSTICE CATLETTSBURG, KENTUCKY

SCALLOPS WITH CHIPOTLE-ORANGE SAUCE

> I keep several cans of salmon in my pantry at all times so I never have to worry about drop-in guests. This recipe is so tasty and quick...and it doubles easily for company.
>
> —**KATNEE CABECEIRAS** SOUTH PRAIRIE, WASHINGTON

EAT SMART Open-Faced Salmon Sandwiches

PREP/TOTAL TIME: 25 MIN.
MAKES: 4 SERVINGS

- 1 egg, lightly beaten
- 1 small onion, finely chopped
- 1 small green pepper, finely chopped
- ⅓ cup soft bread crumbs
- 1 tablespoon lemon juice
- 1 teaspoon reduced-sodium teriyaki sauce
- ¼ teaspoon dried parsley flakes
- ¼ teaspoon dried basil
- ¼ teaspoon pepper
- 1 can (14¾ ounces) salmon, drained, bones and skin removed
- 2 English muffins, split and toasted Lettuce leaves and tomato slices, optional

1. In a small bowl, combine the first nine ingredients. Fold in salmon. Shape into four patties.

2. In a large nonstick skillet coated with cooking spray, cook patties over medium heat for 4-5 minutes on each side or until lightly browned. Serve on English muffin halves with lettuce and tomato if desired.

PER SERVING *270 cal., 10 g fat (2 g sat. fat), 99 mg chol., 757 mg sodium, 19 g carb., 2 g fiber, 26 g pro.* **Diabetic Exchanges:** *3 lean meat, 1 starch.*

Nicoise Salad

This garden-fresh salad is a feast for the eyes as well as the palate. Add some crusty bread and you have a great meal perfect for summer.

—**MARLA FOGDERUD** MASON, MICHIGAN

PREP: 40 MIN. + COOLING
MAKES: 2 SERVINGS

- ⅓ cup olive oil
- 3 tablespoons white wine vinegar
- 1½ teaspoons Dijon mustard
- ⅛ teaspoon each salt, onion powder and pepper

SALAD

- 2 small red potatoes
- ½ cup cut fresh green beans
- 3½ cups torn Bibb lettuce
- ½ cup cherry tomatoes, halved
- 10 Greek olives, pitted and halved
- 2 hard-cooked eggs, quartered
- 1 can (5 ounces) albacore white tuna in water, drained and flaked

1. In a small bowl, whisk the oil, vinegar, mustard, salt, onion powder and pepper; set aside.

2. Place potatoes in a small saucepan and cover with water. Bring to a boil. Reduce heat; cover and simmer for 15-20 minutes or until tender. Drain and cool; cut into quarters.

3. Place beans in another saucepan and cover with water. Bring to a boil. Cover and cook for 3-5 minutes or until crisp-tender; drain and rinse in cold water.

4. Divide lettuce between two salad plates; top with potatoes, beans, tomatoes, olives, eggs and tuna. Drizzle with dressing.

Shrimp Scampi

Shrimp scampi looks like you fussed, but it's actually a snap to prepare. Lemon and herbs enhance the shrimp, and bread crumbs add a pleasing crunch. Served over pasta, the main dish is pretty enough for company.

—LORI PACKER OMAHA, NEBRASKA

PREP/TOTAL TIME: 20 MIN.
MAKES: 4 SERVINGS

- 3 to 4 garlic cloves, minced
- ¼ cup butter, cubed
- ¼ cup olive oil
- 1 pound uncooked medium shrimp, peeled and deveined
- ¼ cup lemon juice
- ½ teaspoon pepper
- ¼ teaspoon dried oregano
- ½ cup grated Parmesan cheese
- ¼ cup dry bread crumbs
- ¼ cup minced fresh parsley
  Hot cooked angel hair pasta

1. In a 10-in. ovenproof skillet, saute garlic in butter and oil until fragrant. Add the shrimp, lemon juice, pepper and oregano; cook and stir until shrimp turn pink. Sprinkle with cheese, bread crumbs and parsley.
2. Broil 6 in. from the heat for 2-3 minutes or until topping is golden brown. Serve with pasta.

Crab Salad Shells

I received this recipe from a friend and adjusted the ingredients to suit my family's tastes. It's a fun and flavorful way to enjoy crab salad. Serve it over lettuce for a refreshing summer meal.

—JO ANNE ANDERSON KNOXVILLE, IOWA

PREP: 35 MIN. + CHILLING
MAKES: 30 STUFFED SHELLS

- 30 uncooked jumbo pasta shells
- 1 cup finely chopped fresh broccoli florets
- 1 garlic clove, minced
- 2 packages (8 ounces each) imitation crabmeat, chopped
- 1 cup (8 ounces) sour cream
- ½ cup mayonnaise
- ¼ cup finely shredded carrot
- ¼ cup diced seeded peeled cucumber
- 1 tablespoon chopped green onion
- 1 teaspoon dill weed

1. Cook pasta according to package directions; rinse in cold water and drain well.
2. Meanwhile, in a small microwave-safe bowl, combine the broccoli and garlic. Cover and microwave on high for 1 minute or until crisp-tender.
3. Transfer to a large bowl; stir in the remaining ingredients. Stuff into pasta shells. Cover and refrigerate overnight.

Here's an easy way to enjoy fish tacos. I tuck golden-brown catfish nuggets into tortillas with a quick coleslaw filling. —MONICA PERRY BOISE, IDAHO

CATFISH SOFT TACOS

Catfish Soft Tacos

PREP: 10 MIN. + CHILLING **COOK:** 10 MIN.
MAKES: 2 SERVINGS

- 1½ cups coleslaw mix
- 2 tablespoons finely chopped onion
- ⅛ teaspoon pepper
- 1 teaspoon Creole or Cajun seasoning, divided
- ¼ cup coleslaw salad dressing
- 2 tablespoons pancake mix
- ½ pound catfish fillets, cut into 2-inch pieces
- 1 teaspoon canola oil
- 4 flour tortillas (6 inches), warmed

1. Combine the coleslaw mix, onion, pepper and ¼ teaspoon seasoning. Stir in dressing. Cover and refrigerate for at least 30 minutes.
2. In a resealable plastic bag, combine the pancake mix and remaining seasoning. Add fish and toss to coat.
3. In a small nonstick skillet over medium heat, cook fish in oil until light golden brown on all sides and fish flakes easily with a fork.
4. Spoon coleslaw mixture onto tortillas; top with fish and roll up.

Linguine With Clam Sauce

Keep the ingredients for this 30-minute dish handy for a fresh and fast dinner.
—PERLENE HOEKEMA LYNDEN, WASHINGTON

PREP/TOTAL TIME: 30 MIN.
MAKES: 4 SERVINGS

- 1 package (8 ounces) linguine
- 2 to 3 garlic cloves, minced
- 5 tablespoons butter
- ¼ cup olive oil
- 1 tablespoon all-purpose flour
- 2 cans (6½ ounces each) minced clams
- 1 cup (4 ounces) shredded Monterey Jack cheese
- ¼ cup minced fresh parsley

1. Cook linguine according to package directions. Meanwhile, in a large skillet over medium heat, cook the garlic in butter and oil until fragrant. Stir in flour until blended. Drain the clams, reserving juice; set clams aside.

SALMON WITH VEGETABLE SALSA

This salsa recipe is great not only with salmon, but also with grilled chicken breasts and barbecued shrimp kabobs. The only fresh ingredient not available in my son's garden was the avocado!

—PRISCILLA GILBERT INDIAN HARBOUR BEACH, FLORIDA

2. Gradually stir juice into the pan. Bring to a boil; cook and stir for 2 minutes or until thickened. Reduce heat; add the clams, cheese and parsley. Cook and stir until cheese is melted. Drain linguine; serve with clam sauce.

Salmon With Vegetable Salsa

PREP/TOTAL TIME: 30 MIN.
MAKES: 4 SERVINGS

- 1½ cups grape tomatoes, halved
- 1½ cups chopped peeled cucumber
- 1 medium ripe avocado, peeled and cubed
- 1 small red onion, chopped
- 2 tablespoons minced fresh cilantro
- 1 jalapeno pepper, seeded and minced
- 2 tablespoons lime juice
- ½ teaspoon salt

FISH
- 4 salmon fillets (6 ounces each)
- 1 tablespoon lime juice
- ½ teaspoon salt
- ¼ teaspoon cayenne pepper
- 1 tablespoon butter

1. In a large bowl, combine the tomatoes, cucumber, avocado, onion, cilantro, jalapeno, lime juice and salt; set aside.
2. Drizzle salmon with lime juice. Sprinkle with salt and cayenne pepper. In a large skillet, cook fillets in butter for 3-4 minutes on each side or until fish flakes easily with a fork. Serve with salsa.
NOTE *Wear disposable gloves when cutting hot peppers; the oils can burn skin. Avoid touching your face.*

MEXICAN CARNITAS, PAGE 199

Oven Entrees

Beef & Ground Beef

175   181   167

Nothing satisfies hungry bellies like baked dishes containing hearty beef. This chapter includes **slow-roasted beef stew** and Swiss steak, **classic noodle casseroles**, meat loaf, pot roasts and **taste-tempting lasagna**. Find the perfect remedy to any chilly day.

> A friend shared the recipe for this cheesy baked pasta years ago. I love to serve it with a salad and garlic bread. It's great for entertaining.
>
> —MARGARET MCNEIL GERMANTOWN, TENNESSEE

EAT SMART Mostaccioli

PREP: 25 MIN. **BAKE:** 25 MIN.
MAKES: 2 CASSEROLES (6 SERVINGS EACH)

- 1 package (16 ounces) mostaccioli
- 1½ pounds ground beef
- 1¼ cups chopped green pepper
- 1 cup chopped onion
- 1 jar (26 ounces) spaghetti sauce
- 1 can (10¾ ounces) condensed cheddar cheese soup, undiluted
- 1½ teaspoons Italian seasoning
- ¾ teaspoon pepper
- 2 cups (8 ounces) shredded part-skim mozzarella cheese, divided

1. Cook mostaccioli according to package directions. Meanwhile, in a large skillet, cook the beef, green pepper and onion over medium heat until meat is no longer pink; drain. Stir in the spaghetti sauce, soup, Italian seasoning and pepper.
2. Drain mostaccioli. Add mostaccioli and 1½ cups cheese to beef mixture. Transfer to two greased 11-in. x 7-in. baking dishes. Sprinkle with remaining cheese.
3. Cover and freeze one casserole for up to 3 months. Cover and bake the remaining casserole at 350° for 20 minutes. Uncover; bake 5-10 minutes longer or until bubbly and cheese is melted.
TO USE FROZEN CASSEROLE *Thaw in the refrigerator overnight. Remove from the refrigerator 30 minutes before baking. Cover and bake at 350° for 50-60 minutes or until heated through and cheese is melted.*
PER SERVING *1 cup equals 351 cal., 12 g fat (5 g sat. fat), 42 mg chol., 633 mg sodium, 39 g carb., 3 g fiber, 22 g pro.* **Diabetic Exchanges:** *2½ starch, 2 lean meat, 1 fat.*

Taco Pie

Here's a fun way to serve tacos without the mess. Crushed corn chips provide a lively crunch, and you can customize the pie with your own favorite toppings.

—MARGERY BRYAN

MOSES LAKE, WASHINGTON

PREP: 15 MIN. **BAKE:** 20 MIN.
MAKES: 6 SERVINGS

- 1½ pounds ground beef
- 1 envelope taco seasoning
- ½ cup water
- 1 can (2¼ ounces) sliced ripe olives, drained
- 1 cup crushed corn chips, divided
- 1 unbaked pastry shell (9 inches)
- 1 cup (8 ounces) sour cream
- 1 cup (4 ounces) shredded cheddar cheese
  Shredded lettuce and sliced avocado, optional

1. In a large skillet, cook beef until no longer pink; drain. Stir in the taco seasoning, water and olives. Simmer mixture, uncovered, for 5 minutes, stirring frequently.
2. Sprinkle half of the corn chips into pastry shell. Top with meat mixture, sour cream and cheese. Cover with remaining corn chips.
3. Bake at 375° for 20-25 minutes or until crust is golden brown. Cut into wedges. Top with lettuce and avocado if desired.

This zippy Mexican casserole is a real winner at our house. If your family has spicier tastes, increase the chili powder and choose a medium or hot salsa.

—**JULIE HUFFMAN** NEW LEBANON, OHIO

ENCHILADA CASSEROLE

Enchilada Casserole

PREP: 20 MIN. **BAKE:** 40 MIN.
MAKES: 2 CASSEROLES (4 SERVINGS EACH)

- 1½ pounds ground beef
- 1 large onion, chopped
- 1 cup water
- 2 to 3 tablespoons chili powder
- 1½ teaspoons salt
- ½ teaspoon pepper
- ¼ teaspoon garlic powder
- 2 cups salsa, divided
- 10 flour tortillas (8 inches), cut into ¾-inch strips, divided
- 1 cup (8 ounces) sour cream
- 2 cans (15¼ ounces each) whole kernel corn, drained
- 4 cups (16 ounces) shredded part-skim mozzarella cheese

1. In a large skillet, cook beef and onion over medium heat until meat is no longer pink; drain. Stir in the water, chili powder, salt, pepper and garlic powder. Bring to a boil. Reduce heat; simmer, uncovered, for 10 minutes.

2. Place ¼ cup salsa in each of two greased 8-in. square baking dishes. Top each with a fourth of the tortillas and ¼ cup salsa.

3. Divide the meat mixture, sour cream and corn between the two casseroles. Top with remaining tortillas, salsa and cheese.

4. Cover and freeze one casserole for up to 1 month. Cover and bake second casserole at 350° for 35 minutes. Uncover; bake 5-10 minutes longer or until heated through.

TO USE FROZEN CASSEROLE *Thaw in the refrigerator for 24 hours. Remove from the refrigerator 30 minutes before baking. Bake as directed above.*

HEARTY MEAT PIE

A rich mushroom gravy makes my potpie extra-special. I spend a little more time to make two of them, but the reward comes later when I pull the second pie out of the freezer and pop it in the oven.

—**TWILA BURKHOLDER** MIDDLEBURG, PENNSYLVANIA

Hearty Meat Pie

PREP: 40 MIN. **BAKE:** 1¼ HOURS
MAKES: 2 PIES (6-8 SERVINGS EACH)

- Pastry for two double-crust pies
- 2 cups grated peeled potatoes
- 1¼ cups diced celery
- 1 cup grated carrots
- ¼ cup chopped onion
- 2 tablespoons Worcestershire sauce
- 1 teaspoon salt
- ¼ teaspoon pepper
- ¾ pound lean ground beef (90% lean)

MUSHROOM GRAVY (FOR EACH PIE)
- 1 can (4 ounces) mushroom stems and pieces
- 2 tablespoons all-purpose flour
- 2 tablespoons canola oil
- 1 teaspoon beef bouillon granules
- 4 drops browning sauce, optional

1. Divide pastry into fourths. On a lightly floured surface, roll out one portion to fit a 9-in. pie plate. In a large bowl, combine the next seven ingredients; crumble beef over mixture and mix well. Spoon half into crust.

2. Roll out another portion of pastry to fit top of pie; place over filling and seal edges. Cut vents in top pastry. Repeat with remaining pastry and filling. Cover and freeze one pie for up to 3 months.

3. Bake second pie at 375° for 15 minutes. Reduce heat; bake at 350° for 1 hour. Meanwhile, drain mushrooms, reserving liquid. Add water to the liquid to measure 1 cup; set aside.

4. In a small saucepan, cook mushrooms and flour in oil until bubbly. Remove from the heat; stir in bouillon and reserved mushroom liquid. Bring to a boil; cook and stir for 1 minute or until thickened. Stir in browning sauce if desired. Serve with pie.

TO USE FROZEN PIE *Bake at 375° for 70 minutes. Prepare gravy as directed. Serve with pie.*

GRANDMA'S RICE DISH

Sweet-and-Sour Meatballs

These tasty homemade meatballs are popular at parties and so simple to make. They're also delicious prepared with ground venison instead of beef.

—KIMMY HUBBARD LODI, OHIO

PREP: 20 MIN. **BAKE:** 50 MIN.
MAKES: 6-8 SERVINGS

- 2 **eggs, lightly beaten**
- ¾ **cup seasoned bread crumbs**
- 2 **tablespoons finely chopped onion**
- 1½ **teaspoons brown sugar**
- 1 **teaspoon salt**
- ¼ **teaspoon ground nutmeg**
- ⅛ **teaspoon pepper**
- 1½ **pounds lean ground beef (90% lean)**

SAUCE
- ½ **cup packed brown sugar**
- 2 **tablespoons cornstarch**
- 1 **can (20 ounces) pineapple chunks, undrained**
- ⅓ **cup sliced green onions**
- ⅓ **cup cider vinegar**
- 1 **tablespoon soy sauce**
- 1 **medium green pepper, cut into strips**
   Hot cooked rice, optional

1. In a large bowl, combine the first seven ingredients. Crumble beef over mixture and mix well. Shape into 2 dozen 1½-in. balls. Place in a greased 2-qt. baking dish.
2. For sauce, combine brown sugar and cornstarch in a saucepan. Add pineapple and juice, green onions, vinegar and soy sauce; cook and stir until thickened and bubbly. Pour over meatballs.
3. Cover and bake at 350° for 40 minutes. Stir in green pepper. Cover and bake 10 minutes longer or until meat is no longer pink. Serve with rice if desired.

Grandma's Rice Dish

My grandmother often made this casserole when I was young. I had forgotten all about it until one day, when I found myself adding the same ingredients to some leftover rice. The memories came flooding back.

—LORNA MOORE GLENDORA, CALIFORNIA

PREP: 20 MIN. **BAKE:** 15 MIN.
MAKES: 4 SERVINGS

- 1 **pound ground beef**
- ⅓ **cup chopped onion**
- ½ **cup chopped green pepper**
- 2 **cups cooked long grain rice**
- 1 **can (14½ ounces) diced tomatoes, undrained**
- 1 **can (11 ounces) whole kernel corn, drained**
- 1 **can (2¼ ounces) sliced ripe olives, drained**
- 6 **bacon strips, cooked and crumbled**
- 2 **teaspoons chili powder**
- 1 **teaspoon garlic powder**
- ½ **teaspoon salt**
- 1½ **cups (6 ounces) shredded cheddar cheese, divided**
- ½ **cup dry bread crumbs**
- 1 **tablespoon butter, melted**

1. In a large skillet, cook the beef, onion and green pepper over medium heat until meat is no longer pink; drain.
2. Stir in the rice, tomatoes, corn, olives, bacon and seasonings; heat through. Stir in 1 cup cheese until melted.
3. Transfer to a greased 11-in. x 7-in. baking dish. Sprinkle with remaining cheese. Toss the bread crumbs with butter; sprinkle over top.
4. Bake, uncovered, at 350° for 15-20 minutes or until heated through and cheese is melted.

Garlic Roast Beef Sandwiches

Here's an amazing sandwich that will knock your socks off with just one bite. Using garlic bread really boosts the flavor.
—**BRIDGET EVANS** FORRESTON, ILLINOIS

PREP/TOTAL TIME: 25 MIN.
MAKES: 6 SERVINGS

- 1 loaf (10 ounces) frozen garlic bread
- ½ pound sliced fresh mushrooms
- ⅔ cup sliced onion
- 4 teaspoons butter
- 1 teaspoon minced garlic
- 1 teaspoon Worcestershire sauce
- 1 pound shaved deli roast beef
- 6 slices Colby cheese

1. Bake garlic bread according to package directions. Meanwhile, in a large skillet, saute mushrooms and onion in butter until tender. Add garlic; cook 1 minute longer. Stir in Worcestershire sauce.
2. Layer each half of garlic bread with roast beef, mushroom mixture and cheese. Return to oven; bake for 3-5 minutes or until heated through and cheese is melted.

Beef Potpie With Biscuits

I home-school our three daughters, so my days are busy. I often rely on good, simple recipes like this hurried-up potpie.
—**DOLORES JENSEN** ARNOLD, MISSOURI

PREP: 15 MIN. **BAKE:** 35 MIN.
MAKES: 6-8 SERVINGS

- 1½ pounds beef top round steak, cut into ½-inch cubes
- 2 cups frozen peas and carrots, thawed
- 1 large potato, peeled, cooked and diced
- 1 medium onion, chopped
- 1 jar (18 ounces) beef gravy
- ½ teaspoon dried thyme
- ¼ teaspoon pepper
- 1 tube (12 ounces) refrigerated buttermilk biscuits

1. In a large skillet, cook beef over medium heat until no longer pink; drain. Stir in the vegetables, gravy, thyme and pepper.
2. Transfer to a greased 9-in. deep-dish pie plate or 11-in. x 7-in. baking dish. Bake, uncovered, at 400° for 25 minutes.

3. Place the biscuits in a single layer over meat mixture. Bake 10-15 minutes longer or until biscuits are golden brown.

Make the potpie your own by substituting your favorite frozen veggies for the peas and carrots. Top the filling with spoonfuls of your favorite drop biscuits instead of using refrigerated ones.

Classic Beef Stew

Here's a good old-fashioned stew with lots of veggies in a rich beef gravy. It's the perfect dish for a blustery winter day.

—ALBERTA MCKAY

BARTLESVILLE, OKLAHOMA

PREP: 15 MIN. **BAKE:** 2½ HOURS
MAKES: 6-8 SERVINGS

- 2 **pounds beef stew meat, cut into 1-inch cubes**
- 1 **to 2 tablespoons canola oil**
- 1½ **cups chopped onions**
- 1 **can (14½ ounces) diced tomatoes, undrained**
- 1 **can (10½ ounces) condensed beef broth, undiluted**
- 3 **tablespoons quick-cooking tapioca**
- 1 **garlic clove, minced**
- 1 **tablespoon dried parsley flakes**
- 1 **teaspoon salt**
- ¼ **teaspoon pepper**
- 1 **bay leaf**
- 6 **medium carrots, cut into 2-inch pieces**
- 3 **medium potatoes, peeled and cut into 2-inch pieces**
- 1 **cup sliced celery (1-inch lengths)**

1. In an oven-proof Dutch oven, brown beef in batches in oil; drain. Return all meat to the pan. Add onions, tomatoes, broth, tapioca, garlic, parsley, salt, pepper and bay leaf. Bring to a boil.

2. Cover stew and bake at 350° for 1½ hours. Stir in carrots, potatoes and celery. Bake, covered, 1 hour longer or until meat and vegetables are tender. Discard bay leaf.

GREEK MEAT LOAVES

Flavored with sun-dried tomatoes and Greek olives, this twist on traditional meat loaf will be a hit, especially when served with a Greek salad and crusty bread. **—RADELLE KNAPPENBERGER** OVIEDO, FLORIDA

Greek Meat Loaves

PREP: 20 MIN. **BAKE:** 50 MIN.
MAKES: 2 LOAVES (6 SERVINGS EACH)

- 2 **eggs, lightly beaten**
- ½ **cup ketchup**
- ¼ **cup 2% milk**
- 1 **large red onion, finely chopped**
- ¾ **cup quick-cooking oats**
- ⅓ **cup oil-packed sun-dried tomatoes, patted dry and finely chopped**
- ⅓ **cup pitted Greek olives, chopped**
- 2 **garlic cloves, minced**
- 1 **teaspoon salt**
- 1 **teaspoon pepper**
- 2 **pounds lean ground beef (90% lean)**
- ½ **cup crumbled feta cheese**

1. In a large bowl, combine the first 10 ingredients. Crumble beef over mixture and mix well. Pat into two greased 8-in. x 4-in. loaf pans. Cover and freeze one meat loaf for up to 3 months.

2. Bake remaining meat loaf, uncovered, at 350° for 50-60 minutes or until no pink remains and a thermometer reads 160°. Let stand for 5 minutes. Transfer to a serving plate; sprinkle with cheese.

TO USE FROZEN MEAT LOAF *Thaw in the refrigerator overnight. Bake as directed; sprinkle with cheese.*

MAPLE-ORANGE POT ROAST

EAT SMART Maple-Orange Pot Roast

This tender roast is a wonderful reminder of New England's autumn flavors. It always brings back memories of a friend's maple sap house in New Hampshire, where we're originally from.

—CHRISTINA MARQUIS

ORLANDO, FLORIDA

PREP: 25 MIN. **BAKE:** 3 HOURS + STANDING
MAKES: 8 SERVINGS

- 1 beef rump roast or bottom round roast (3 pounds)
- ½ cup orange juice
- ¼ cup sugar-free maple-flavored syrup
- ¼ cup white wine or chicken broth
- 2 tablespoons balsamic vinegar
- 1 tablespoon Worcestershire sauce
- 1 teaspoon grated orange peel
- 1 bay leaf
- ½ teaspoon salt
- ¼ teaspoon pepper
- 1½ pounds red potatoes, cut into large chunks
- 5 medium carrots, cut into 2-inch pieces
- 2 celery ribs, cut into 2-inch pieces
- 2 medium onions, cut into wedges
- 4 teaspoons cornstarch
- ¼ cup cold water

1. In a large nonstick skillet coated with cooking spray, brown roast on all sides. Place in a roasting pan coated with cooking spray.

2. In the same skillet, combine the orange juice, syrup, wine, vinegar, Worcestershire sauce, orange peel, bay leaf, salt and pepper. Bring to a boil, stirring frequently; pour over the meat.

3. Place the potatoes, carrots, celery and onions around roast. Cover and bake at 325° for 3 hours or until meat is tender.

4. Remove meat and vegetables; keep warm. Pour pan juices into a measuring cup. Discard bay leaf and skim fat. Pour into a small saucepan.

5. In a small bowl, combine cornstarch and water until smooth. Gradually stir into juices. Bring to a boil; cook and stir for 2 minutes or until thickened. Let stand for 10 minutes before slicing. Serve with pot roast and vegetables.

PER SERVING *335 cal., 8 g fat (3 g sat. fat), 102 mg chol., 264 mg sodium, 27 g carb., 4 g fiber, 36 g pro.* **Diabetic Exchanges:** *3 lean meat, 2 vegetable, 1 starch.*

CREAMY LASAGNA CASSEROLE

> Satisfy your gang easily with this casserole. I can whip up two rich, amazing mini lasagnas in almost no time. The best part is being able to enjoy the second casserole with virtually no work at all!
>
> —SHELLY KORELL EATON, COLORADO

Creamy Lasagna Casserole

PREP: 30 MIN. **BAKE:** 25 MIN. + STANDING
MAKES: 2 CASSEROLES
(4-6 SERVINGS EACH)

- 2 **pounds ground beef**
- 1 **can (29 ounces) tomato sauce**
- 1 **teaspoon salt**
- ½ **teaspoon pepper**
- ½ **teaspoon garlic powder**
- 2 **packages (3 ounces each) cream cheese, softened**
- 2 **cups (16 ounces) sour cream**
- 2 **cups (8 ounces) shredded cheddar cheese, divided**
- 4 **green onions, chopped**
- 12 **to 14 lasagna noodles, cooked and drained**

1. In a Dutch oven, cook beef over medium heat until no longer pink; drain. Add the tomato sauce, salt, pepper and garlic powder. Bring to a boil. Reduce heat; simmer, uncovered, for 15 minutes.

2. In a large bowl, beat cream cheese until smooth. Add the sour cream, 1 cup cheddar cheese and onions; mix well.

3. Spread about ½ cup meat sauce into each of two greased 8-in. square baking dishes. Place two to three noodles in each dish, trimming to fit as necessary. Top each with about ½ cup cream cheese mixture and ⅔ cup meat sauce. Repeat layers twice. Sprinkle ½ cup cheddar cheese over each.

4. Cover and freeze one casserole for up to 1 month. Bake remaining casserole, uncovered, at 350° for 25-30 minutes or until bubbly and heated through. Let stand for 15 minutes before cutting.

TO USE FROZEN CASSEROLE *Thaw in the refrigerator for 18 hours. Remove from the refrigerator 30 minutes before baking. Bake, uncovered, at 350° for 40-50 minutes or until heated through.*

Greek Pasta and Beef

PREP: 35 MIN. **BAKE:** 45 MIN.
MAKES: 12 SERVINGS

- 1 **package (16 ounces) elbow macaroni**
- 1 **pound ground beef**
- 1 **large onion, chopped**
- 1 **garlic clove, minced**
- 1 **can (8 ounces) tomato sauce**
- ½ **cup water**
- 1 **teaspoon salt**
- ½ **teaspoon ground cinnamon**
- ¼ **teaspoon ground nutmeg**
- ¼ **teaspoon pepper**
- 1 **egg, lightly beaten**
- ½ **cup grated Parmesan cheese**

SAUCE

- ¼ **cup butter**
- ¼ **cup all-purpose flour**
- ¼ **teaspoon ground cinnamon**
- 3 **cups 2% milk**
- 2 **eggs, lightly beaten**
- ⅓ **cup grated Parmesan cheese**

1. Cook macaroni according to package directions. In a large skillet, cook beef and onion over medium heat until meat is no longer pink. Add garlic; cook 1 minute longer. Drain. Stir in the tomato sauce, water and seasonings. Cover and simmer for 10 minutes, stirring occasionally.

2. Drain macaroni; place in a large bowl. Add egg and cheese; set aside.

3. For sauce, in a large saucepan, melt butter; stir in flour and cinnamon until smooth. Gradually add milk. Bring to a boil over medium heat; cook and stir for 2 minutes or until slightly thickened. Remove from the heat. Stir a small amount of hot mixture into eggs; return all to pan, stirring constantly. Stir in cheese.

4. In a greased 3-qt. baking dish, spread half of the macaroni mixture. Top with beef mixture and remaining macaroni mixture. Pour sauce over the top. Bake, uncovered, at 350° for 45-50 minutes or until a thermometer reads 160°. Let stand for 5 minutes before serving.

Here's a dish that gives everyday macaroni and cheese an international flavor. A co-worker who's a pro at Greek cooking shared the recipe.

—**DOROTHY BATEMAN** CARVER, MASSACHUSETTS

GREEK PASTA AND BEEF

EGGPLANT PARMIGIANA

Eggplant Parmigiana

I developed this recipe one summer when my husband grew eggplant in the garden. I was thrilled when it won high honors at a national beef contest.

—CELESTE COPPER

BATON ROUGE, LOUISIANA

PREP: 50 MIN. + SIMMERING
BAKE: 35 MIN. + STANDING
MAKES: 8 SERVINGS

- ⅓ cup chopped onion
- ¼ cup finely chopped celery
- ⅛ teaspoon garlic powder
- 2 tablespoons canola oil
- 1 can (14½ ounces) Italian stewed tomatoes
- ¼ cup tomato paste
- 1 teaspoon dried parsley flakes
- ½ teaspoon dried oregano
- 1¼ teaspoons salt, divided
- ½ teaspoon pepper, divided

- 1 bay leaf
- ¾ cup all-purpose flour
- 1 cup buttermilk
- 1 medium eggplant, peeled and cut into ½-inch slices
  Additional canola oil
- ½ cup grated Parmesan cheese
- 1 pound ground beef, cooked and drained
- 2 cups (8 ounces) shredded part-skim mozzarella cheese, divided
  Minced fresh parsley

1. In a large saucepan, saute onion, celery and garlic powder in oil until tender. Stir in the tomatoes, tomato paste, parsley, oregano, ½ teaspoon salt, ¼ teaspoon pepper and bay leaf. Bring to a boil. Reduce heat; cover and simmer for 1 hour. Discard bay leaf.

2. In a shallow dish, combine flour and remaining salt and pepper. Place buttermilk in another shallow dish. Dip eggplant in buttermilk, then in flour mixture.

3. In a large skillet, cook eggplant in batches in ½ in. of hot oil until golden brown on each side; drain.

4. Place half of eggplant in a greased 13-in. x 9-in. baking dish. Top with half of Parmesan cheese, beef and tomato mixture. Sprinkle with 1 cup mozzarella cheese. Top with remaining eggplant, Parmesan cheese, beef and tomato mixture.

5. Bake, uncovered, at 350° for 30 minutes or until heated through. Sprinkle with the remaining mozzarella cheese. Bake 5-10 minutes longer or until cheese is melted. Let stand for 10 minutes before serving. Sprinkle with parsley.

Western Chili Casserole

In our busy household, easy yet scrumptious meals are a must. This crunchy casserole fits the bill. The children love it.

—**TERRI MOCK** AMERICAN FALLS, IDAHO

PREP/TOTAL TIME: 25 MIN.
MAKES: 4 SERVINGS

- 1 **pound ground beef**
- 1 **cup chopped onion**
- ½ **cup chopped celery**
- 1 **can (15 ounces) chili with beans**
- 1½ **cups coarsely crushed corn chips, divided**
- ¾ **cup shredded cheddar cheese**

1. In a large skillet, cook the beef, onion and celery over medium heat until meat is no longer pink and vegetables are tender; drain. Stir in chili and ½ cup corn chips.

2. Transfer to a greased 1½-qt. baking dish. Sprinkle remaining chips around edge of dish; fill center with cheese. Bake, uncovered, at 350° for 10 minutes or until casserole is heated through.

Baked Swiss Steak

Our ladies' group at church used to hold fundraising dinners every month, and Swiss steak was one of our regular main dishes. The recipe is easy, popular and always delicious.

—**ELAINE DE WITT** LAKE CITY, MINNESOTA

PREP: 20 MIN. **BAKE:** 1½ HOURS
MAKES: 6-8 SERVINGS

- 2 **pounds beef top round steak**
- ½ **cup all-purpose flour**
- ½ **teaspoon salt**
- ½ **teaspoon pepper, divided**
- 2 **tablespoons canola oil**
- 1 **cup chopped onion**
- ½ **cup chopped green pepper**
- ¼ **cup soy sauce**
- ½ **teaspoon garlic salt**
  Hot cooked noodles, optional

1. Cut steak into serving-size pieces. Combine flour, salt and ¼ teaspoon pepper; sprinkle over steak and pound into both sides. In a skillet over medium heat, brown steak on both sides in oil.

2. Transfer to a greased 13-in. x 9-in. baking dish; top with onion and green pepper. Drizzle with soy sauce; sprinkle with garlic salt and the remaining pepper.

3. Cover and bake at 325° for 1½ hours or until meat is tender. Serve with noodles if desired.

Herbed Italian Rib Roast

This amazing recipe has been a family favorite for years. Any leftover vegetables make a quick full-flavored hash for breakfast the next day.

—**LILY JULOW** GAINESVILLE, FLORIDA

PREP: 30 MIN.
BAKE: 1¾ HOURS + STANDING
MAKES: 10 SERVINGS

- 1 **bone-in beef rib roast (4 to 5 pounds)**
- 2 **pounds Yukon gold potatoes, peeled and quartered**
- 1 **pound parsnips, quartered**
- 1 **pound carrots, quartered**
- 2 **large onions, cut into wedges**
- ½ **cup butter, melted**
- 2 **tablespoons dried rosemary, crushed**
- 2 **tablespoons dried oregano**
- 1 **teaspoon salt**
- ¼ **teaspoon pepper**

1. Place roast in a large shallow roasting pan. Bake, uncovered, at 350° for 45 minutes.

2. In a large bowl, combine the potatoes, parsnips, carrots and onions. Drizzle with butter; toss to coat. Spoon vegetables around roast; sprinkle with rosemary, oregano, salt and pepper.

3. Bake 1 to 1¼ hours longer or until meat reaches desired doneness (for medium-rare, a thermometer should read 145°; medium, 160°; well-done, 170°), stirring vegetables occasionally. Let stand for 10 minutes before slicing.

HERBED ITALIAN RIB ROAST

Tender zucchini boats are great holders for an ample beef and cheese filling. Jalapeno peppers add a little kick! Here's a great way to use up zucchini.

—TRACEY ROSATO MARKHAM, ONTARIO

INTERNATIONAL STUFFED ZUCCHINI

International Stuffed Zucchini

PREP: 20 MIN. **BAKE:** 20 MIN.
MAKES: 4 SERVINGS

- 2 **large zucchini**
- 1 **pound ground beef**
- 1 **garlic clove, minced**
- 1 **cup (4 ounces) shredded Havarti cheese with jalapeno or Havarti cheese**
- ¾ **cup crumbled feta cheese, divided**
- 2 **tablespoons minced fresh basil or oregano**
- ¼ **teaspoon salt**
- ⅛ **teaspoon pepper**

1. Cut each zucchini in half lengthwise; cut a thin slice from the bottoms so they sit flat. Scoop out pulp, leaving ¼-in. shells. Place zucchini shells in a small microwave- and oven-safe dish. Cover and microwave on high for 3 minutes or until crisp-tender; drain and set aside.
2. In a large skillet over medium heat, cook beef and garlic until meat is no longer pink; drain. Stir in the Havarti cheese, ½ cup feta cheese, basil, salt and pepper.
3. Fill zucchini with meat mixture. Bake at 400° for 15 minutes. Top with remaining feta; bake 5 minutes longer or until zucchini is tender and cheese is melted.

NOTE *This recipe was tested in a 1,100-watt microwave.*

You can **save time and money** by purchasing ground beef on sale. Brown the beef in 1-pound batches, then cool and freeze. Later on, you'll have recipe-ready beef!

BAKED LASAGNA IN A BUN

Baked Lasagna in a Bun

My family loves the meat sauce and cheeses tucked into the hollowed-out buns. Add a crisp green salad for a complete meal.

—**CINDY MORELOCK** AFTON, TENNESSEE

PREP: 20 MIN. **BAKE:** 25 MIN.
MAKES: 8 SERVINGS

- 8 **submarine or hoagie buns (8 inches)**
- 1 **pound ground beef**
- 1 **cup spaghetti sauce**
- 1 **tablespoon garlic powder**
- 1 **tablespoon Italian seasoning**
- 1 **cup ricotta cheese**
- ¼ **cup grated Parmesan cheese**
- 1 **cup (4 ounces) shredded cheddar cheese, divided**
- 1 **cup (4 ounces) shredded part-skim mozzarella cheese, divided**

1. Preheat oven to 350°. Make a 2-in.-wide V-shaped cut in the center of each bun to within 1 inch of bottom. Remove cut portion and save for another use. Place buns on an ungreased baking sheet.
2. In a large skillet, cook beef over medium heat 6-8 minutes or until no longer pink, breaking into crumbles; drain. Stir in spaghetti sauce, garlic powder and Italian seasoning; heat through.
3. Meanwhile, in a small bowl, mix ricotta cheese, Parmesan cheese and half of the cheddar and mozzarella cheeses. Spoon meat sauce into buns; top with ricotta mixture. Cover loosely with foil.
4. Bake 20 minutes. Sprinkle tops with the remaining cheeses; bake sandwiches, uncovered, 3-5 minutes or until cheese is melted.

HOLIDAY BRISKET

Roasted Tenderloin and Red Potatoes

I love thyme and cracked black peppercorns on beef, so I combined them in one easy yet impressive recipe. Family and friends have commented that this is the best beef they've ever tasted.
—KATHYRN HEFT BULLHEAD CITY, ARIZONA

PREP: 25 MIN. **BAKE:** 25 MIN.
MAKES: 4 SERVINGS

- 1 beef tenderloin roast (1½ pounds)
- 2 garlic cloves, thinly sliced
- 1 tablespoon minced fresh thyme or 1 teaspoon dried thyme
- 1½ teaspoons coarsely ground pepper, divided
- 3 tablespoons olive oil
- 8 small red potatoes, cut into chunks
- ½ cup reduced-sodium beef broth

1. Cut small slits in the tenderloin; place a garlic slice in each slit. Combine thyme and 1 teaspoon pepper; rub over beef. In a skillet, brown beef in oil on all sides. Place in a small shallow roasting pan. Sprinkle potatoes with remaining pepper; add to skillet. Cook and stir until lightly browned. Remove to the roasting pan.
2. Gradually add broth to skillet, stirring to loosen browned bits. Pour over meat and potatoes.
3. Bake, uncovered, at 375° for 25-40 minutes or until meat reaches desired doneness (for medium-rare, a thermometer should read 145°; medium, 160°; well-done, 170°) and potatoes are tender.

Holiday Brisket

When I was a child, my mom would make brisket on Jewish holidays and other special occasions. Everyone gathered around the table to enjoy the tender slices of meat with browned carrots, celery and potatoes.
—CHERI BRAGG VIOLA, DELAWARE

PREP: 15 MIN. **BAKE:** 2¾ HOURS + STANDING
MAKES: 6 SERVINGS

- 2 large onions, sliced
- 1 fresh beef brisket (3 pounds)
- ¾ cup ketchup
- 1 teaspoon paprika
- ½ teaspoon garlic powder
- 2 beef bouillon cubes
- 1½ cups hot water
- 5 small potatoes, peeled and cut into chunks
- 4 medium carrots, cut into chunks
- 2 celery ribs, cut into chunks

1. Place onions in a greased shallow roasting pan; top with brisket. Combine the ketchup, paprika and garlic powder; spread over brisket. Dissolve bouillon in hot water; pour into pan. Cover and bake at 325° for 1½ hours.
2. Add the potatoes, carrots and celery. Cover and bake 1¼ to 1½ hours longer or until meat and vegetables are tender.
3. Remove brisket to a serving platter; let stand for 10 minutes. Thinly slice meat across the grain. Serve with vegetables.
NOTE *This is a fresh beef brisket, not corned beef.*

> I layer cabbage with tomato sauce and beef to create a hearty casserole that tastes like cabbage rolls, but without all the work.
>
> —**DOREEN MARTIN** KITIMAT, BRITISH COLUMBIA

EAT SMART Cabbage Roll Casserole

PREP: 20 MIN. **BAKE:** 55 MIN.
MAKES: 12 SERVINGS

- 2 **pounds ground beef**
- 1 **large onion, chopped**
- 3 **garlic cloves, minced**
- 2 **cans (15 ounces each) tomato sauce, divided**
- 1 **teaspoon dried thyme**
- ½ **teaspoon dill weed**
- ½ **teaspoon rubbed sage**
- ¼ **teaspoon salt**
- ¼ **teaspoon pepper**
- ¼ **teaspoon cayenne pepper**
- 2 **cups cooked rice**
- 4 **bacon strips, cooked and crumbled**
- 1 **medium head cabbage (2 pounds), shredded**
- 1 **cup (4 ounces) shredded part-skim mozzarella cheese**

1. In a large skillet, cook beef and onion over medium heat until meat is no longer pink. Add garlic; cook 1 minute longer. Drain. Stir in one can of tomato sauce and seasonings. Bring to a boil. Reduce heat; cover and simmer for 5 minutes. Stir in rice and bacon; heat through. Remove from the heat.
2. Layer a third of the cabbage in a greased 13-in. x 9-in. baking dish. Top with half of the meat mixture. Repeat layers; top with remaining cabbage. Pour remaining tomato sauce over top.
3. Cover and bake at 375° for 45 minutes. Uncover; sprinkle with cheese. Bake 10 minutes longer or until cheese is melted. Let stand for 5 minutes before serving.
PER SERVING *230 cal., 8 g fat (4 g sat. fat), 44 mg chol., 620 mg sodium, 18 g carb., 3 g fiber, 20 g pro.* **Diabetic Exchanges:** *3 vegetable, 2½ lean meat, ½ fat.*

Cheesy Stuffed Peppers

This is my favorite summertime dinner because I can use peppers and tomatoes fresh from my garden.
—**BETTY DERAAD**
SIOUX FALLS, SOUTH DAKOTA

PREP: 20 MIN. **BAKE:** 20 MIN.
MAKES: 6 SERVINGS

- 6 **medium green peppers**
- 1½ **pounds ground beef**
- 1 **medium onion, chopped**
- ½ **teaspoon salt**
- 2 **cups (8 ounces) shredded cheddar cheese**
- 2½ **cups chopped tomatoes (3 medium)**
- 1½ **cups cooked rice**

1. Cut tops off peppers and remove seeds. In a Dutch oven, cook peppers in boiling water 6-8 minutes or until crisp-tender.
2. Meanwhile, brown beef, onion and salt in a skillet; drain. Cool slightly. Stir in the cheese, tomatoes and rice.
3. Drain peppers and stuff with meat mixture. Place in a baking dish. Bake, uncovered, at 350° for 20 minutes or until heated through.

TEX-MEX LASAGNA

> This yummy dish combines my love of lasagna with my love of Mexican food. I made the recipe healthier by using lean ground beef and reduced-fat cheese. And I increased the fiber by adding beans.
>
> —**ATHENA RUSSELL** FLORENCE, SOUTH CAROLINA

Tex-Mex Lasagna

PREP: 20 MIN. **BAKE:** 45 MIN. + STANDING
MAKES: 12 SERVINGS

- 1 **pound lean ground beef (90% lean)**
- 1 **can (16 ounces) refried black beans**
- 1 **can (15 ounces) black beans, rinsed and drained**
- ½ **cup frozen corn, thawed**
- 1 **jalapeno pepper, seeded and chopped**
- 1 **envelope taco seasoning**
- 1 **can (15 ounces) tomato sauce, divided**
- 2½ **cups salsa**
- 12 **no-cook lasagna noodles**
- 1½ **cups (6 ounces) shredded reduced-fat Monterey Jack cheese or Mexican cheese blend**
- 1½ **cups (6 ounces) shredded reduced-fat cheddar cheese**
- 1 **cup (8 ounces) fat-free sour cream**
- 1 **medium ripe avocado, peeled and cubed**
- 4 **green onions, thinly sliced**

1. In a large nonstick skillet, cook beef over medium heat until no longer pink; drain. Stir in the beans, corn, jalapeno, taco seasoning and ¾ cup tomato sauce.
2. Combine salsa and remaining tomato sauce. Spread ¼ cup into a 13-in. x 9-in. baking dish coated with cooking spray. Layer with four noodles (noodles will overlap slightly), half of the meat sauce, 1 cup salsa mixture, ½ cup Monterey Jack cheese and ½ cup cheddar cheese. Repeat layers. Top with the remaining noodles, salsa mixture and cheeses.
3. Cover and bake at 350° for 45-50 minutes or until edges are bubbly and cheese is melted. Let stand for 10 minutes before cutting. Serve with sour cream, avocado and onions.
NOTE *Wear disposable gloves when cutting hot peppers; the oils can burn skin. Avoid touching your face.*

Refried Bean-Taco Pizza

PREP: 30 MIN. **BAKE:** 20 MIN.
MAKES: 8 SERVINGS

- 1¼ **pounds ground beef**
- 1 **small onion, chopped**
- ½ **cup water**
- 1 **envelope taco seasoning**
- 1 **prebaked 12-inch pizza crust**
- 1 **can (16 ounces) refried beans**
- 2 **taco shells, coarsely crushed**
- 1 **cup (4 ounces) shredded cheddar cheese**
- 1 **cup (4 ounces) shredded part-skim mozzarella cheese**
- 2 **cups torn iceberg lettuce**
- 2 **medium tomatoes, chopped**
- 1 **tablespoon sliced ripe olives**

1. In a large skillet, cook beef and onion over medium heat until no longer pink; drain. Stir in water and taco seasoning. Bring to a boil. Reduce heat; simmer, uncovered, for 5 minutes.
2. Meanwhile, place crust on an ungreased baking sheet. Spread with refried beans. Top with the beef mixture, taco shells and cheeses.
3. Bake at 450° for 10-15 minutes or until cheese is melted. Top with lettuce, tomatoes and olives.

For a little extra heat, try making the pizza with refried beans flavored with **smoky, slightly sweet** chipotle peppers.

I like to make pizzas, and a fun taco version is my favorite. You can't beat ready-to-use pizza crust when time is tight. If you like taco salad, you'll love this pizza.
—**MARY DETWEILER** MIDDLEFIELD, OHIO

REFRIED BEAN-TACO PIZZA

Sloppy Joe Under a Bun

I usually keep a can of sloppy joe sauce in the pantry because our kids love sloppy joes. But I don't always have buns on hand. With this fun casserole, we can enjoy the flavor they adore any time.

—**TRISH BLOOM** RAY, MICHIGAN

PREP: 10 MIN. **BAKE:** 25 MIN.
MAKES: 8 SERVINGS

- 1½ **pounds ground beef**
- 1 **can (15½ ounces) sloppy joe sauce**
- 2 **cups (8 ounces) shredded cheddar cheese**
- 2 **cups biscuit/baking mix**
- 2 **eggs, lightly beaten**
- 1 **cup 2% milk**
- 1 **tablespoon sesame seeds**

1. In a large skillet, cook ground beef over medium heat until no longer pink; drain. Stir in the sloppy joe sauce. Transfer to a lightly greased 13-in. x 9-in. baking dish; sprinkle with cheese.

2. In a large bowl, combine the biscuit mix, eggs and milk just until blended. Pour over cheese; sprinkle with sesame seeds. Bake, uncovered, at 400° for 25 minutes or until golden brown.

Sesame seeds make the biscuit topping feel more like a bun for these **easy sloppy joes**. But if you'll be serving picky eaters, you might wish to omit them.

COBRE VALLEY CASSEROLE

We live in southeastern Arizona, in a part of the state known as Cobre Valley. "Cobre" is a Spanish word for copper, which is mined here. Variations of this recipe have been enjoyed in this area for many years.

—**CAROLYN DEMING** MIAMI, ARIZONA

Cobre Valley Casserole

PREP: 15 MIN. **BAKE:** 30 MIN.
MAKES: 8 SERVINGS

- 1 **pound ground beef**
- 1 **medium onion, chopped**
- 1 **celery rib, chopped**
- 1 **envelope taco seasoning**
- ¼ **cup water**
- 2 **cans (16 ounces each) refried beans**
- 1 **can (4 ounces) chopped green chilies, optional**
- 1 **cup (4 ounces) shredded cheddar cheese**
- 2 **green onions, sliced**
- 1 **large tomato, peeled, seeded and chopped**
- ⅓ **cup sliced ripe olives**
- 1-½ **cups crushed tortilla chips**

1. In a large skillet, cook the beef, onion and celery over medium heat until meat is no longer pink; drain. Stir in the taco seasoning, water, beans and green chilies if desired.

2. Transfer mixture to a greased 11-in. x 7-in. baking dish.

3. Bake, uncovered, at 350° for 30 minutes or until heated through. Top with cheese, green onions, tomato, olives and chips.

EAT SMART Hamburger Noodle Casserole

People have a hard time believing my homey and hearty casserole uses lighter ingredients. The taste is so rich and creamy...what a great weeknight meal!

—**MARTHA HENSON** WINNSBORO, TEXAS

PREP: 30 MIN. **BAKE:** 35 MIN.
MAKES: 10 SERVINGS

- 5 cups uncooked yolk-free noodles
- 1¼ pounds lean ground beef (90% lean)
- 2 garlic cloves, minced
- 3 cans (8 ounces each) tomato sauce
- ½ teaspoon sugar
- ½ teaspoon salt
- ⅛ teaspoon pepper
- 1 package (8 ounces) reduced-fat cream cheese
- 1 cup reduced-fat ricotta cheese
- ¼ cup fat-free sour cream
- 3 green onions, thinly sliced, divided
- ⅔ cup shredded reduced-fat cheddar cheese

1. Cook noodles according to package directions. Meanwhile, in a large nonstick skillet over medium heat, cook beef until no longer pink. Add garlic; cook 1 minute longer. Drain. Stir in the tomato sauce, sugar, salt and pepper; heat through. Drain noodles; stir into beef mixture.
2. In a small bowl, beat cream cheese, ricotta cheese and sour cream until blended. Stir in half of the onions.

3. Spoon half of the noodle mixture into a 13-in. x 9-in. baking dish coated with cooking spray. Top with cheese mixture and remaining noodle mixture.
4. Cover and bake at 350° for 30 minutes. Uncover; sprinkle with cheddar cheese. Bake 5-10 minutes longer or until heated through and cheese is melted. Sprinkle with remaining onions.
PER SERVING *290 cal., 12 g fat (7 g sat. fat), 56 mg chol., 650 mg sodium, 23 g carb., 2 g fiber, 22 g pro.* **Diabetic Exchanges:** *2 lean meat, 1½ starch, 1 fat.*

HAMBURGER NOODLE CASSEROLE

Poultry

185   190   194

Potpie, stuffed chicken, casseroles and more...there is much to love about home-style **baked chicken and turkey entrees**. You're sure to discover a new family favorite among these classic comfort foods.

EAT SMART Hazelnut & Lemon-Crusted Turkey Breast

Here is proof that simple recipes can still be special. Placing the turkey breast over sliced fresh lemon results in a sensational main course.

—LORRAINE CALAND SHUNIAH, ONTARIO

PREP: 15 MIN.
BAKE: 1¼ HOURS + STANDING
MAKES: 6 SERVINGS

- ½ cup hazelnuts, toasted
- ¼ cup olive oil
- 3 tablespoons minced fresh rosemary or 1 tablespoon dried rosemary, crushed
- 3 tablespoons lemon juice
- 2 tablespoons butter, softened
- 2 garlic cloves, minced
- 2 teaspoons grated lemon peel
- ¼ teaspoon salt
- ¼ teaspoon pepper
- 1 boneless skinless turkey breast half (2 pounds)
- 1 medium lemon, thinly sliced

1. Place the first nine ingredients in a food processor; cover and process until finely chopped. Rub mixture over turkey.

2. Arrange lemon slices in a foil-lined 13-in. x 9-in. baking pan; top with turkey.

3. Bake, uncovered, at 325° for 1¼ to 1½ hours or until a thermometer reads 170°. Let stand for 10 minutes before slicing.

PER SERVING *346 cal., 19 g fat (2 g sat. fat), 94 mg chol., 174 mg sodium, 5 g carb., 2 g fiber, 39 g pro.* **Diabetic Exchanges:** *5 lean meat, 2½ fat.*

Feta cheese takes this chicken and potato dinner over the top. Serve with a side salad tossed with pepperoncini, black olives and low-fat vinaigrette for a fresh and healthy meal. **—TASTE OF HOME TEST KITCHEN**

EAT SMART Greek Chicken Dinner

PREP: 15 MIN. **BAKE:** 50 MIN.
MAKES: 6 SERVINGS

- 7 medium red potatoes, cut into 1-inch cubes
- 6 boneless skinless chicken thighs (about 1½ pounds)
- ½ cup reduced-fat sun-dried tomato salad dressing
- 2 teaspoons Greek seasoning
- 1 teaspoon dried basil
- ½ cup crumbled reduced-fat feta cheese

1. In a large bowl, combine the first five ingredients. Transfer to a 13-in. x 9-in. baking dish coated with cooking spray.

2. Cover and bake at 400° for 40 minutes. Sprinkle with cheese. Bake, uncovered, 10-15 minutes longer or until chicken juices run clear and potatoes are tender.

PER SERVING *316 cal., 12 g fat (3 g sat. fat), 79 mg chol., 767 mg sodium, 25 g carb., 2 g fiber, 26 g pro.* **Diabetic Exchanges:** *3 lean meat, 1½ starch, 1 fat.*

If you don't have Greek seasoning, try mixing your own with **a blend of lemon, garlic, salt and oregano.**

If you're looking for an elegant dinner for two, we suggest these Cornish game hens. A blend of sage, lemon, onion and garlic gives this entree outstanding flavor.

—TASTE OF HOME COOKING SCHOOL

HERB-STUFFED CORNISH HENS

Herb-Stuffed Cornish Hens

PREP: 20 MIN. **BAKE:** 70 MIN.
MAKES: 2 SERVINGS

- 2 **Cornish game hens (20 to 24 ounces each)**
- 12 **fresh sage leaves**
- 4 **lemon wedges**
- 6 **green onions, cut into 2-inch lengths, divided**
- 2 **tablespoons butter, melted**
- 1 **tablespoon olive oil**
- 1 **tablespoon lemon juice**
- 2 **garlic cloves, minced**
- 1 **teaspoon kosher salt or sea salt**
- ¼ **teaspoon coarsely ground pepper**
- 6 **small red potatoes, halved**

1. Gently lift skin from hen breasts and place sage leaves under the skin. Place lemon wedges and a third of the onions in the cavities. Tuck wings under hens; tie legs together. Place in a small greased roasting pan.
2. Combine the butter, oil, lemon juice and garlic; spoon half over hens. Sprinkle with salt and pepper.
3. Bake at 375° for 30 minutes. Add potatoes and remaining onions to pan. Brush hens with remaining butter mixture. Bake 40-45 minutes longer or until meat juices run clear and potatoes are tender.
4. Remove hens to serving platter. Stir potatoes and onions to coat with pan drippings. Serve with hens.

Chicken Potpie

PREP: 40 MIN. **BAKE:** 35 MIN. + STANDING
MAKES: 2 POTPIES (8 SERVINGS EACH)

- 2 **cups diced peeled potatoes**
- 1¾ **cups sliced carrots**
- 1 **cup butter, cubed**
- ⅔ **cup chopped onion**
- 1 **cup all-purpose flour**
- 1¾ **teaspoons salt**
- 1 **teaspoon dried thyme**
- ¾ **teaspoon pepper**
- 3 **cups chicken broth**
- 1½ **cups milk**
- 4 **cups cubed cooked chicken**
- 1 **cup frozen peas**
- 1 **cup frozen corn**
- 2 **packages (14.1 ounces each) refrigerated pie pastry**

CHICKEN POTPIE

Chock-full of chicken, potatoes and peas, this autumn favorite makes two golden pies, so you can serve one at dinner and save the other for a busy night. These potpies are perfect for company or a potluck. —**KAREN JOHNSON** BAKERSFIELD, CALIFORNIA

1. Preheat oven to 425°. Place potatoes and carrots in a large saucepan; add water to cover. Bring to a boil. Reduce heat; cook, covered, 8-10 minutes or until vegetables are crisp-tender; drain.
2. In a large skillet, heat butter over medium-high heat. Add onion; cook and stir until tender. Stir in flour and seasonings until blended. Gradually stir in broth and milk. Bring to a boil, stirring constantly; cook and stir 2 minutes or until thickened. Stir in chicken, peas, corn and potato mixture; remove from heat.
3. Unroll a pastry sheet into each of two 9-in. pie plates; trim even with rims. Add chicken mixture. Unroll remaining pastry; place over filling. Trim, seal and flute edges. Cut slits in tops.
4. Bake 35-40 minutes or until crust is lightly browned. Let stand 15 minutes before cutting.
FREEZE OPTION *Cover and freeze unbaked pies. To use, remove from freezer 30 minutes before baking (do not thaw). Preheat oven to 425°. Place pies on baking sheets; cover edges loosely with foil. Bake 30 minutes. Reduce oven setting to 350°; bake 70-80 minutes longer or until crust is golden brown and a thermometer inserted in center reads 165°.*

SAUSAGE SPINACH PASTA BAKE

> I've made this pasta many times and in different ways over the years. I've swapped in other meats, such as chicken sausage, veal or ground pork, and added in summer squash, zucchini, green beans and mushrooms, depending on what I have. Fresh herbs also perk up the flavor.
>
> **—KIM FORNI** CLAREMONT, NEW HAMPSHIRE

3. Drain pasta; stir into turkey mixture. Add spinach and cream; heat through. Transfer to a 13-in. x 9-in. baking dish coated with cooking spray. Sprinkle with cheeses. Bake, uncovered, at 350° for 25-30 minutes or until golden brown.

PER SERVING *377 cal., 11 g fat (5 g sat. fat), 50 mg chol., 622 mg sodium, 45 g carb., 8 g fiber, 25 g pro.* **Diabetic Exchanges:** *3 lean meat, 2 starch, 2 vegetable, ½ fat.*

Turkey With Sausage Stuffing

Here's a super way to savor roast turkey and stuffing without having to cook the big holiday bird. The stuffing is hearty, and the turkey always comes out juicy.

—AURA LEE JOHNSON VERMILION, OHIO

PREP: 30 MIN. **BAKE:** 2 HOURS + STANDING
MAKES: 10-14 SERVINGS

- 1 **bone-in turkey breast (5 to 7 pounds)**
- ¼ **cup butter, melted**
- 1½ **pounds bulk pork sausage**
- 2 **cups sliced celery**
- 2 **medium onions, chopped**
- 4 **cups dry bread cubes**
- 2 **cups pecan halves**
- 1 **cup raisins**
- ⅔ **cup chicken broth**
- 2 **eggs, beaten**
- 1 **teaspoon salt**
- ½ **teaspoon rubbed sage**
- ¼ **teaspoon pepper**

1. Place turkey breast side up in a shallow roasting pan. Brush with butter. Bake, uncovered, at 325° for 2 to 2½ hours or until a thermometer reads 170° (cover loosely with foil to prevent overbrowning if necessary).
2. Meanwhile, in a large skillet over medium heat, cook the sausage, celery and onions until meat is no longer pink; drain. Transfer to a bowl; stir in the bread cubes, pecans, raisins, broth, eggs, salt, sage and pepper.
3. Spoon into a greased 3-qt. baking dish. Cover and bake at 325° for 1 hour. Let turkey stand for 10 minutes before slicing. Serve with the stuffing.

EAT SMART Sausage Spinach Pasta Bake

PREP: 35 MIN. **BAKE:** 25 MIN.
MAKES: 10 SERVINGS

- 1 **package (16 ounces) whole wheat spiral pasta**
- 1 **pound Italian turkey sausage links, casings removed**
- 1 **medium onion, chopped**
- 5 **garlic cloves, minced**
- 1 **can (28 ounces) crushed tomatoes**
- 1 **can (14½ ounces) diced tomatoes, undrained**
- 1 **teaspoon dried oregano**
- 1 **teaspoon dried basil**
- ¼ **teaspoon pepper**

- 1 **package (10 ounces) frozen chopped spinach, thawed and squeezed dry**
- ½ **cup half-and-half cream**
- 2 **cups (8 ounces) shredded part-skim mozzarella cheese**
- ½ **cup grated Parmesan cheese**

1. Cook pasta according to package directions.
2. Meanwhile, in a large skillet, cook turkey and onion over medium heat until meat is no longer pink. Add garlic. Cook 1 minute longer; drain. Stir in the tomatoes, oregano, basil and pepper. Bring to a boil. Reduce heat; simmer, uncovered, for 10 minutes.

APPLE-BRINED CHICKEN THIGHS

Apple-Brined Chicken Thighs

I love the flavor of chicken baked with apples, and when I had a bumper crop of green beans, I wanted to include them, too. This recipe is the tasty result.

—**KATHY RAIRIGH** MILFORD, INDIANA

PREP: 30 MIN. + CHILLING **BAKE:** 55 MIN.
MAKES: 5 SERVINGS

- 3 cups apple cider or juice
- 1 medium onion, sliced
- 1 medium lemon, sliced
- 4 fresh rosemary sprigs
- ⅓ cup kosher salt
- ½ cup packed brown sugar, divided
- 4 garlic cloves, minced
- 1 bay leaf
- 1 teaspoon whole peppercorns
- 2 cups cold water
- 10 bone-in chicken thighs (about 3¾ pounds)
- 1 two-gallon resealable plastic bag
- 1 pound fresh green beans, trimmed
- 3 medium tart apples, cut into wedges
- 1 tablespoon minced fresh rosemary or 1 teaspoon dried rosemary, crushed
- 1 tablespoon olive oil
- ¼ teaspoon pepper

1. In a Dutch oven, combine the cider, onion, lemon, rosemary sprigs, salt, ¼ cup brown sugar, garlic, bay leaf and peppercorns. Bring to a boil. Cook and stir until salt and brown sugar are dissolved. Remove from the heat; stir in water. Cool brine to room temperature.

2. Place chicken in the 2-gallon resealable plastic bag. Carefully pour cooled brine into bag. Squeeze out as much air as possible; seal bag and turn to coat. Place in a roasting pan. Refrigerate for 2 hours, turning occasionally.

3. Place beans and apples in a greased roasting pan. Drain chicken; place in prepared pan. Bake, uncovered, at 400° for 40 minutes.

4. Combine the minced rosemary, oil, pepper and remaining brown sugar; sprinkle over chicken. Bake 15-25 minutes longer or until a thermometer reads 180° and beans are tender.

POTATO-TOPPED CHICKEN CASSEROLE

2. Meanwhile, in a Dutch oven, cook the chicken, carrots and onions over medium heat until meat is no longer pink; drain. Stir in the flour, tomato paste, salt, pepper and thyme. Add chicken broth; bring to a boil. Reduce heat; simmer, uncovered, for 6-8 minutes or until thickened.

3. Divide mixture between two greased 13-in. x 9-in. baking dishes. Drain potatoes; place in a large bowl. Add milk and butter; mash until smooth. Stir in cheese. Spread over chicken mixture.

4. Cover and freeze one casserole for up to 3 months. Bake the remaining casserole, uncovered, at 400° for 15-20 minutes or until bubbly.

TO USE FROZEN CASSEROLE *Thaw in the refrigerator overnight. Remove from the refrigerator 30 minutes before baking. Bake, uncovered, at 400° for 50-55 minutes or until bubbly.*

PER SERVING *412 cal., 20 g fat (10 g sat. fat), 110 mg chol., 636 mg sodium, 33 g carb., 4 g fiber, 26 g pro.*

Sunday Chicken

PREP: 15 MIN. **BAKE:** 2 HOURS
MAKES: 4-6 SERVINGS

- 1 **can (10¾ ounces) condensed cream of mushroom soup, undiluted**
- 1 **can (10¾ ounces) condensed cream of celery soup, undiluted**
- 1 **can (10¾ ounces) condensed cream of chicken soup, undiluted**
- ⅓ **cup butter, melted, divided**
- 1¼ **cups quick-cooking rice**
- 1 **broiler/fryer chicken (3 to 4 pounds), cut up Salt and pepper to taste Paprika**

1. In a large bowl, combine the soups, ¼ cup butter and rice. Pour into a greased 13-in. x 9-in. baking dish. Top with chicken pieces. Drizzle chicken with remaining butter. Sprinkle with salt, pepper and paprika.

2. Bake, uncovered, at 350° for 2 hours or until chicken juices run clear and rice is tender.

> A friend gave me this easy and delicious recipe. Any cheese you have on hand will work fine. The extra casserole is perfect for those nights when you want something hearty and homemade, but know you won't have much time.
>
> —MARY ANN DELL PHOENIXVILLE, PENNSYLVANIA

EAT SMART Potato-Topped Chicken Casserole

PREP: 45 MIN. **BAKE:** 15 MIN.
MAKES: 2 CASSEROLES (6 SERVINGS EACH)

- 4 **pounds medium red potatoes, quartered**
- 3 **pounds ground chicken**
- 4 **medium carrots, finely chopped**
- 2 **medium onions, finely chopped**
- ¼ **cup all-purpose flour**
- 2 **tablespoons tomato paste**
- 1½ **teaspoons salt**
- ¾ **teaspoon pepper**
- ¼ **teaspoon minced fresh thyme**
- 1¼ **cups chicken broth**
- 1 **cup milk**
- 6 **tablespoons butter, cubed**
- 1¾ **cups (7 ounces) shredded cheddar cheese**

1. Place potatoes in a Dutch oven and cover with water. Bring to a boil. Reduce heat; cover and simmer for 15-20 minutes or until tender.

This was my mother's favorite recipe for Sundays—hence the name. It can be prepared ahead of time and left to bake while you attend church. The leftovers also freeze well. —DON HARKSEN DOTHAN, ALABAMA

SUNDAY CHICKEN

CHICKEN CAESAR FLORENTINE

I adapted this dish from my favorite chicken Caesar salad recipe. It has many of the same ingredients as the salad: croutons, grated Parmesan, chicken, and creamy Caesar dressing. These chicken breasts are perfect for company, even on a busy weeknight.

—JOYCE CONWAY WESTERVILLE, OHIO

Chicken Caesar Florentine

PREP: 15 MIN. **BAKE:** 40 MIN.
MAKES: 4 SERVINGS

- 2 cups grated Parmesan cheese, divided
- 2 cups Caesar salad croutons, coarsely crushed, divided
- 1 cup fresh baby spinach
- 1 cup creamy Caesar salad dressing, divided
- 4 bone-in chicken breast halves, skin removed (8 ounces each)

1. In a large bowl, combine 1 cup cheese, 1 cup crushed croutons, spinach and ½ cup salad dressing. Cut a pocket in the thickest part of each chicken breast; fill with cheese mixture.

2. Place remaining dressing and crushed croutons in separate shallow bowls. Dip chicken in dressing, then roll in croutons.

3. Transfer to a greased 13-in. x 9-in. baking dish. Bake, uncovered, at 375° for 30 minutes. Sprinkle with remaining cheese; bake 10-15 minutes longer or until a thermometer reads 170°.

Spanish Rice and Chicken

My mother has always been an avid cook, and my sister, two brothers and I were raised on this casserole. When I polled our family to see which recipe I should share, this fresh-tasting, well-seasoned chicken casserole came out on top. I know you'll enjoy is as much as we do.

—CINDY CLARK
MECHANICSBURG, PENNSYLVANIA

PREP: 20 MIN. **BAKE:** 65 MIN.
MAKES: 4-6 SERVINGS

- 1 broiler/fryer chicken (3 pounds), cut up
- 1 teaspoon garlic salt
- 1 teaspoon celery salt
- 1 teaspoon paprika
- 1 cup uncooked rice
- ¾ cup chopped onion
- ¾ cup chopped green pepper
- ¼ cup minced fresh parsley
- 1½ cups chicken broth
- 1 cup chopped tomatoes
- 1½ teaspoons chili powder
- 1 teaspoon salt

1. Place chicken in a greased 13-in. x 9-in. baking pan. Combine garlic salt, celery salt and paprika; sprinkle over chicken. Bake, uncovered, at 425° for 20 minutes.

2. Remove chicken from pan. Combine rice, onion, green pepper and parsley; spoon into the pan. In a saucepan, bring broth, tomatoes, chili powder and salt to a boil. Pour over rice mixture; mix well. Place chicken pieces on top. Cover and bake for 45 minutes or until chicken and rice are tender.

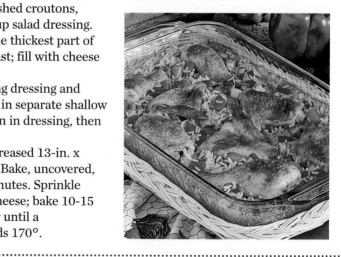

Italian Baked Chicken

For a casual get-together, this saucy herbed chicken is a terrific choice. Serve it over angel hair pasta for a delicious dinner that's special enough for company.

—MARCELLO BASCO

DEERFIELD BEACH, FLORIDA

PREP: 25 MIN. **BAKE:** 35 MIN.
MAKES: 4 SERVINGS

½ cup all-purpose flour
½ teaspoon salt
⅛ teaspoon pepper
4 boneless skinless chicken breast halves (6 ounces each)
3 tablespoons olive oil, divided
5 garlic cloves, minced
2 cups chicken broth
1 cup tomato puree
1 teaspoon dried basil
1 teaspoon dried oregano
4 slices mozzarella cheese
4 tomato slices
4 teaspoons grated Parmesan cheese
Hot cooked angel hair pasta
Minced fresh parsley

1. In a large resealable plastic bag, combine the flour, salt and pepper; add chicken, one piece at a time, and shake to coat. In a large skillet over medium heat, brown chicken in 2 tablespoons oil on each side. Transfer to a greased 11-in. x 7-in. baking dish.
2. In the same skillet, saute garlic in remaining oil for 1 minute. Stir in the broth, tomato puree, basil and oregano. Bring to a boil. Pour mixture over chicken.
3. Cover and bake at 400° for 25-30 minutes or until a thermometer reads 170°.
4. Remove chicken and set aside. Pour sauce into a small bowl and keep warm. Return chicken to the pan; top with mozzarella and tomato. Sprinkle with Parmesan.
5. Bake, uncovered, for 6-8 minutes or until cheese is melted. Arrange pasta on a large serving platter; top with chicken. Pour sauce over chicken and sprinkle with parsley.

Leftover **tomato puree and paste** freeze well. Place any **leftovers** in a freezer container; label, date and mark the volume being **frozen**.

A handful of Italian-style pantry staples team up with chicken for this hearty entree that the entire family will love. Just add breadsticks!

—**KRISTIN MILLER** CARMEL, INDIANA

BRAVO ITALIAN CHICKEN

Bravo Italian Chicken

PREP: 20 MIN. + STANDING
BAKE: 35 MIN. **MAKES:** 4 SERVINGS

- 1 **medium eggplant, peeled and cut into 1-inch cubes**
- 1 **teaspoon salt**
- 4 **boneless skinless chicken breast halves (5 ounces each)**
- ¼ **teaspoon Italian seasoning**
- ¼ **teaspoon pepper**
- 1½ **cups (6 ounces) shredded part-skim mozzarella cheese**
- 1 **jar (24 ounces) tomato basil pasta sauce**

1. Place eggplant in a colander over a plate; sprinkle with salt and toss. Let stand for 30 minutes.
2. Meanwhile, sprinkle the chicken with Italian seasoning and pepper. In a large nonstick skillet coated with cooking spray, brown chicken on both sides. Transfer chicken to a greased 13-in. x 9-in. baking dish and sprinkle with ¾ cup of mozzarella cheese.
3. Rinse the eggplant; pat dry with paper towels. Transfer to a large bowl; add pasta sauce and toss to coat. Spoon over chicken; top with remaining cheese.
4. Cover and bake at 350° for 35-40 minutes or until a thermometer inserted into the chicken reads 170°.

CHICKEN IN PUFF PASTRY

You'll never believe a dish this scrumptious, comforting and impressive-looking could be made with just five ingredients! It offers such an easy way to entertain friends. —**GINA HOBBS** TIFTON, GEORGIA

Pesto-Olive Chicken

Give weeknight dining a lift with this amazingly easy dressed-up chicken. You can keep the ingredients handy right in your pantry.
—**CRISTY KING** SCOTT DEPOT, WEST VIRGINIA

PREP/TOTAL TIME: 30 MIN.
MAKES: 4 SERVINGS

- 4 **boneless skinless chicken breast halves (6 ounces each)**
- ½ **cup prepared pesto**
- 2 **jars (4½ ounces each) sliced mushrooms, drained**
- 1 **can (4½ ounces) chopped ripe olives**
- 1 **cup (4 ounces) shredded provolone cheese**

1. Flatten chicken slightly. Place in an ungreased 13-in. x 9-in. baking dish. Spoon pesto over chicken; top with mushrooms and olives.
2. Bake, uncovered, at 400° for 15-18 minutes or until a thermometer reads 170°. Sprinkle with cheese; bake 1-2 minutes longer or until cheese is melted.

Chicken in Puff Pastry

PREP: 15 MIN. **BAKE:** 20 MIN.
MAKES: 4 SERVINGS

- 4 **chicken tenderloins**
- ⅛ **teaspoon salt**
- ⅛ **teaspoon pepper**
- 1 **sheet frozen puff pastry, thawed**
- ½ **cup spreadable spinach and artichoke cream cheese**
- 4 **slices Muenster cheese, halved**
- 1 **egg**
- 1 **tablespoon water**

1. Sprinkle chicken with salt and pepper; set aside. On a lightly floured surface, roll puff pastry into a 14-in. square. Cut into four squares.
2. Spoon 2 tablespoons cream cheese into the center of each square; top with Muenster cheese and chicken.
3. Whisk egg and water; lightly brush over edges. Bring opposite corners of pastry over each bundle; pinch seams to seal. Place seam side down on a greased baking sheet; brush with remaining egg mixture.
4. Bake at 400° for 18-22 minutes or until golden brown.

BROCCOLI CHICKEN CASSEROLE

All ages really seem to go for this comforting, scrumptious meal in one. It takes just a handful of ingredients and minutes to prepare. I sometimes add dried cranberries to the stuffing mix for a zing of tartness and color. —JENNIFER SCHLACHTER BIG ROCK, ILLINOIS

Broccoli Chicken Casserole

PREP: 15 MIN. **BAKE:** 30 MIN.
MAKES: 6 SERVINGS

- 1½ **cups water**
- 1 **package (6 ounces) chicken stuffing mix**
- 2 **cups cubed cooked chicken**
- 1 **cup frozen broccoli florets, thawed**
- 1 **can (10¾ ounces) condensed broccoli cheese soup, undiluted**
- 1 **cup (4 ounces) shredded cheddar cheese**

1. In a small saucepan, bring water to a boil. Stir in stuffing mix. Remove from the heat; cover and let stand for 5 minutes.
2. Meanwhile, layer chicken and broccoli in a greased 11-in. x 7-in. baking dish. Top with soup. Fluff stuffing with a fork; spoon over soup. Sprinkle with cheese.
3. Bake, uncovered, at 350° for 30-35 minutes or until heated through.

Cranberry-Stuffed Chicken

My grandma used to roast stuffed chicken for our family, and now I do the same for our grandchildren. Everyone relishes the tempting stuffing.
—**CHERE BELL**
COLORADO SPRINGS, COLORADO

PREP: 20 MIN.
BAKE: 2½ HOURS + STANDING
MAKES: 6-8 SERVINGS

- 1 **cup chopped celery**
- 1 **cup chopped onion**
- ⅔ **cup dried cranberries**
- ½ **cup plus 2 tablespoons butter, divided**
- 1 **garlic clove, minced**
- 3 **cups herb-seasoned stuffing croutons**
- 1 **cup crushed corn bread stuffing or crumbled corn bread**
- 1½ **to 2 cups chicken broth**
- 1 **roasting chicken (5 to 7 pounds)**
- ½ **teaspoon salt**
- ½ **teaspoon pepper**
- ¼ **teaspoon poultry seasoning**
- ¼ **teaspoon rubbed sage**

1. In a large skillet, saute the celery, onion and cranberries in ½ cup butter until tender. Stir in the garlic, croutons, corn bread stuffing and enough broth to moisten; set aside.
2. Place chicken with breast side up on a rack in a roasting pan. Combine salt, pepper, poultry seasoning and sage; sprinkle over inside and outside of chicken. Loosely stuff with cranberry mixture. Melt remaining butter; brush over chicken.
3. Bake, uncovered, at 350° for 2½ to 3 hours or until a thermometer reads 180° for chicken and 165° for the stuffing, basting occasionally with pan juices.
4. Remove chicken from the oven and tent with foil. Let stand 15 minutes before removing stuffing and carving.

Alfredo Chicken Lasagna

My easy recipe is elegant enough for a special-occasion dinner. I've served it often, and the rich flavor is everyone's favorite part. I personally love the fact that it can be made ahead.

—BRIDGETTE MONAGHAN
MASONVILLE, IOWA

PREP: 25 MIN.
BAKE: 40 MIN. + STANDING
MAKES: 3 SERVINGS

- **6** ounces boneless skinless chicken breast, cut into bite-size pieces
- **1** cup sliced fresh mushrooms
- **2** tablespoons chopped onion
- **1** tablespoon olive oil
- **1** garlic clove, minced
- **1** tablespoon all-purpose flour
- **1** cup Alfredo sauce
- **¾** cup 2% cottage cheese
- **¼** cup plus 2 tablespoons shredded Parmesan cheese, divided
- **1** egg, lightly beaten
- **½** teaspoon Italian seasoning
- **½** teaspoon dried parsley flakes
- **4** lasagna noodles, cooked and drained
- **1½** cups (6 ounces) shredded part-skim mozzarella cheese

1. In a large skillet, saute the chicken, mushrooms and onion in oil until chicken is no longer pink. Add garlic; cook 1 minute longer. Stir in flour until blended; gradually stir in Alfredo sauce. Bring to a boil. Reduce heat; simmer, uncovered, for 3-5 minutes or until thickened.
2. In a small bowl, combine the cottage cheese, ¼ cup Parmesan cheese, egg, Italian seasoning and parsley.
3. Spread ½ cup Alfredo mixture in an 8-in. x 4-in. loaf pan coated with cooking spray. Layer with two noodles (trimmed to fit pan), half of the cottage cheese mixture, half of the remaining Alfredo mixture and ¾ cup mozzarella cheese. Sprinkle with remaining Parmesan cheese. Repeat layers.
4. Cover and bake at 350° for 30 minutes. Uncover; bake 10 minutes longer or until bubbly. Let stand for 10 minutes before cutting.

EAT SMART Pepperoni Baked Ziti

I took a favorite family recipe and put my own nutritious spin on it to create a kid-friendly casserole. The pepperoni and cheeses add traditional Italian flair.

—ANDREA ABRAHAMSEN
BRENTWOOD, CALIFORNIA

PREP: 20 MIN. **BAKE:** 30 MIN.
MAKES: 10 SERVINGS

- **1** package (1 pound) uncooked ziti or small tube pasta
- **½** pound lean ground turkey
- **2** cans (one 29 ounces, one 8 ounces) tomato sauce, divided
- **1½** cups (6 ounces) shredded part-skim mozzarella cheese, divided
- **1** can (8 ounces) mushroom stems and pieces, drained
- **5** ounces frozen chopped spinach, thawed and squeezed dry
- **½** cup reduced-fat ricotta cheese
- **4** teaspoons Italian seasoning
- **2** garlic cloves, minced
- **½** teaspoon garlic powder
- **½** teaspoon crushed red pepper flakes
- **¼** teaspoon pepper
- **½** cup water
- **1** tablespoon grated Parmesan cheese
- **1½** ounces sliced turkey pepperoni

1. Cook pasta according to package directions.
2. Meanwhile, in a large nonstick skillet, cook turkey over medium heat until no longer pink; drain. Transfer to a large bowl. Add the 29-oz. can tomato sauce, 1 cup mozzarella cheese, mushrooms, spinach, ricotta cheese, Italian seasoning, garlic, garlic powder, pepper flakes and pepper. Drain pasta; fold into turkey mixture.
3. Transfer to a 13-in. x 9-in. baking dish coated with cooking spray. Combine the water and remaining tomato sauce; pour over pasta mixture. Sprinkle with Parmesan cheese and remaining mozzarella cheese. Top with pepperoni.
4. Cover and bake at 350° for 25-30 minutes or until bubbly. Uncover; bake 5 minutes longer or until cheese is melted.

PER SERVING 306 cal., 7 g fat (3 g sat. fat), 37 mg chol., 795 mg sodium, 42 g carb., 4 g fiber, 20 g pro. **Diabetic Exchanges:** 2½ starch, 2 lean meat, 1 vegetable.

PEPPERONI BAKED ZITI

Country Roasted Chicken

Easy home-style chicken gets wonderful flavor from the celery, onion and parsley tucked inside. When my daughter was away at school, she even called home for the recipe so she could make it herself.

—JUDY PAGE EDENVILLE, MICHIGAN

PREP: 10 MIN. **BAKE:** 65 MIN.
MAKES: 4 SERVINGS

- 1 broiler/fryer chicken (3 pounds)
- ½ teaspoon dried thyme
- 2 teaspoons salt, divided
- 1 large onion, cut into eighths
- 2 celery ribs with leaves, cut into 4-inch pieces
- 4 fresh parsley sprigs
- 8 small red potatoes
- ¼ cup chicken broth
  Minced fresh parsley

1. Sprinkle inside of chicken with thyme and 1 teaspoon salt. Stuff chicken with the onion, celery and parsley sprigs. Place in a greased oven-proof Dutch oven.

2. Cover and bake at 375° for 30 minutes. Sprinkle remaining salt over chicken. Add potatoes and broth to pan. Cover and bake 25 minutes longer.

3. Increase oven temperature to 400°. Bake, uncovered, for 10-15 minutes or until potatoes are tender and a thermometer inserted in chicken reads 180°. Remove chicken from oven; tent with foil. Let stand 15 minutes before carving. Sprinkle with minced parsley.

CORDON BLEU CASSEROLE

> I got this cherished recipe from a friend many years ago. I freeze several disposable pans to share with neighbors or for when I am scrambling for time but still want a good meal. **—REA NEWELL** DECATUR, ILLINOIS

Cordon Bleu Casserole

PREP: 20 MIN. **BAKE:** 40 MIN.
MAKES: 2 CASSEROLES (6 SERVINGS EACH)

- 2 packages (6 ounces each) reduced-sodium stuffing mix
- 1 can (10¾ ounces) condensed cream of chicken soup, undiluted
- 1 cup milk
- 8 cups cubed cooked chicken
- ½ teaspoon pepper
- ¾ pound sliced deli ham, cut into 1-inch strips
- 1 cup (4 ounces) shredded Swiss cheese
- 3 cups (12 ounces) shredded cheddar cheese

1. Prepare stuffing mixes according to package directions. Meanwhile, in a large bowl, combine soup and milk; set aside.

2. Divide the chicken between two greased 13-in. x 9-in. baking dishes. Sprinkle with pepper. Layer with ham, Swiss cheese, 1 cup cheddar cheese, soup mixture and stuffing. Sprinkle with remaining cheddar cheese.

3. Cover and freeze one casserole for up to 3 months. Cover and bake the remaining casserole at 350° for 30 minutes. Uncover; bake 10-15 minutes longer or until cheese is melted.

TO USE FROZEN CASSEROLE *Thaw in the refrigerator overnight. Remove from the refrigerator 30 minutes before baking. Cover and bake at 350° for 45 minutes. Uncover; bake 10-15 minutes longer or until heated through and cheese is melted.*

Turkey Enchilada Casserole

Every time I make this hearty and tasty entree for guests, I end up sharing my well-worn, well-loved recipe!

—**DEBRA MARTIN** BELLEVILLE, MICHIGAN

PREP: 30 MIN. **BAKE:** 25 MIN.
MAKES: 10 SERVINGS

- 1 **pound lean ground turkey**
- 1 **medium green pepper, chopped**
- 1 **medium onion, chopped**
- 3 **garlic cloves, minced**
- 2 **cans (15 ounces each) black beans, rinsed and drained**
- 1 **jar (16 ounces) salsa**
- 1 **can (15 ounces) tomato sauce**
- 1 **can (14½ ounces) Mexican stewed tomatoes**
- 1 **teaspoon each onion powder, garlic powder and ground cumin**
- 12 **corn tortillas (6 inches)**
- 2 **cups (8 ounces) shredded reduced-fat cheddar cheese, divided**

1. In a large nonstick saucepan coated with cooking spray, cook the turkey, green pepper and onion over medium heat until meat is no longer pink. Add garlic; cook 1 minute longer. Drain. Stir in the beans, salsa, tomato sauce, tomatoes, onion powder, garlic powder and cumin. Bring to a boil. Reduce heat; simmer, uncovered, for 10 minutes.

2. Spread 1 cup meat sauce into a 13-in. x 9-in. baking dish coated with cooking spray. Top with six tortillas. Spread with half of the remaining meat sauce; sprinkle with 1 cup cheese. Layer with remaining tortillas and meat sauce.

3. Cover and bake at 350° for 20 minutes. Uncover; sprinkle with remaining cheese. Bake 5-10 minutes longer or until bubbly and cheese is melted.

TURKEY ENCHILADA CASSEROLE

Crispy Buffalo Chicken Roll-ups

These winning chicken rolls with a crispy crust are both impressive and easy to make. My family and friends absolutely love them!

—**LISA KEYS**

KENNET SQUARE, PENNSYLVANIA

PREP: 15 MIN. **BAKE:** 30 MIN.
MAKES: 4 SERVINGS

- 4 **boneless skinless chicken breast halves (6 ounces each)**
- ¾ **teaspoon salt**
- ½ **teaspoon pepper**
- ¼ **cup crumbled blue cheese**
- ¼ **cup hot pepper sauce**
- 2 **tablespoons mayonnaise**
- 1 **cup crushed cornflakes**

1. Flatten chicken breasts to ¼-in. thickness. Season with salt and pepper; sprinkle with blue cheese. Roll up each from a short side and secure with toothpicks.

2. In a shallow bowl, combine pepper sauce and mayonnaise. Place cornflakes in a separate shallow bowl. Dip chicken in pepper sauce mixture, then coat with cornflakes. Place seam side down in a greased 11-in. x 7-in. baking dish.

3. Bake, uncovered, at 400° for 30-35 minutes or until chicken is no longer pink. Discard toothpicks.

Pork

203 200 209

Taking a break from beef and chicken? Consider pork!
Try other home cooks' tasty twists on **pasta**, **pizzas**,
Southwestern fare and more. You'll find new ways to
serve **pork chops**, spice up meals with **sausage** and bake
tender **ham** dishes that come together in a pinch!

> Here's a great way to mix up dinner! Carnitas come together with little work and simply bake up on their own in the oven. —**PATRICIA COLLINS** IMBLER, OREGON

Mexican Carnitas

PREP: 40 MIN. **BAKE:** 2 HOURS
MAKES: 12-16 SERVINGS

- 1 boneless pork shoulder butt roast (3 to 4 pounds), cut into 1-inch cubes
- 6 large garlic cloves, minced
- ½ cup fresh cilantro leaves, chopped
- 1 teaspoon salt
  Pepper to taste
- 3 large oranges, divided
- 1 large lemon
  Oil for frying
- 12 to 16 flour tortillas (8 inches), warmed
  Optional toppings: shredded cheddar cheese, salsa and guacamole

1. Place meat in a medium-size roasting pan. Sprinkle with garlic and cilantro. Season with salt and pepper. Squeeze the juice from one orange and the lemon over the meat. Slice the remaining oranges and place over the meat.
2. Cover and bake at 350° for about 2 hours or until meat is tender. With a slotted spoon, remove meat and drain well on paper towels. Heat a small amount of oil in a skillet and fry meat in batches until browned and crispy.
3. Serve warm in tortillas with toppings of your choice.

Brunch Enchiladas

When I have company for brunch, this tried-and-true casserole is usually on the menu. With ham, eggs and plenty of cheese, the enchiladas are hearty and fun. I like that I can make them the day before.
—**GAIL SYKORA**
MENOMONEE FALLS, WISCONSIN

PREP: 15 MIN. + CHILLING
BAKE: 40 MIN. + STANDING
MAKES: 10 ENCHILADAS

- 2 cups cubed fully cooked ham
- ½ cup chopped green onions
- 10 flour tortillas (8 inches)
- 2 cups (8 ounces) shredded cheddar cheese, divided
- 1 tablespoon all-purpose flour
- 2 cups half-and-half cream
- 6 eggs, lightly beaten
- ¼ teaspoon salt, optional

1. In a large bowl, combine ham and onions; place about ¼ cup down the center of each tortilla. Top with 2 tablespoons cheese. Roll up and place seam side down in a greased 13-in. x 9-in. baking dish.
2. In another large bowl, combine the flour, cream, eggs and salt if desired until smooth. Pour over tortillas. Cover and refrigerate for 8 hours or overnight.
3. Remove from the refrigerator 30 minutes before baking. Cover and bake at 350° for 25 minutes. Uncover; bake for 10 minutes. Sprinkle with remaining cheese; bake 3 minutes longer or until the cheese is melted. Let stand for 10 minutes before serving.

RIGATONI & SAUSAGE

To serve a dozen people without much extra effort, simply double the recipe and prepare two of these hearty pasta casseroles. —ELAINE NEUKIRCH GENOA, ILLINOIS

Rigatoni & Sausage

PREP: 20 MIN. **BAKE:** 15 MIN.
MAKES: 6 SERVINGS

- 3¾ cups uncooked rigatoni
- 5 Italian sausage links (4 ounces each), sliced
- 1 jar (24 ounces) spaghetti sauce
- ¼ cup dry red wine
- 2 cups (8 ounces) shredded Italian cheese blend

1. Cook rigatoni according to package directions. Meanwhile, in a Dutch oven, cook sausage over medium heat until no longer pink; drain. Add spaghetti sauce and wine.
2. Drain rigatoni; add to sausage mixture and toss to coat. Transfer to a greased 13-in. x 9-in. baking dish; sprinkle with cheese. Bake, uncovered, at 350° for 15-20 minutes or until cheese is melted.

Pork with Corn Bread Stuffing

This dish is one of my family's favorites. It's fantastic for holiday gatherings, because it looks just as good as it tastes!
—FERN KLEEMAN TELL CITY, INDIANA

PREP: 25 MIN. **BAKE:** 40 MIN.
MAKES: 6 SERVINGS (CHOPS) OR 8-10 SERVINGS (ROAST)

- ¼ cup boiling water
- ¼ cup raisins
- 2 bacon strips, cut up
- ½ cup diced celery
- 2 tablespoons diced onion
- 1 egg, beaten
- 1 teaspoon salt
- ¼ teaspoon pepper
- 2½ cups corn bread crumbs
- 6 center-cut pork chops (1¼ inches thick) or 1 pork shoulder butt roast (3 to 4 pounds), boned for stuffing

1. Pour water over raisins; set aside. In a saucepan, cook bacon until crisp; add celery and onion. Cook and stir for 2 minutes; remove from the heat. In a small bowl, combine the egg, salt, pepper and bacon and raisin mixtures. Add crumbs and toss lightly.
2. If stuffing pork chops, cut a pocket in each chop by slicing from the fat side almost to the bone. Spoon about ⅓ cup stuffing into each chop; place on a rack in a shallow roasting pan. Bake at 375° for 40-50 minutes or until meat is no longer pink.
3. If stuffing a roast, fill pocket in roast with stuffing. Tie roast with string and place on a rack in a shallow roasting pan. Roast at 325° for 1¾ to 2¼ hours or until a thermometer reads 160°. Cover and let stand 10 minutes before carving.

Pear Pork Chops

PREP: 15 MIN. **BAKE:** 40 MIN.
MAKES: 6 SERVINGS

- 1 can (15 ounces) pear halves
- 6 bone-in pork chops (¾ inch thick)
- 3 tablespoons butter
- ⅓ cup packed brown sugar
- 1 teaspoon prepared mustard

1. Drain pears, reserving the juice; cut pears into slices and set aside. In a large skillet, brown the pork chops in butter. Transfer to a greased 13-in. x 9-in. baking dish.
2. In a small bowl, combine the brown sugar, mustard and reserved pear juice. Pour over chops; top with pear slices.
3. Bake, uncovered, at 350° for 40-45 minutes or until a thermometer reads 160°.

Sliced pears make a satisfying alternative to apples in this rustic pork chop dinner. A hint of brown sugar adds the perfect sweetness.

—**KATHY STOOKSBURY** AIKEN, SOUTH CAROLINA

PEAR PORK CHOPS

My family loves this five-ingredient casserole with hearty chunks of sausage and green pepper. The recipe makes a big pan, so it's nice for gatherings.
—**CAROL CAROLTON** WHEATON, ILLINOIS

SAUSAGE SPAGHETTI SPIRALS

Sausage Spaghetti Spirals

PREP: 15 MIN. **BAKE:** 30 MIN.
MAKES: 6 SERVINGS

- 1 pound bulk Italian sausage
- 1 medium green pepper, chopped
- 5 cups spiral pasta, cooked and drained
- 1 jar (24 ounces) spaghetti sauce
- 1½ cups (6 ounces) shredded part-skim mozzarella cheese

1. In a large skillet, cook sausage and green pepper over medium heat until meat is no longer pink; drain. Stir in pasta and spaghetti sauce.

2. Transfer to a greased 13-in. x 9-in. baking dish. Cover and bake at 350° for 25 minutes. Uncover; sprinkle with cheese. Bake 5-10 minutes longer or until cheese is melted.

EAT SMART Crumb-Crusted Pork Roast With Root Vegetables

PREP: 25 MIN.
BAKE: 1½ HOURS + STANDING
MAKES: 8 SERVINGS

- 1 boneless pork loin roast (2 to 3 pounds)
- 4½ teaspoons honey
- 1 tablespoon molasses
- 1½ teaspoons spicy brown mustard
- 2 teaspoons rubbed sage
- 1 teaspoon dried thyme
- 1 teaspoon dried rosemary, crushed
- ½ cup soft whole wheat bread crumbs
- 2 tablespoons grated Parmesan cheese
- 1 large celery root, peeled and cubed
- 1 large rutabaga, peeled and cubed
- 1 large sweet potato, peeled and cubed
- 1 large onion, cut into wedges
- 2 tablespoons canola oil
- ½ teaspoon salt
- ¼ teaspoon pepper

1. Place roast on a rack in a shallow roasting pan coated with cooking spray. In a small bowl, combine the honey, molasses and mustard; brush over roast. In another small bowl, combine the sage, thyme and rosemary; set aside. Combine the bread crumbs, Parmesan cheese and 2 teaspoons of the herb mixture; press onto roast.

2. In a resealable plastic bag, combine celery root, rutabaga, sweet potato, onion, oil, salt, pepper and remaining herb mixture; toss to coat. Arrange vegetables around roast.

3. Bake, uncovered, at 350° for 1½ to 1¾ hours or until a thermometer reads 160°. Transfer to a warm serving platter. Let stand for 10-15 minutes before slicing.

PER SERVING *302 cal., 10 g fat (2 g sat. fat), 57 mg chol., 313 mg sodium, 29 g carb., 5 g fiber, 25 g pro.* **Diabetic Exchanges:** *3 lean meat, 2 starch, ½ fat.*

Boneless pork loin roast should be cooked to 160°, which may leave a faint pink interior.

Perfect for fall, this combo brings together well-seasoned pork loin with seasonal roasted veggies.
—TASTE OF HOME TEST KITCHEN

SAUSAGE & SPINACH CALZONES

> Ready in just 30 minutes, my calzones are perfect for quick lunches or even late-night snacks. Co-workers ask for them when it's my turn to bring in lunch.
>
> —**KOURTNEY WILLIAMS** MECHANICSVILLE, VIRGINIA

Sausage & Spinach Calzones

PREP/TOTAL TIME: 30 MIN.
MAKES: 4 SERVINGS

- ½ **pound bulk Italian sausage**
- 1 **tube (13.8 ounces) refrigerated pizza crust**
- ¾ **cup shredded part-skim mozzarella cheese**
- 3 **cups fresh baby spinach, chopped**
- ½ **cup part-skim ricotta cheese**
- ¼ **teaspoon salt**
- ¼ **teaspoon pepper**

1. In a large skillet, cook sausage over medium heat until no longer pink. Meanwhile, unroll pizza crust; pat into a 15-in. x 11-in. rectangle. Cut into four rectangles. Sprinkle mozzarella cheese over half of each rectangle to within 1 in. of edges.

2. Drain sausage. Add spinach; cook and stir over medium heat until spinach is wilted. Remove from the heat. Stir in the ricotta cheese, salt and pepper; spread over mozzarella cheese. Fold dough over filling; press edges with a fork to seal.

3. Transfer to a greased baking sheet. Bake at 400° for 10-15 minutes or until lightly browned.

Andouille-Stuffed Peppers

Inspired by the use of green peppers in Cajun dishes, I created this spicy recipe. For a healthier alternative, substitute chicken sausage or cubed cooked chicken breast for the andouille.

—**SARAH LARSON** CARLSBAD, CALIFORNIA

PREP: 40 MIN. **BAKE:** 40 MIN.
MAKES: 4 SERVINGS

- 1 **package (8 ounces) jambalaya mix**
- 4 **small green peppers**
- ¾ **pound fully cooked andouille sausage links, chopped**
- 1 **jalapeno pepper, seeded and minced**
- 1 **can (16 ounces) tomato juice**
  Louisiana-style hot sauce, optional

1. Prepare jambalaya mix according to package directions. Meanwhile, cut peppers lengthwise in half; remove seeds.

2. In a large skillet, cook and stir sausage over medium-high heat until browned. Add jalapeno; cook 1 minute longer.

3. Stir sausage mixture into prepared jambalaya. Spoon into pepper halves. Place in a greased 13-in. x 9-in. baking dish; pour tomato juice over and around peppers.

4. Bake, uncovered, at 350° for 40-45 minutes or until peppers are tender. Serve with hot sauce if desired.

NOTE *Wear disposable gloves when cutting hot peppers; the oils can burn skin. Avoid touching your face.*

ITALIAN QUICHES

Italian Quiches

This recipe makes two quiches, so you can freeze one! Enjoy them for breakfast as well as supper.

—BERNICE HANCOCK

GREENVILLE, PENNSYLVANIA

PREP: 25 MIN. **BAKE:** 35 MIN. + STANDING
MAKES: 2 QUICHES (6 SERVINGS EACH)

- 2 **unbaked pastry shells (9 inches)**
- 1 **pound bulk Italian sausage**
- 4 **cups (16 ounces) finely shredded part-skim mozzarella cheese**
- 1 **medium onion, thinly sliced**
- 1 **medium green pepper, thinly sliced**
- 1 **medium sweet red pepper, thinly sliced**

- 6 **eggs**
- 2 **cups milk**
- 1 **teaspoon minced garlic**
- ¼ **cup grated Parmesan cheese**

1. Line unpricked pastry shells with a double thickness of heavy-duty foil. Bake at 400° for 4 minutes. Remove foil; bake 4 minutes longer.

2. In a large skillet, cook sausage over medium heat until no longer pink; drain. Spoon sausage into pastry shells; sprinkle with mozzarella cheese. Top with onion and peppers. In a large bowl, whisk the eggs, milk and garlic. Pour over peppers; sprinkle with Parmesan cheese.

3. Cover and freeze one quiche for up to 3 months. Cover edges of remaining quiche loosely with foil; place on a baking sheet. Bake at 400° for 35-40 minutes or until a knife inserted near the center comes out clean. Let stand for 10 minutes before cutting.

TO USE FROZEN QUICHE *Remove from the freezer 30 minutes before baking (do not thaw). Cover edges of crust loosely with foil; place on a baking sheet. Bake at 400° for 50-60 minutes or until a knife inserted near the center comes out clean. Let stand for 10 minutes before cutting.*

SOUTHWESTERN POTPIE WITH CORNMEAL BISCUITS

> My Southwestern-inspired potpie is full of sweet and spicy pork, corn, beans and green chilies. It's a sure-fire winner for any gathering. The cornmeal gives the biscuits a delightful little crunch.
>
> —ANDREA BOLDEN UNIONVILLE, TENNESSEE

Southwestern Potpie With Cornmeal Biscuits

PREP: 35 MIN. + SIMMERING
BAKE: 15 MIN. + STANDING
MAKES: 12 SERVINGS

- ¼ cup all-purpose flour
- 1½ pounds boneless pork loin roast, cut into ½-inch cubes
- 2 tablespoons butter
- 1 jalapeno pepper, seeded and chopped
- 2 garlic cloves, minced
- 2 cups beef broth
- 1 can (14½ ounces) diced tomatoes, undrained
- 1 teaspoon ground cumin
- ½ teaspoon chili powder
- ¼ to ½ teaspoon ground cinnamon
- 1 can (15¼ ounces) whole kernel corn, drained
- 1 can (15 ounces) pinto beans, rinsed and drained
- 1 can (4 ounces) chopped green chilies

BISCUITS

- 3 cups biscuit/baking mix
- ¾ cup cornmeal
- ½ cup shredded cheddar cheese
- 4½ teaspoons sugar
- 1 cup 2% milk

1. Place flour in a large resealable plastic bag. Add pork, a few pieces at a time, and shake to coat. In a Dutch oven, brown pork in butter in batches. Remove and set aside.

2. In the same pan, saute jalapeno and garlic in the drippings for 1 minute. Stir in the broth, tomatoes, cumin, chili powder, cinnamon and pork. Bring to a boil. Reduce heat; cover and simmer for 1 hour or until pork is tender.

3. Add the corn, beans and chilies; heat through. Transfer to a greased 13-in. x 9-in. baking dish.

4. In a large bowl, combine the biscuit mix, cornmeal, cheese and sugar; stir in milk just until moistened. Turn onto a lightly floured surface; knead 8-10 times.

5. Pat or roll out to ½-in. thickness; cut with a floured 2½-in. biscuit cutter. Arrange over meat mixture. Bake at 400° for 15-18 minutes or until golden brown. Let stand for 10 minutes before serving.

NOTE *Wear disposable gloves when cutting hot peppers; the oils can burn skin. Avoid touching your face.*

Perfect Pork Chop Bake

PREP: 15 MIN. **BAKE:** 40 MIN.
MAKES: 6 SERVINGS

- 6 boneless pork loin chops (5 ounces each)
- ½ teaspoon salt, divided, optional
- 1 medium onion, thinly sliced and separated into rings
- 3 medium potatoes, peeled and thinly sliced
- 6 medium carrots, thinly sliced
- 1 teaspoon dried marjoram
- 3 tablespoons all-purpose flour
- ¾ cup milk
- 1 can (10¾ ounces) condensed cream of mushroom soup, undiluted

1. Coat a large skillet with cooking spray; cook chops over medium heat for 2-3 minutes on each side or until lightly browned. Place in an ungreased 13-in. x 9-in. baking dish; sprinkle with ¼ teaspoon salt if desired. Layer with onion, potatoes and carrots. Sprinkle with marjoram and remaining salt if desired.

2. In a small bowl, whisk flour and milk until smooth; add soup. Pour over vegetables. Cover and bake at 350° for 30-35 minutes. Uncover; bake 10-15 minutes longer or until meat is tender.

This recipe is useful on busy days when I'm particularly short on time. I love that the one-dish supper bakes in the oven on its own while I tend to other things.
—**JAN LUTZ** STEVENS POINT, WISCONSIN

PERFECT PORK CHOP BAKE

A cranberry and apricot stuffing wonderfully complements pork tenderloin in this impressive entree. The elegant dish is much easier to prepare than it looks.

—**JOANN BROWN** LOS ALAMOS, NEW MEXICO

CRANBERRY-APRICOT PORK TENDERLOINS

Cranberry-Apricot Pork Tenderloins

PREP: 30 MIN. **BAKE:** 30 MIN.
MAKES: 6-8 SERVINGS

- 1 cup dried cranberries
- 1 cup chopped dried apricots
- 3 tablespoons water
- 2 teaspoons dried rosemary, crushed
- ½ teaspoon salt
- ¼ teaspoon pepper
- 2 pork tenderloins (1 pound each)

1. In a small saucepan, bring the first six ingredients to a boil. Reduce heat; cover and simmer 10 minutes or until fruit is softened. Cool.
2. Cut a lengthwise slit down the center of each tenderloin to within ½ in. of bottom. Open tenderloins so they lie flat; cover with plastic wrap. Flatten to ¾-in. thickness; remove plastic. Spread with fruit mixture to within ¾ in. of edges. Roll up jelly-roll style, starting with a long side; tie with kitchen string at 1-½ in. intervals.
3. Line a shallow pan with heavy-duty foil. Place meat on a rack in prepared pan. Bake, uncovered, at 400° for 30-35 minutes or until a thermometer reads 160°.

Tangy Reuben Bake

I created this casserole because my husband's background is Czech, so just about everyone in the family loves sauerkraut. My daughter won a ribbon at the state fair with the recipe.
—JEWELL KRONAIZL
VERMILLION, SOUTH DAKOTA

PREP: 10 MIN. **BAKE:** 30 MIN.
MAKES: 4 SERVINGS

- 3 medium potatoes, peeled, sliced and cooked
- ½ pound smoked kielbasa or Polish sausage, thinly sliced
- 1 can (8 ounces) sauerkraut, rinsed and drained
- ½ cup Thousand Island salad dressing
- 2 tablespoons sugar
- 2 tablespoons minced fresh parsley
- 1 tablespoon dried minced onion
- ½ to 1 teaspoon caraway seeds
- ¾ cup shredded cheddar cheese

BIG KAHUNA PIZZA

1. In a bowl, combine the first eight ingredients. Transfer to a greased 8-in. square baking dish.
2. Bake, uncovered, at 350° for 25 minutes. Sprinkle with cheese. Bake until cheese is melted.

Big Kahuna Pizza

A prebaked pizza crust and refrigerated barbecued pork make this five-ingredient supper so fast and easy!
—JONI HILTON ROCKLIN, CALIFORNIA

PREP/TOTAL TIME: 30 MIN.
MAKES: 6 SERVINGS

- 1 prebaked 12-inch pizza crust
- 1 carton (18 ounces) refrigerated fully cooked barbecued shredded pork
- 1 can (20 ounces) pineapple chunks, drained
- ⅓ cup chopped red onion
- 2 cups (8 ounces) shredded part-skim mozzarella cheese

1. Place pizza crust on an ungreased 12-in. pizza pan. Spread shredded pork over crust; top with pineapple and onion. Sprinkle with cheese.
2. Bake at 350° for 20-25 minutes or until cheese is melted.

ANTIPASTO PIZZA

Mama's Spaghetti Pie

This savory pie for two has a simple pasta crust and satisfying Italian filling. It freezes well before baking, too.

—KATHLEEN WILLIAMS LEESBURG, FLORIDA

PREP: 20 MIN. **BAKE:** 20 MIN.
MAKES: 2 SERVINGS

- 3 ounces uncooked spaghetti or angel hair pasta
- 1 egg, beaten
- ¼ cup grated Parmesan cheese
- ⅓ pound bulk pork sausage
- ¼ cup chopped onion
- ½ cup Italian tomato sauce
- ⅓ cup sour cream
- ½ teaspoon Italian seasoning
- ½ cup shredded part-skim mozzarella cheese

1. Cook spaghetti according to package directions; drain. In a small bowl, combine the pasta, egg and Parmesan cheese. Press onto the bottom and up the sides of a 7-in. pie plate or shallow 2-cup round baking dish coated with cooking spray; set aside.

2. Crumble sausage into a small skillet; add onion. Cook over medium heat until meat is no longer pink; drain. Stir in the tomato sauce, sour cream and Italian seasoning. Spoon into crust.

3. Bake, uncovered, at 350° for 15-20 minutes or until heated through. Sprinkle with mozzarella cheese; bake 2-3 minutes longer or until cheese is melted. Serve immediately.

> You'll need less than half an hour to whip up this deliciously different and versatile pizza. Deli ham, hard salami and prepared sauce make it a snap.
> **—MINDEE CURTIS** OMAHA, NEBRASKA

Antipasto Pizza

PREP/TOTAL TIME: 25 MIN.
MAKES: 8 SLICES

- 1 prebaked 12-inch pizza crust
- ¾ cup pizza sauce
- 2 cups (8 ounces) shredded part-skim mozzarella cheese, divided
- ½ cup julienned roasted sweet red peppers
- ½ cup marinated quartered artichoke hearts, drained
- ¼ pound thinly sliced hard salami, julienned
- ¼ pound sliced deli ham, julienned
- ¼ cup minced fresh basil

1. Place crust on an ungreased pizza pan. Spread sauce over crust; sprinkle with 1 cup cheese. Top with red peppers, artichokes, salami and ham; sprinkle with remaining cheese.

2. Bake at 450° for 10-12 minutes or until cheese is melted. Sprinkle with basil.

BOW TIES & HAM

Bow Ties & Ham

We love casseroles! Here's one from our family cookbook that's filled with recipes from generations of women. Just pop it in the oven to warm your home and fill your stomach.
—**SUZETTE JURY** KEENE, CALIFORNIA

PREP: 20 MIN. **BAKE:** 25 MIN.
MAKES: 2 CASSEROLES (6 SERVINGS EACH)

- 4 **cups uncooked bow tie pasta**
- 6 **cups frozen broccoli florets**
- 4 **cups cubed fully cooked ham**
- 2 **cartons (10 ounces each) refrigerated Alfredo sauce**
- 2 **cups (8 ounces) shredded Swiss cheese**
- 1 **can (8 ounces) mushroom stems and pieces, drained**

1. Cook pasta according to package directions, adding the broccoli during the last 5 minutes of cooking. Meanwhile, in a large bowl, combine the ham, Alfredo sauce, cheese and mushrooms. Drain pasta mixture; add to ham mixture and toss to coat.
2. Transfer to two greased 11-in. x 7-in. baking dishes. Cover and freeze one casserole for up to 3 months. Cover and bake remaining casserole at 375° for 20 minutes. Uncover; bake 5-10 minutes longer or until bubbly.
TO USE FROZEN CASSEROLE *Thaw in the refrigerator overnight. Remove from the refrigerator 30 minutes before heating. Cover and microwave on high for 8-10 minutes or until heated through, stirring once.*
NOTE *This recipe was tested in a 1,100-watt microwave.*

Fully cooked ham is ham that has been **cooked and smoked and/or cured**. It can be eaten without heating but is generally heated to a minimum of 140° for **optimal flavor**.

Deep-Dish Sausage Pizza

This impressive pizza pie is sure to become a staple in your house. Prepared bread dough is pressed into a springform pan to make an easy crust, and Italian sausage creates a hearty filling with plenty of flavor. What's not to like?

—TASTE OF HOME TEST KITCHEN

PREP: 30 MIN. **BAKE:** 20 MIN.
MAKES: 6 SERVINGS

- 1 loaf (1 pound) frozen bread dough, thawed
- 2 teaspoons cornmeal
- 1¾ cups pizza sauce
- ½ pound bulk Italian sausage, cooked and drained
- 1½ cups (6 ounces) shredded part-skim mozzarella cheese
- 1 teaspoon dried oregano
  Green pepper rings

1. On a lightly floured surface, roll and stretch dough into a 9-in. circle. Cover with plastic wrap; let rest for 10 minutes. Roll and stretch the dough into a 12-in. circle. Sprinkle cornmeal into a greased 9-in. springform pan. Place dough in pan and press 1 in. up the sides of the pan.

2. Spread pizza sauce over crust. Top with sausage, 1 cup of cheese, oregano and green pepper. Sprinkle with remaining cheese.

3. Bake at 425° for 20-25 minutes or until crust is golden brown. Remove to a wire rack; let stand for 5 minutes before removing sides of pan.

You can **customize the pizza** with sliced fresh **mushrooms**, chopped **onions** or sweet yellow **peppers**. How about some **pepperoni?**

HOT HAM & CHEESE ROLL-UPS

Here's a fast yet fun twist on traditional hot ham and cheese sandwiches. Kids love to help make them!

—KATHERINE DESROSIERS TRAIL, BRITISH COLUMBIA

Hot Ham & Cheese Roll-Ups

PREP/TOTAL TIME: 20 MIN.
MAKES: 4 SERVINGS

- 2 tablespoons olive oil, divided
- 4 flour tortillas (10 inches)
- ½ cup grated Parmesan cheese, divided
- ¼ pound thinly sliced deli ham
- ¼ pound thinly sliced provolone cheese
- ¼ pound thinly sliced hard salami
- ½ cup julienned roasted sweet red peppers
- 1 cup (4 ounces) shredded part-skim mozzarella cheese
  Marinara sauce, optional

1. Brush 1 tablespoon oil on one side of tortillas. Sprinkle with ¼ cup Parmesan cheese. Layer tortillas with ham, provolone cheese, salami, red peppers and mozzarella cheese. Fold in sides of tortillas; roll up.

2. Place seam side down on a parchment paper-lined baking sheet. Brush with remaining oil; sprinkle with remaining Parmesan cheese. Bake at 425° for 9-12 minutes or until golden brown. Serve with marinara sauce if desired.

Italian Pork and Potato Casserole

The aroma of this hearty dish baking brings back fond memories of home. My mother created the recipe years ago, using ingredients she had on hand.

—**THERESA KREYCHE** TUSTIN, CALIFORNIA

PREP: 10 MIN. **BAKE:** 45 MIN.
MAKES: 6 SERVINGS

- 6 **cups sliced red potatoes**
- 3 **tablespoons water**
- 1 **garlic clove, minced**
- ½ **teaspoon salt**
- ⅛ **teaspoon pepper**
- 6 **boneless pork loin chops (6 ounces each)**
- 1 **jar (24 ounces) marinara sauce**
- ¼ **cup shredded Parmesan cheese**

1. Place potatoes and water in a microwave-safe dish. Cover and microwave on high for 5 minutes or until almost tender; drain.
2. Place potatoes in a 13-in. x 9-in. baking dish coated with cooking spray. Sprinkle with garlic, salt and pepper. Top with pork chops and marinara sauce. Cover and bake at 350° for 40-45 minutes or until a thermometer inserted in pork reads 145° and potatoes are tender.
3. Sprinkle with cheese. Bake, uncovered, 3-5 minutes longer or until cheese is melted. Let stand 5 minutes before serving.
NOTE *This recipe was tested in a 1,100-watt microwave.*

ITALIAN PORK AND POTATO CASSEROLE

Baked Apple Ham Steaks

When my mother wanted to serve ham, she went to the smokehouse, took one down from the rafters and sliced off as much as was needed. The rest was hung up again. This recipe is especially sweet and buttery if you use real smoked ham with no water added.

—**MARJORIE SCHMIDT** ST. MARYS, OHIO

PREP: 10 MIN. **BAKE:** 1¼ HOURS
MAKES: 6-8 SERVINGS

- 2 **fully cooked bone-in ham steaks (1 pound each)**
- 2 **teaspoons ground mustard**
- ½ **cup packed brown sugar**
- 3 **medium tart apples**
- 2 **tablespoons butter**
  Pepper to taste

1. Place ham in an ungreased 13-in. x 9-in. baking dish. Rub with mustard and sprinkle with brown sugar. Core apples and cut into ¾-in. slices; arrange in a single layer over ham. Dot with butter and sprinkle with pepper.
2. Cover and bake at 400° for 15 minutes. Reduce heat to 325°; bake for 45 minutes. Uncover and bake 15 minutes longer or until apples are tender.

SWEET-SOUR HAM BALLS

> Pineapple, brown sugar and mustard create a delightful sauce for this unique dish, particularly when served over rice. I use the ham balls for appetizers, too. —DOROTHY PRITCHETT WILLS POINT, TEXAS

Sweet-Sour Ham Balls

PREP: 20 MIN. **BAKE:** 45 MIN. **MAKES:**
2 BATCHES (ABOUT 30 HAM BALLS EACH)

- 4 eggs, lightly beaten
- ¼ cup chopped onion
- 1½ cups soft bread crumbs
- 2 pounds ground ham
- 1 pound ground pork
- 2 cans (8 ounces each) crushed pineapple, undrained
- 1 cup packed brown sugar
- ¼ cup prepared mustard
- 2 tablespoons cider vinegar

1. In a large bowl, combine the eggs, onion and bread crumbs. Crumble meat over mixture and mix well. Shape into 1½-in. balls. Place in two greased 13-in. x 9-in. baking dishes.
2. In a blender, combine the pineapple, brown sugar, mustard and vinegar; cover and process until smooth. Pour over ham balls. Transfer to freezer bags; seal and freeze. Or, bake, uncovered, at 350° for 45-50 minutes or until a thermometer reads 160°, basting occasionally with sauce.

TO USE FROZEN HAM BALLS
Completely thaw uncooked ham balls with sauce in the refrigerator. Bake as directed in recipe.

Unstuffed Pork Chops

Now this is comfort food! The savory flavors of sage and onion in the stuffing infuse the chops while they bake. The pork comes out tender and moist.
—**SHERRI MELOTIK** OAK CREEK, WISCONSIN

PREP: 15 MIN. **BAKE:** 30 MIN.
MAKES: 2 SERVINGS

- 2 bone-in pork loin chops (8 ounces each)
- 2 teaspoons olive oil

- 1½ cups crushed chicken stuffing mix
- ¾ cup 2% milk
- ⅔ cup condensed cream of mushroom soup, undiluted
- ⅛ teaspoon pepper

1. In a large skillet, brown pork chops in oil. Transfer to an 8-in. square baking dish; sprinkle with stuffing mix. In a small bowl, combine the milk, soup and pepper; pour over top.
2. Cover and bake at 350° for 30-35 minutes or until a thermometer reads 160°.

EAT SMART Winter Delight Stew

My easy home-style stew is loaded with sausage, beans and vegetables. It wins rave reviews from everyone who tries it.
—**LEE SAUERS**
MIFFLINBURG, PENNSYLVANIA

PREP: 20 MIN. **BAKE:** 1½ HOURS
MAKES: 16 SERVINGS (4 QUARTS)

- 1 pound bulk Italian sausage
- 4 cups chopped cabbage
- 2 cups sliced fresh carrots
- 2 medium potatoes, chopped
- 1 cup chopped onion
- 2 cups beef or chicken broth
- 1 can (16 ounces) kidney beans, rinsed and drained
- 1 can (14½ ounces) diced tomatoes, undrained
- ½ cup tomato juice
- ⅛ teaspoon salt

1. In an ovenproof Dutch oven, cook the sausage over medium heat until no longer pink; drain.
2. Stir in the remaining ingredients. Cover and bake at 350° for 1½ to 2 hours or until vegetables are tender.
PER SERVING *116 cal., 4 g fat (1 g sat. fat), 11 mg chol., 378 mg sodium, 15 g carb., 3 g fiber, 6 g pro.* **Diabetic Exchanges:** *1 vegetable, 1 fat, ½ starch.*

BEANS AND FRANKS BAKE

Beans and Franks Bake

I have made this casserole several times, and it's always a hit. The kid-pleasing dish has a delicious corn bread topping and a tangy-sweet flavor from the baked beans.

—ROXANNE VANGELDER
ROCHESTER, NEW HAMPSHIRE

PREP: 20 MIN. **BAKE:** 40 MIN.
MAKES: 2 CASSEROLES (4 SERVINGS EACH)

- 2 packages (8½ ounces each) corn bread/muffin mix
- 1 can (28 ounces) baked beans
- 4 hot dogs, sliced
- ½ pound sliced bacon, cooked and crumbled
- 1 cup ketchup
- ½ cup packed brown sugar
- ½ cup chopped onion
- 2 cups (8 ounces) shredded part-skim mozzarella cheese

1. Prepare corn bread batter according to package directions; set aside. In a large bowl, combine the beans, hot dogs, bacon, ketchup, brown sugar and onion. Transfer to two greased 8-in. square baking dishes. Sprinkle with cheese; top with corn bread batter.

2. Cover and freeze one casserole for up to 3 months. Bake the second casserole, uncovered, at 350° for 40-45 minutes or until a toothpick inserted near the center comes out clean.

TO USE FROZEN CASSEROLE
Remove from the freezer 30 minutes before baking. Cover and bake at 350° for 40 minutes. Uncover; bake 15-20 minutes longer or until heated through.

Always check the date stamp on packages of bacon. Once the package is opened, **bacon should be used within a week.** For longer storage, you can **freeze bacon** for up to 1 month.

Fish & Seafood

222   229   219

Switch up your dinner routine with **refreshing choices** such as stuffed trout and **baked fish with a pretty fruit relish**. You'll also find quiche, **fresh takes** on tuna casserole and a seafood lasagna that's a true **showstopper!**

> A nice way to dress up this favorite feel-good food is to add scallops. They transform mac and cheese into a delicious and sophisticated dish.
>
> **—LAURIE LUFKIN** ESSEX, MASSACHUSETTS

Scallop Mac & Cheese

PREP: 35 MIN. **BAKE:** 15 MIN.
MAKES: 5 SERVINGS

- 2 cups uncooked medium pasta shells
- ½ cup butter, divided
- 1 cup French bread baguette crumbs
- 1 pound bay scallops
- 1 cup sliced fresh mushrooms
- 1 small onion, chopped
- 3 tablespoons all-purpose flour
- ¾ teaspoon dried thyme
- ¼ teaspoon salt
- ⅛ teaspoon pepper
- 2 cups whole milk
- ½ cup white wine or chicken broth
- 2 tablespoons sherry or chicken broth
- 1 cup (4 ounces) shredded Swiss cheese
- 1 cup (4 ounces) shredded sharp cheddar cheese

1. Cook pasta according to package directions. Meanwhile, in a small skillet, melt 4 tablespoons butter. Add bread crumbs; cook and stir until lightly toasted.

2. In a large skillet over medium heat, melt 2 tablespoons butter. Add scallops; cook and stir for 2 minutes or until firm and opaque. Remove and keep warm. Melt remaining butter in the pan; add mushrooms and onion. Cook and stir until tender. Stir in the flour, thyme, salt and pepper until blended.

3. Gradually add the milk, wine and sherry. Bring to a boil; cook and stir for 1-2 minutes or until thickened. Stir in cheeses until melted. Drain pasta; stir pasta and scallops into sauce.

4. Divide among five 10-oz. ramekins or custard cups. Sprinkle with bread crumbs. Place ramekins on a baking sheet. Bake, uncovered, at 350° for 15-20 minutes or until heated through. Spoon onto plates if desired.

Tuna Mushroom Bake

Since I usually have the ingredients on hand, this recipe is a great standby for an easy supper.
—CONNIE MOORE MEDWAY, OHIO

PREP: 20 MIN. **BAKE:** 35 MIN.
MAKES: 6 SERVINGS

- 6½ cups uncooked egg noodles
- 1 can (12 ounces) light water-packed tuna, drained and flaked
- 1 can (4 ounces) mushroom stems and pieces, drained
- 1 can (10¾ ounces) condensed cream of mushroom soup, undiluted
- 1⅓ cups 2% milk
- ½ teaspoon salt
- ¼ teaspoon pepper
- ½ cup crushed saltines
- 3 tablespoons butter, melted

1. Cook egg noodles according to package directions; stir in tuna and mushrooms. Combine the soup, milk, salt and pepper; add to noodle mixture and mix well.

2. Pour into a greased 2½-qt. baking dish. Combine saltines and butter; sprinkle over noodles. Bake, uncovered, at 350° for 35-45 minutes or until heated through.

BAKED ITALIAN TILAPIA

Pasta Crab Casserole

Here is a yummy combination of spiral pasta, crab and sauteed veggies. It's coated with buttery sauce then covered with cheddar cheese. Mmm!

—GEORGIA MOUNTAIN TAMPA, FLORIDA

PREP: 25 MIN. **BAKE:** 25 MIN.
MAKES: 2 CASSEROLES
(3-4 SERVINGS EACH)

- 8   ounces uncooked spiral pasta
- 2   large onions, chopped
- ½   pound sliced fresh mushrooms
- ½   cup chopped green pepper
- ½   cup butter
- 2   garlic cloves, minced
- 1   pound imitation crabmeat, chopped
- ½   cup sour cream
- 2   teaspoons salt
- 1½ teaspoons dried basil
- 1½ cups (6 ounces) shredded cheddar cheese

1. Cook pasta according to package directions. Meanwhile, in a skillet, saute onions, mushrooms and green pepper in butter until crisp-tender. Add garlic; cook 1 minute longer. Remove from the heat. Drain pasta; add to vegetable mixture. Stir in the crab, sour cream, salt and basil.

2. Transfer to two greased 8-in. square baking dishes. Sprinkle with cheese. Cover and freeze one casserole for up to 3 months. Cover and bake the second casserole at 350° for 20 minutes. Uncover and bake 5 minutes longer.

TO USE FROZEN CASSEROLE *Thaw in the refrigerator overnight. Remove from the refrigerator 30 minutes before baking. Cover and bake at 350° for 55-60 minutes or until heated through.*

It's easy to include healthful fish in your weekly menus with recipes as tasty and simple as this one!

—KIMBERLY MCGEE MOSHEIM, TENNESSEE

EAT SMART Baked Italian Tilapia

PREP: 10 MIN. **BAKE:** 40 MIN.
MAKES: 4 SERVINGS

- 4   tilapia fillets (6 ounces each)
- ¼   teaspoon pepper
- 1   can (14½ ounces) diced tomatoes with basil, oregano and garlic, drained
- 1   large onion, halved and thinly sliced
- 1   medium green pepper, julienned
- ¼   cup shredded Parmesan cheese

1. Place tilapia in a 13-in. x 9-in. baking dish coated with cooking spray; sprinkle with pepper. Spoon tomatoes over tilapia; top with onion and green pepper.

2. Cover and bake at 350° for 30 minutes. Uncover; sprinkle with cheese. Bake 10-15 minutes longer or until fish flakes easily with a fork.

PER SERVING *215 cal., 4 g fat (2 g sat. fat), 86 mg chol., 645 mg sodium, 12 g carb., 2 g fiber, 36 g pro.*

TANGERINE CASHEW SNAPPER

Tangerine Cashew Snapper

Delicious toppings make healthy snapper fillets pleasing to both the palate and the eye.

—**CRYSTAL BRUNS** ILIFF, COLORADO

PREP/TOTAL TIME: 30 MIN.
MAKES: 4 SERVINGS

- 4 **tangerines**
- 2 **tablespoons lime juice**
- 2 **tablespoons reduced-sodium soy sauce**
- 1 **tablespoon brown sugar**
- 2 **teaspoons minced fresh gingerroot**
- 1 **teaspoon sesame oil**
- ⅛ **teaspoon crushed red pepper flakes**
- 4 **red snapper fillets (4 ounces each)**
- ⅓ **cup chopped unsalted cashews**
- 2 **green onions, thinly sliced**

1. Peel, slice and remove seeds from 2 tangerines; chop the fruit and place in a small bowl. Squeeze juice from remaining tangerines; add to bowl. Stir in the lime juice, soy sauce, brown sugar, ginger, sesame oil and pepper flakes.

2. Place fillets in a 13-in. x 9-in. baking dish coated with cooking spray. Pour tangerine mixture over fillets; sprinkle with cashews and green onions. Bake, uncovered, at 425° for 15-20 minutes or until fish flakes easily with a fork.

PER SERVING *260 cal., 8 g fat (2 g sat. fat), 40 mg chol., 358 mg sodium, 22 g carb., 2 g fiber, 26 g pro.* **Diabetic Exchanges:** *3 lean meat, 1 fruit, 1 fat.*

Sesame oil provides a distinct Asian flavor, and a little goes a long way. But if you prefer, you can use **olive or canola** oil in the topping. Sprinkle the fish with **sesame seeds** if you have them!

ORANGE TILAPIA IN PARCHMENT

Sweet orange juice and spicy cayenne pepper give this no-fuss dish fabulous flavor. A bonus? Cleanup is effortless, too! —**TIFFANY DIEBOLD** NASHVILLE, TENNESSEE

EAT SMART Orange Tilapia in Parchment

PREP/TOTAL TIME: 30 MIN.
MAKES: 4 SERVINGS

- ¼ **cup orange juice**
- 4 **teaspoons grated orange peel**
- ¼ **teaspoon salt**
- ¼ **teaspoon cayenne pepper**
- ¼ **teaspoon pepper**
- 4 **tilapia fillets (6 ounces each)**
- ½ **cup julienned carrot**
- ½ **cup julienned zucchini**

1. In a small bowl, combine the first five ingredients; set aside. Cut parchment paper or heavy-duty foil into four 18-in. x 12-in. lengths; place a fish fillet on each. Top with carrot and zucchini; drizzle with orange juice mixture.

2. Fold parchment paper over fish. Working from the bottom inside corner, fold up about ¾ in. of the paper and crimp both layers to seal. Repeat, folding edges up and crimping, until a half-moon-shaped packet is formed. Repeat for the remaining packets. Place packets on baking sheets.

3. Bake at 450° for 12-15 minutes or until fish flakes easily with a fork. Open packets carefully to allow steam to escape.

PER SERVING *158 cal., 2 g fat (1 g sat. fat), 83 mg chol., 220 mg sodium, 4 g carb., 1 g fiber, 32 g pro.* **Diabetic Exchange:** *5 lean meat.*

Shrimp-Stuffed Poblano Peppers

PREP: 35 MIN. **BAKE:** 10 MIN.
MAKES: 8 SERVINGS

- 4 **large poblano peppers**
- 2 **tablespoons butter, melted, divided**
- 1 **teaspoon coarsely ground pepper**
- ½ **teaspoon kosher salt**
- 1 **small onion, finely chopped**
- 2 **celery ribs, chopped**
- 4 **ounces cream cheese, softened**
- 1 **pound chopped cooked peeled shrimp**
- 1¾ **cups shredded Mexican cheese blend**
- 1½ **cups cooked rice**
- 2 **tablespoons lemon juice**
- 2 **teaspoons dried cilantro flakes**
- ½ **teaspoon onion powder**
- ½ **teaspoon garlic powder**

TOPPING

- 1 **cup panko (Japanese) bread crumbs**
- ¼ **cup grated Parmesan cheese**
- 2 **tablespoons butter, melted**

1. Cut peppers in half lengthwise and discard seeds. Place peppers, cut side down, in an ungreased 15-in. x 10-in. x 1-in. baking pan. Brush with 1 tablespoon butter; sprinkle with pepper and salt. Bake, uncovered, at 350° for 10-15 minutes or until tender.

2. Meanwhile, in a large skillet, saute onion and celery in remaining butter until tender. Stir in cream cheese until melted. Add the shrimp, cheese blend, rice, lemon juice and seasonings; heat through. Spoon into pepper halves.

3. Place in an ungreased 15-in. x 10-in. x 1-in. baking pan. Combine topping ingredients; sprinkle over peppers. Bake, uncovered, at 350° for 10-15 minutes or until topping is golden brown.

NOTE *Wear disposable gloves when cutting hot peppers; the oils can burn skin. Avoid touching your face.*

I created this dish to celebrate my mother's moving back to our hometown. She stayed with me until her house was ready for her to move in. Since my mom enjoys shrimp and slightly spicy food, I decided to create shrimp-stuffed poblanos to surprise her. She was delighted with my creation. —TINA GARCIA-ORTIZ TAMPA, FLORIDA

SHRIMP-STUFFED POBLANO PEPPERS

TILAPIA WITH TOMATO-ORANGE RELISH

The mild flavor and tender texture of tilapia goes beautifully with this garden-fresh relish. It makes a big impression with only a little work!

—HELEN CONWELL PORTLAND, OREGON

EAT SMART Tilapia with Tomato-Orange Relish

PREP/TOTAL TIME: 25 MIN.
MAKES: 6 SERVINGS

- 6 tilapia fillets (6 ounces each)
- 3 tablespoons butter, melted
- ½ teaspoon salt, divided
- ½ teaspoon lemon-pepper seasoning
- 1 medium tomato, seeded and chopped
- 1 medium orange, peeled, sectioned and chopped
- ⅓ cup finely chopped red onion
- 1 tablespoon capers, drained
- 1½ tablespoons brown sugar
- 1 tablespoon red wine vinegar

1. Place fish in a greased 15-in. x 10-in. x 1-in. baking pan. Drizzle with butter; sprinkle with ¼ teaspoon salt and the lemon-pepper. Bake at 425° for 10 minutes or until fish flakes easily with a fork.
2. In a small bowl, combine the tomato, orange, onion, capers, brown sugar, vinegar and remaining salt. Serve with fish.
PER SERVING *219 cal., 7 g fat (4 g sat. fat), 98 mg chol., 381 mg sodium, 7 g carb., 1 g fiber, 32 g pro. Diabetic Exchanges: 5 lean meat, 1 fat, ½ starch.*

Seafood Pizza

Thick and creamy cheese sauce is an ideal match for the scallops, shrimp and imitation crabmeat.

—SARA WATTERS BOSCOBEL, WISCONSIN

PREP: 35 MIN. **BAKE:** 15 MIN.
MAKES: 4 SERVINGS

- 1 package (6½ ounces) pizza crust mix
- 3 tablespoons butter, divided
- 2 tablespoons all-purpose flour
- ¾ cup milk
- ¼ cup chicken broth
- ¼ cup shredded Monterey Jack cheese
- ¼ cup shredded Swiss cheese
- ¼ pound uncooked bay scallops, chopped
- ¼ pound peeled and deveined cooked shrimp, chopped
- ¼ pound imitation crabmeat, chopped
- 2 cups (8 ounces) shredded part-skim mozzarella cheese Paprika, optional

1. Prepare pizza dough according to package directions. Press onto a lightly greased 12-in. pizza pan; build up edges slightly. Prick dough thoroughly with a fork. Bake at 400° for 5-6 minutes or until crust is firm and begins to brown.
2. Meanwhile, in a large saucepan, melt 2 tablespoons butter over medium heat. Stir in flour until smooth. Gradually stir in milk and broth. Bring to a boil; cook and stir for 2 minutes or until thickened. Reduce heat. Stir in Monterey Jack and Swiss cheeses until melted. Remove from the heat.
3. In a large skillet, melt the remaining butter over medium heat. Add scallops; cook and stir for 3-4 minutes or until firm and opaque. Stir in the shrimp, crab and 3 tablespoons cheese sauce. Remove from the heat.
4. Spread remaining cheese sauce over the crust. Top with the seafood mixture; sprinkle with mozzarella cheese and paprika if desired. Bake for 13-16 minutes or until golden brown. Let stand for 5-10 minutes before cutting.

EAT SMART Creamy Tuna-Noodle Casserole

Tuna fish is an excellent standby when you need supper on the table in a hurry. You'll love my casserole packed with peas, peppers and onions. No tuna on hand? Try making it with chicken instead!

—EDIE DESPAIN LOGAN, UTAH

PREP: 25 MIN. **BAKE:** 25 MIN.
MAKES: 6 SERVINGS

- 5 cups uncooked egg noodles
- 1 can (10¾ ounces) reduced-fat reduced-sodium condensed cream of mushroom soup, undiluted
- 1 cup (8 ounces) fat-free sour cream
- ⅔ cup grated Parmesan cheese
- ⅓ cup 2% milk
- ¼ teaspoon salt
- 2 cans (5 ounces each) light water-packed tuna, drained and flaked
- 1 cup frozen peas, thawed
- ¼ cup finely chopped onion
- ¼ cup finely chopped green pepper

TOPPING
- ½ cup soft bread crumbs
- 1 tablespoon butter, melted

1. Cook noodles according to package directions.
2. Meanwhile, in a large bowl, combine the soup, sour cream, cheese, milk and salt. Stir in the tuna, peas, onion and pepper. Drain noodles; add to soup mixture.
3. Transfer to an 11-in. x 7-in. baking dish coated with cooking spray. Combine topping ingredients; sprinkle over top. Bake, uncovered, at 350° for 25-30 minutes or until bubbly.

PER SERVING *340 cal., 8 g fat (4 g sat. fat), 63 mg chol., 699 mg sodium, 41 g carb., 3 g fiber, 25 g pro. **Diabetic Exchanges:** 3 starch, 2 lean meat, ½ fat.*

Check to see if your local grocery store offers its own **grated Parmesan cheese**. You can save money and get a **fresher, higher-quality** product.

Make tuna salad special with this great sub sandwich. Peas and celery give it crunch and color while Swiss cheese adds rich, distinctive flavor. Consider mixing the tuna filling ahead of time so you can just assemble, heat and enjoy!

—**CAROLE LANTHIER** COURTICE, ONTARIO

HOT TUNA HEROES

Hot Tuna Heroes

PREP/TOTAL TIME: 30 MIN.
MAKES: 6 SERVINGS

- 2 pouches (7.06 ounces each) light water-packed tuna
- 1 cup chopped celery
- 1 cup frozen peas, thawed
- ¾ cup mayonnaise
- 4 slices Swiss cheese, cut into ½-inch strips
- ¼ cup minced fresh parsley
- ¼ cup butter, melted
- 6 hoagie buns, split

1. In a large bowl, combine the first six ingredients. Brush butter over cut sides of buns. Spoon tuna mixture onto bun bottoms; replace tops.
2. Place each sandwich on a piece of heavy-duty foil (about 12 in. square). Fold foil around sandwich and seal tightly. Bake at 400° for 15-20 minutes or until heated through.

Seafood Lasagna

PREP: 40 MIN. **BAKE:** 45 MIN. + STANDING
MAKES: 12 SERVINGS

- 2 cans (6 ounces each) lump crabmeat, drained
- 1 package (5 ounces) frozen cooked salad shrimp, thawed and patted dry
- 1 carton (15 ounces) ricotta cheese
- 2 eggs, lightly beaten
- 1 tablespoon Italian seasoning
- 1 pound sliced fresh mushrooms
- 1 large onion, chopped
- 6 tablespoons butter
- 2 garlic cloves, minced
- ½ cup all-purpose flour
- 2 cans (12 ounces each) evaporated milk
- 1 cup milk
- 1 cup grated Parmesan cheese, divided
  Salt and pepper to taste
- 9 lasagna noodles, cooked and drained
- 1 package (10 ounces) frozen chopped spinach, thawed and squeezed dry
- 4 cups (16 ounces) shredded part-skim mozzarella cheese
- 3 cups frozen chopped broccoli, thawed

SEAFOOD LASAGNA

Once, when expecting a visit from a college friend, I wanted to serve something different. So I came up with a creamy crab and shrimp lasagna. It's perfect for company because it can be assembled in advance.

—**DOLORES JENSEN** ARNOLD, MISSOURI

1. In a small bowl, combine crab and shrimp; set aside. In another bowl, combine the ricotta cheese, eggs and Italian seasoning until smooth; set aside.
2. In a large skillet, saute the mushrooms and onion in butter until tender. Add garlic; cook 1 minute longer. Stir in flour until blended. Gradually add evaporated milk and milk. Bring to a boil; cook and stir for 2 minutes or until thickened. Reduce heat; stir in ½ cup Parmesan cheese, salt and pepper until cheese is melted.
3. Spread 1 cup mushroom sauce in a greased shallow 4-qt. baking dish. Layer with three noodles and the spinach. Top with a third of the ricotta mixture, a third of the mozzarella cheese and a third of the mushroom sauce.
4. Top with three noodles and crab mixture. Repeat with ricotta mixture, mozzarella cheese and mushroom sauce. Layer with remaining noodles and the broccoli. Repeat with remaining ricotta mixture, mozzarella and mushroom sauce. Sprinkle with remaining Parmesan cheese.
5. Bake, uncovered, at 350° for 45-55 minutes or until a thermometer reads 160°. Let stand for 10 minutes before cutting.

CHEDDAR SALMON QUICHE

> My mother-in-law shared the recipe for her pretty salmon quiche with me. It dresses up canned salmon in a very satisfying way. We frequently enjoy the dish during Lent. —**JANE HORN** BELLEVUE, OHIO

Cheddar Salmon Quiche

PREP: 25 MIN. **BAKE:** 50 MIN. + STANDING
MAKES: 6 SERVINGS

- 1 cup all-purpose flour
- ¼ teaspoon salt
- 3 tablespoons cold butter
- 3 tablespoons shortening
- ¼ cup milk

FILLING

- 1 can (14¾ ounces) salmon, drained, bones and skin removed
- 1 cup (4 ounces) shredded cheddar cheese
- ¼ cup chopped green pepper
- ¼ cup chopped onion
- 1 tablespoon all-purpose flour
- ½ teaspoon salt
- ⅛ teaspoon pepper
- 3 eggs
- 1¼ cups milk

1. In a large bowl, combine the flour and salt; cut in butter and shortening until crumbly. Stir in milk.
2. On a floured surface, roll dough to fit a 9-in. pie plate. Transfer pastry to an ungreased pie plate; trim and flute edges. Bake the crust at 350° for 10 minutes.
3. In a large bowl, combine salmon, cheese, green pepper, onion, flour, salt and pepper; spoon into crust. Combine the eggs and milk; pour over salmon mixture.
4. Bake for 50-55 minutes or until a knife inserted near the center comes out clean. Let stand for 10 minutes before cutting.

Southwest Tuna-Noodle Casserole

PREP: 20 MIN. **BAKE:** 30 MIN.
MAKES: 6 SERVINGS

- 1 package (16 ounces) egg noodles
- 2½ cups milk
- 1 can (12 ounces) light water-packed tuna, drained
- 1 can (10¾ ounces) condensed cream of chicken soup, undiluted
- 1 can (10¾ ounces) condensed cream of mushroom soup, undiluted
- 1 cup (4 ounces) shredded cheddar cheese
- 1 can (4 ounces) chopped green chilies
- 2 cups crushed tortilla chips

1. Cook noodles according to package directions. Meanwhile, in a large bowl, combine the milk, tuna, soups, cheese and chilies. Drain noodles; gently stir into tuna mixture.
2. Transfer to an ungreased 13-in. x 9-in. baking dish. Sprinkle with tortilla chips. Bake, uncovered, at 350° for 30-35 minutes or until bubbly.

Pepper and Salsa Cod

My husband created this recipe after he sampled something like it at the grocery store. I love when he makes it for us.

—**ROBYN GALLAGHER** YORKTOWN, VIRGINIA

PREP/TOTAL TIME: 30 MIN.
MAKES: 2 SERVINGS

- 1 teaspoon olive oil
- ½ pound cod or haddock fillet
- ¼ teaspoon salt
  Dash pepper
- ⅓ cup orange juice
- ¼ cup salsa
- ⅓ cup julienned green pepper
- ⅓ cup julienned sweet red pepper
  Hot cooked rice

1. Coat a small baking dish with oil. Place fish in dish; sprinkle with salt and pepper. Pour orange juice over fish. Top with salsa and peppers.
2. Cover and bake at 350° for 18-22 minutes or until peppers are tender and fish flakes easily with a fork. Serve with rice.

None of my co-workers had ever tried tuna-noodle casserole. Since we live near the Mexican border, they challenged me to make a Southwest version. After trying the tasty results, everyone wanted the recipe! —SANDRA CRANE LAS CRUCES, NEW MEXICO

SOUTHWEST TUNA-NOODLE CASSEROLE

Mac and cheese goes upscale in this deliciously cheesy variation. The shrimp gives a unique twist to the popular standard. —**MICHAEL COHEN** LOS ANGELES, CALIFORNIA

SHRIMP & MACARONI CASSEROLE

Shrimp & Macaroni Casserole

PREP: 20 MIN. **BAKE:** 20 MIN.
MAKES: 3 SERVINGS

- 1 cup uncooked elbow macaroni
- 1 egg
- ¼ cup half-and-half cream
- 2 tablespoons butter, melted
- ½ cup grated Parmesan cheese
- ¾ cup shredded part-skim mozzarella cheese, divided
- 1 garlic clove, minced
- ¼ teaspoon salt
- ⅛ teaspoon pepper
- ¼ pound uncooked shrimp, peeled, deveined and chopped
- ¾ cup chopped fresh spinach

1. Cook macaroni according to package directions. Meanwhile, in a bowl, combine the egg, cream and butter; set aside. Drain macaroni; transfer to a small bowl. Add the Parmesan cheese, ½ cup mozzarella cheese, garlic, salt, pepper and reserved egg mixture; toss to coat. Stir in shrimp and spinach.
2. Transfer to a 1-qt. baking dish coated with cooking spray. Sprinkle with remaining mozzarella cheese. Bake, uncovered, at 350° for 20-25 minutes or until shrimp turn pink and cheese is melted.

Stuffed Trout

Fish is perfect for a busy cook like me, since it's so quick and easy to prepare.
—SHIRLEY COLEMAN MONKTON, VERMONT

PREP: 15 MIN. **BAKE:** 35 MIN.
MAKES: 4 SERVINGS

- 2 bacon strips, cooked and crumbled
- ½ cup fresh coarse bread crumbs
- ¼ cup chopped onion
- 2 tablespoons chopped fresh parsley
- ⅛ teaspoon salt
- ⅛ teaspoon pepper
- 4 dressed trout (½ pound each)

In a small bowl, combine the first six ingredients. Stuff into trout. Place on a lightly greased baking sheet. Bake at 350° for 30-35 minutes or until fish flakes easily with a fork.

SPINACH SALMON BUNDLES

Here's an elegant entree that'll turn a weeknight dinner into a fancy occasion. Rich salmon and flaky golden-brown pastry will delight family and guests—and no one has to know how easy it is.

—LARISSA GEDNEY MYRTLE BEACH, SOUTH CAROLINA

Spinach Salmon Bundles

PREP/TOTAL TIME: 30 MIN.
MAKES: 4 SERVINGS

- 2 tubes (8 ounces each) refrigerated crescent rolls
- 4 salmon fillets (6 ounces each)
- ¼ teaspoon salt
- ¼ teaspoon pepper
- ⅓ cup garlic-herb spreadable cheese
- 1 package (10 ounces) frozen chopped spinach, thawed and squeezed dry

1. Unroll crescent dough and separate into four rectangles; seal perforations. Place a salmon fillet in the center of each rectangle; sprinkle with salt and pepper. Spoon spreadable cheese over each; top with spinach. Fold dough over filling and pinch edges to seal.
2. Place on an ungreased baking sheet. Bake at 400° for 20-25 minutes or until golden brown.
NOTE *This recipe was tested with Alouette spreadable cheese.*

Breads &Salads

239

233

240

Round out any meal with **crispy vegetable salads, flavorful, homey biscuits**, potluck favorites, **savory yeast rolls**, fluffy, fruity creations and more—all thanks to the **delightful recipes in this bonus chapter.**

LAYERED SALAD FOR A CROWD

My sons love this salad. I took it to a luncheon honoring our school district's food-service manager, and she did, too—and asked for the recipe! I like to make the dressing the day before so the flavors blend together. **—LINDA ASHLEY** LEESBURG, GEORGIA

Layered Salad For a Crowd

PREP/TOTAL TIME: 20 MIN.
MAKES: 20 SERVINGS

  1 **cup mayonnaise**
  ¼ **cup milk**
  2 **teaspoons dill weed**
  ½ **teaspoon seasoning blend**
  1 **bunch romaine, torn**
  2 **medium carrots, grated**
  1 **cup chopped red onion**
  1 **medium cucumber, sliced**
  1 **package (10 ounces) frozen peas, thawed**
  1½ **cups (6 ounces) shredded cheddar cheese**
  8 **bacon strips, cooked and crumbled**

1. For dressing, in a small bowl, whisk the mayonnaise, milk, dill and seasoning blend.
2. In a 4-qt. clear glass serving bowl, layer the romaine, carrots, onion and cucumber (do not toss). Pour dressing over the top; sprinkle with peas, cheese and bacon. Cover and refrigerate until serving.
NOTE *This recipe was tested with Nature's Seasons seasoning blend by Morton. Look for it in the spice aisle.*

EAT SMART **Blueberry Corn Muffins**

Sweet blueberries really jazz up an ordinary box of corn muffin mix. These are perfect for on-the-go snacking or as an addition to any summer potluck.
—DIANE HIXON NICEVILLE, FLORIDA

PREP/TOTAL TIME: 25 MIN.
MAKES: 8 MUFFINS

  1 **package (8½ ounces) corn bread/ muffin mix**
  1 **tablespoon brown sugar**
  1 **egg, lightly beaten**
  ⅓ **cup milk**
  ½ **cup fresh or frozen blueberries**

1. In a large bowl, combine the muffin mix and brown sugar. Combine the egg and milk; stir into dry ingredients just until moistened. Fold in blueberries.
2. Coat muffin cups with cooking spray or use paper liners. Fill half full with batter. Bake at 400° for 12-15 minutes or until a toothpick inserted in muffin comes out clean. Cool for 5 minutes before removing from pan to a wire rack. Serve warm.
NOTE *If using frozen blueberries, use without thawing to avoid discoloring the batter.*
PER SERVING *146 cal., 4 g fat (1 g sat. fat), 33 mg chol., 264 mg sodium, 25 g carb., 1 g fiber, 3 g pro.* **Diabetic Exchanges:** *1½ starch, ½ fat.*

Try layering in your own favorite toppings to the salad. Sliced cucumbers, chopped hard-cooked eggs, broccoli florets or flaked imitation crabmeat are nice options.

I learned how to cook from the two best cooks I know: my mom, Arline, and my Grandma Etta. Friends and family always request this recipe, which I got from my sister-in-law. The salad is quick and easy, just what I need in my busy life.
—**GINGER CUSANO** SANDUSKY, OHIO

ROASTED RED POTATO SALAD

Roasted Red Potato Salad

PREP: 40 MIN. + CHILLING
MAKES: 6-8 SERVINGS

- 2 pounds red potatoes, cut into 1-inch cubes
- 1 medium onion, chopped
- 4 hard-cooked eggs, sliced
- 6 bacon strips, cooked and crumbled
- 1 cup mayonnaise
- ½ teaspoon salt
- ¼ teaspoon pepper
  Paprika, optional

1. Place the potatoes in a greased 15-in. x 10-in. x 1-in. baking pan. Bake, uncovered, at 400° for 25-30 minutes or until tender and golden brown, stirring occasionally. Cool for 15 minutes.

2. Transfer to a large bowl; add onion, eggs, bacon, mayonnaise, salt and pepper. Toss to coat. Cover and refrigerate for several hours or overnight. Sprinkle with paprika if desired.

Bing Cherry Salad

For a sweet, fruity salad at your next get-together, my recipe will surely delight. Cherries makes it irresistible.

—CINDY MAHN HUNTLEY, MONTANA

PREP/TOTAL TIME: 15 MIN.
MAKES: 6-8 SERVINGS

- 1 can (16 ounces) pitted dark sweet cherries, juice reserved
- 1 package (8 ounces) cream cheese, softened
- 1 cup drained crushed pineapple
- 1 carton (8 ounces) frozen whipped topping, thawed
- 2 cups miniature marshmallows

Drain cherries, reserving ¼ cup juice. In a bowl, whip juice with cream cheese. Stir in cherries, pineapple, whipped topping and marshmallows. Chill until serving.

ARTICHOKE BREAD

A creamy, rich artichoke spread tops these warm, crusty bites that folks just love. You won't find a quicker or more delicious way to round out your menu. It's especially good with Italian food.

—SHERRY CAMPBELL SAINT AMANT, LOUISIANA

EAT SMART Artichoke Bread

PREP: 30 MIN. + COOLING **BAKE:** 15 MIN.
MAKES: 1 LOAF (12 SLICES)

- 1 tube (11 ounces) refrigerated crusty French loaf
- 1 can (14 ounces) water-packed artichoke hearts, rinsed, drained and chopped
- ½ cup seasoned bread crumbs
- ⅓ cup grated Parmesan cheese
- ⅓ cup reduced-fat mayonnaise
- 2 garlic cloves, minced
- 1 cup (4 ounces) shredded part-skim mozzarella cheese

1. Bake loaf according to package directions; cool. Cut bread in half lengthwise; place on an ungreased baking sheet.

2. In a small bowl, combine the artichokes, bread crumbs, Parmesan cheese, mayonnaise and garlic; spread evenly over cut sides of bread. Sprinkle with mozzarella cheese.

3. Bake at 350° for 15-20 minutes or until cheese is melted. Serve warm.

PER SERVING *151 cal., 5 g fat (2 g sat. fat), 10 mg chol., 456 mg sodium, 18 g carb., 1 g fiber, 7 g pro.* **Diabetic Exchanges:** *1 starch, 1 fat.*

Frosted Strawberry Salad

My daughter has always requested this sweet strawberry gelatin salad with its fluffy topping for every family get-together. It even graced the buffet table at her wedding.

—**BARBARA TOWLER** DERBY, OHIO

PREP: 15 MIN. + CHILLING
MAKES: 16-20 SERVINGS

- 2 **packages (6 ounces each) strawberry gelatin**
- 3 **cups boiling water**
- 2 **packages (10 ounces each) frozen sweetened sliced strawberries, thawed**
- 1 **can (20 ounces) crushed pineapple, undrained**
- 1 **cup chopped pecans**
- ½ **cup chopped maraschino cherries**

TOPPING
- 1 **package (8 ounces) cream cheese, softened**
- 1 **jar (7 ounces) marshmallow creme**
- 1 **carton (8 ounces) frozen whipped topping, thawed**
  Fresh strawberries and mint

1. In a large bowl, dissolve gelatin in boiling water. Stir in strawberries and pineapple. Refrigerate until partially set.

2. Stir in pecans and cherries. Transfer to a 13-in. x 9-in. dish. Chill for 2 hours or until firm.

3. For topping, in a small bowl, beat cream cheese and marshmallow creme just until combined; fold in whipped topping. Spread over salad. Chill for several hours or overnight. Cut into squares. Garnish with strawberries and mint.

SESAME BREADSTICKS

Thanks to refrigerated dough, tender "homemade" breadsticks come together in a jiffy. They make an easy accompaniment to any meal.

—**DEE DREW** ALISO VIEJO, CALIFORNIA

Sesame Breadsticks

PREP/TOTAL TIME: 20 MIN.
MAKES: 1 DOZEN

- 1 **tube (11 ounces) refrigerated breadsticks**
- 1 **tablespoon butter, melted**
- 2 **tablespoons sesame seeds**

Unroll and separate breadsticks; place on an ungreased baking sheet. Brush with butter and sprinkle with sesame seeds. Bake at 400° for 12-14 minutes or until golden brown. Serve warm.

Herbed Asparagus Salad

Here's a wonderful way to serve fresh-cut asparagus. The tarragon and oregano are a nice surprise, and sliced cooked eggs make a pretty garnish.

—**DAWN SZALAI** EDWARDSBURG, MICHIGAN

PREP: 20 MIN. + CHILLING
MAKES: 6-8 SERVINGS

- 2 **pounds fresh asparagus, cut into 1-inch pieces**
- ¾ **cup canola oil**
- ½ **cup lemon juice**
- 1½ **teaspoons sugar**
- 1 **teaspoon salt**
- ½ **teaspoon dried oregano**
- ½ **teaspoon dried tarragon**
- ½ **teaspoon coarsely ground pepper**
- 1 **garlic clove, minced**
- 8 **cups torn mixed salad greens**
- 3 **hard-cooked eggs, sliced**

1. In a large saucepan, bring ½ in. of water to a boil. Add asparagus; cover and boil for 3 minutes. Drain and immediately place asparagus in ice water. Drain and pat dry. Place in a large bowl.

2. In a small bowl, whisk the oil, lemon juice, sugar, salt, oregano, tarragon, pepper and garlic. Pour over asparagus; cover and refrigerate for at least 2 hours.

3. Place salad greens on a serving platter. With a slotted spoon, arrange asparagus over greens. Garnish with egg slices.

EAT SMART Tomato-Basil Couscous Salad

It's hard to believe that tossing a few pantry ingredients with summer's fresh best can yield such a lovely salad. Pair it with grilled lemon chicken for a light lunch.

—SONYA LABBE

WEST HOLLYWOOD, CALIFORNIA

PREP: 20 MIN. + CHILLING
MAKES: 8 SERVINGS

- 1½ cups water
- 1½ cups uncooked couscous
- 2 medium tomatoes, seeded and chopped
- ¼ cup fresh basil leaves, thinly sliced
- ½ cup olive oil
- ¼ cup balsamic vinegar
- ½ teaspoon salt
- ¼ teaspoon pepper

1. In a small saucepan, bring water to a boil. Stir in couscous. Remove from the heat; cover and let stand for 5-10 minutes or until water is absorbed. Fluff with a fork; cool.

2. In a large bowl, combine the couscous, tomatoes and basil. In a small bowl, whisk the oil, vinegar, salt and pepper. Pour over salad; toss to coat. Refrigerate until chilled.

PER SERVING *255 cal., 14 g fat (2 g sat. fat), 0 chol., 155 mg sodium, 29 g carb., 2 g fiber, 5 g pro.* **Diabetic** *Exchanges: 2 starch, 2 fat.*

To quickly seed tomatoes, cut them into four or six wedges. Then **swipe the wedges** with your fingers to **remove the gel pockets.** Then chop the wedges.

DIJON-WALNUT SPINACH SALAD

> This family favorite of ours has a great fresh taste, lots of different textures and can be tossed together in a heartbeat. For variety, change up the dressing to honey mustard or any other favorite.
>
> —**CHRIS DEMONTRAVEL** MOHEGAN LAKE, NEW YORK

PER SERVING *80 cal., 1 g fat (trace sat. fat), 0 chol., 217 mg sodium, 16 g carb., 2 g fiber, 2 g pro.* **Diabetic Exchanges:** *1 starch.*

Crab Crescent Loaf

PREP: 20 MIN. **BAKE:** 20 MIN.
MAKES: 1 LOAF (12 SLICES)

- 1 tube (8 ounces) refrigerated crescent rolls
- 2 packages (3 ounces each) cream cheese, softened
- ⅓ cup chopped onion
- ½ teaspoon dill weed
- 1 cup chopped imitation crabmeat or 1 can (6 ounces) lump crabmeat, drained
- 1 egg yolk, lightly beaten

1. On a greased baking sheet, unroll crescent dough into one long rectangle; seal seams and perforations. In a small bowl, beat the cream cheese, onion and dill until blended. Spread mixture lengthwise over half of the dough to within ½ in. of edges. Top with crab.
2. Fold dough over filling; pinch seam to seal. Brush the top with egg yolk. Bake at 375° for 18-22 minutes or until golden brown.

Pizza-Style Tossed Salad

If you love pizza, you'll enjoy an easy salad that tastes just like pizza in a bowl.
—**PAT HABIGER** SPEARVILLE, KANSAS

PREP/TOTAL TIME: 10 MIN.
MAKES: 8 SERVINGS

- 1 package (10 ounces) Italian blend salad greens
- 1 cup (4 ounces) shredded part-skim mozzarella cheese
- 1 package (3½ ounces) sliced pepperoni
- 1 can (2¼ ounces) sliced ripe olives, drained
- ½ cup Italian salad dressing
- 1 cup onion and garlic salad croutons

In a salad bowl, combine the greens, cheese, pepperoni and olives. Drizzle with dressing; toss to coat. Sprinkle with croutons.

EAT SMART Dijon-Walnut Spinach Salad

PREP/TOTAL TIME: 10 MIN.
MAKES: 13 SERVINGS

- 1 package (9 ounces) fresh baby spinach
- 1 package (4 ounces) crumbled feta cheese
- 1 cup dried cranberries
- 1 cup walnut halves, toasted
- ½ cup honey Dijon vinaigrette

In a salad bowl, combine the spinach, cheese, cranberries and walnuts. Drizzle with vinaigrette; toss to coat. Serve immediately.
PER SERVING *120 cal., 7 g fat (1 g sat. fat), 5 mg chol., 177 mg sodium, 12 g carb., 2 g fiber, 3 g pro.* **Diabetic Exchanges:** *1 vegetable, 1 fat, ½ starch.*

EAT SMART Colorful Corn and Bean Salad

My quick recipe couldn't be easier...the liquid from the corn relish serves as the fuss-free dressing!
—**TERRYANN MOORE** VINELAND, NEW JERSEY

PREP/TOTAL TIME: 15 MIN.
MAKES: 12 SERVINGS

- 1 can (15 ounces) black beans, rinsed and drained
- 1 jar (13 ounces) corn relish
- ½ cup canned kidney beans
- ½ cup quartered cherry tomatoes
- ½ cup chopped celery
- ¼ cup chopped sweet orange pepper
- ¼ cup sliced pimiento-stuffed olives
- 2 teaspoons minced fresh parsley

In a large bowl, combine all ingredients. Cover and refrigerate until serving.

Golden crescent dough is scrumptious filled with dilled cream cheese and tender crab. You're sure to appreciate the rich flavor and easy preparation.

—**MAUREEN DONGOSKI** PETERSBURG, WEST VIRGINIA

CRAB CRESCENT LOAF

Serve this with a slotted spoon as an appetizer or over torn romaine lettuce as a salad. I like it with toasted baguette slices on the side.

—**TAMRA DUNCAN** LINCOLN, ARKANSAS

ANTIPASTO APPETIZER SALAD

Antipasto Appetizer Salad

PREP: 10 MIN. + CHILLING
MAKES: 6 CUPS

- 1 jar (16 ounces) roasted sweet red pepper strips, drained
- ½ pound part-skim mozzarella cheese, cubed
- 1 cup grape tomatoes
- 1 jar (7½ ounces) marinated quartered artichoke hearts, undrained
- 1 jar (7 ounces) pimiento-stuffed olives, drained
- 1 can (6 ounces) pitted ripe olives, drained
- 1 teaspoon dried basil
- 1 teaspoon dried parsley flakes
  Pepper to taste
  Toasted baguette slices or romaine lettuce, torn

1. In a large bowl, combine the first nine ingredients; toss to coat. Cover and refrigerate for at least 4 hours before serving.
2. Serve with baguette slices or over lettuce.

Ranch Biscuits

I dress up biscuit mix with my favorite ranch salad seasonings, then brush the golden bites with garlic butter after baking. The parsley-flecked biscuits go with any entree.
—CHRISTI GILLENTINE TULSA, OKLAHOMA

PREP/TOTAL TIME: 25 MIN.
MAKES: 9 BISCUITS

- 2 cups biscuit/baking mix
- 4 teaspoons dry ranch salad dressing mix
- ⅔ cup milk
- 2 tablespoons butter, melted
- 1 teaspoon dried parsley flakes
- ⅛ teaspoon garlic powder

1. In a large bowl, stir the biscuit mix, salad dressing mix and milk until combined. Drop 2 in. apart onto a greased baking sheet.
2. Bake at 425° for 10-15 minutes or until golden brown. In a small bowl, combine the butter, parsley and garlic powder; brush over warm biscuits. Serve warm.

BACON SCONES

I grew up with this popular scone recipe in Scotland. It pairs great with a salad.
—TERESA ROYSTON SEABECK, WASHINGTON

Bacon Scones

PREP: 20 MIN. **BAKE:** 15 MIN.
MAKES: 8 SCONES

- 1¾ cups all-purpose flour
- 2¼ teaspoons baking powder
- 1 teaspoon ground mustard
- ½ teaspoon salt
- ¼ teaspoon pepper
- 6 tablespoons cold butter
- 2 eggs
- ⅓ cup 2% milk
- ½ cup chopped onion
- ¼ cup shredded cheddar cheese
- 6 bacon strips, cooked and crumbled, divided

1. In a large bowl, combine the first five ingredients. Cut in butter until mixture resembles coarse crumbs. In a small bowl, whisk eggs and milk. Stir into dry ingredients just until moistened. Fold in the onion, cheese and two-thirds of the bacon.
2. Transfer dough to a greased baking sheet. Pat into a 7½-in. circle. Cut into eight wedges, but do not separate. Sprinkle with remaining bacon. Bake at 400° for 15-20 minutes or until golden brown. Serve warm.

RAISIN BRAN BREAD

You won't even realize you're getting bran cereal in your diet when you sample this yummy bread. It's moist and slightly sweet from raisins.

—**JEAN DAVIAU** SAN JACINTO, CALIFORNIA

Raisin Bran Bread

PREP: 10 MIN. **BAKE:** 3 HOURS
MAKES: 1 LOAF (1½ POUNDS, 16 SLICES)

- 1 **cup plus 1 tablespoon water (70° to 80°)**
- ¼ **cup packed brown sugar**
- 2 **tablespoons butter, softened**
- 1½ **cups raisin bran**
- ½ **teaspoon salt**
- ¼ **teaspoon baking soda**
- 2¼ **cups bread flour**
- 2¼ **teaspoons active dry yeast**
- ½ **cup raisins**

1. In bread machine pan, place the first eight ingredients in order suggested by manufacturer. Select basic bread setting. Choose crust color and loaf size if available.
2. Bake according to bread machine directions (check dough after 5 minutes of mixing; add 1 to 2 tablespoons of water or flour if needed).
3. Just before the final kneading (your machine may audibly signal this), add the raisins.

PREP: 45 MIN. + RISING **BAKE:** 20 MIN.
MAKES: 2 DOZEN

- 2½ to 2¾ **cups all-purpose flour**
- ¾ **cup whole wheat flour**
- ½ **cup old-fashioned oats**
- 2 **packages (¼ ounce each) active dry yeast**
- 1 **teaspoon salt**
- 1 **cup water**
- ¼ **cup honey**
- 5 **tablespoons butter, divided**
- 1 **egg**

1. In a large bowl, combine 1 cup all-purpose flour, whole wheat flour, oats, yeast and salt.
2. In a small saucepan, heat the water, honey and 4 tablespoons butter to 120°-130°. Add to dry ingredients; beat just until moistened. Add egg; beat until combined. Stir in enough of the remaining all-purpose flour to form a soft dough.
3. Turn onto a floured surface; knead until smooth and elastic, about 6-8 minutes. Place in a greased bowl, turning once to grease top. Cover and let rise in a warm place until doubled, about 1 hour.
4. Punch dough down. Turn onto a lightly floured surface; divide into 24 pieces. Shape each into a ball. Place in a greased 13-in. x 9-in. baking pan. Cover and let rise until doubled, about 30 minutes.
5. Bake at 375° for 20-22 minutes or until golden brown. Melt remaining butter; brush over rolls. Remove from pan to a wire rack.
PER SERVING *103 cal., 3 g fat (2 g sat. fat), 15 mg chol., 126 mg sodium, 17 g carb., 1 g fiber, 3 g pro.* **Diabetic Exchanges:** *1 starch, ½ fat.*

These tender rolls are a welcome addition to any meal. Whole wheat flour and oats make them nutritious, too. —ARLENE BUTLER OGDEN, UTAH

HONEY-OAT PAN ROLLS

Made with just five ingredients, this special salad is a cinch to put together. Chopped pear balances the rich blue cheese while almonds lend crunch and sweetness. —**GINGER SMISER** BLANCO, TEXAS

BLUE CHEESE PEAR SALAD

Blue Cheese Pear Salad

PREP/TOTAL TIME: 10 MIN.
MAKES: 4 SERVINGS

- 3 **cups hearts of romaine salad mix**
- 1 **large pear, chopped**
- ⅓ **cup slivered almonds**
- ½ **cup crumbled blue cheese**
- ⅓ **cup Italian salad dressing**

In a large bowl, combine the salad mix, pear, almonds and blue cheese. Drizzle with dressing and toss to coat. Serve immediately.

Tomato-Green Bean Salad

Feta cheese adds a salty kick to a quick veggie salad. It tastes even better the next day, when the flavors all have a chance to blend.
—ESTELLE LAULETTA
BOSTON, MASSACHUSETTS

PREP/TOTAL TIME: 20 MIN.
MAKES: 4 SERVINGS

- ½ **pound fresh green beans, trimmed**
- 1½ **cups cherry tomatoes, halved**
- ¾ **cup pitted ripe olives, halved**
- ¼ **cup Italian salad dressing**
- ⅔ **cup crumbled feta cheese**

1. Place beans in a large saucepan and cover with water. Bring to a boil. Cook, uncovered, for 8-10 minutes or until crisp-tender. Drain and immediately place beans in ice water. Drain and pat dry.
2. In a large bowl, combine the beans, tomatoes and olives. Drizzle with dressing; toss to coat. Chill until serving. Just before serving, sprinkle with cheese.

These biscuits couldn't be simpler to make! With from-scratch flavor and a golden-brown cheese topping, they're a ridiculously easy instant hit!
—LYNN TICE OSAGE CITY, KANSAS

Creamy Coleslaw

Packaged coleslaw mix really cuts down on prep time. My recipe is great for potlucks or to serve your family on a busy weeknight.
—RENEE ENDRESS GALVA, ILLINOIS

PREP/TOTAL TIME: 10 MIN.
MAKES: 6 SERVINGS

- 1 **package (14 ounces) coleslaw mix**
- ¾ **cup mayonnaise**
- ⅓ **cup sour cream**
- ¼ **cup sugar**
- ¾ **teaspoon seasoned salt**
- ½ **teaspoon ground mustard**
- ¼ **teaspoon celery salt**

Place coleslaw mix in a large bowl. In a small bowl, combine the remaining ingredients; stir until blended. Pour over coleslaw mix and toss to coat. Refrigerate until serving.

Biscuits Italiano

PREP/TOTAL TIME: 25 MIN.
MAKES: 10 BISCUITS

- 1 **tube (12 ounces) refrigerated buttermilk biscuits**
- ¼ **cup prepared Italian salad dressing**
- ⅓ **cup grated Parmesan cheese**
- ½ **cup shredded part-skim mozzarella cheese**

1. Separate biscuits; dip the top of each in salad dressing, then in Parmesan cheese. Place cheese side up on an ungreased baking sheet; sprinkle with mozzarella cheese.
2. Bake at 400° for 9-11 minutes or until golden brown. Serve warm.

BUTTERHORNS

> I always have to double the recipe because these buttery rolls never last long in our house. You can shape them any way you like, but to me, a crescent shape is so pretty. —KELLY KIRBY WESTVILLE, NOVA SCOTIA

EAT SMART Butterhorns

PREP: 35 MIN. + RISING **BAKE:** 10 MIN.
MAKES: 2 DOZEN

- 1 tablespoon active dry yeast
- 1 teaspoon plus ⅓ cup sugar
- ½ cup warm water (110° to 115°)
- ½ cup butter, softened
- ½ cup warm 2% milk (110° to 115°)
- 1 egg
- ¾ teaspoon salt
- 4 cups all-purpose flour

1. In a large bowl, dissolve yeast and 1 teaspoon sugar in warm water. Add the butter, milk, egg, salt, remaining sugar and 2 cups flour. Beat until smooth. Stir in enough remaining flour to form a soft dough.

2. Turn onto a floured surface; knead until smooth and elastic, about 6-8 minutes. Place in a greased bowl, turning once to grease the top. Cover and let rise in a warm place until doubled, about 1 hour.

3. Punch dough down. Turn onto a lightly floured surface; divide in half. Roll each portion into a 12-in. circle; cut each into 12 wedges. Roll up wedges from the wide end and place point side down 2 in. apart on greased baking sheets. Curve ends to form crescents.

4. Cover and let rise in a warm place until doubled, about 30 minutes. Bake at 350° for 10-12 minutes or until golden brown. Remove from pans to wire racks.
PER SERVING *128 cal., 4 g fat (3 g sat. fat), 19 mg chol., 107 mg sodium, 19 g carb., 1 g fiber, 3 g pro.* ***Diabetic Exchanges:*** *1 starch, 1 fat.*

Cream Cheese Cranberry Muffins

PREP: 15 MIN. **BAKE:** 20 MIN.
MAKES: 2 DOZEN

- 1 cup butter, softened
- 1 package (8 ounces) cream cheese, softened
- 1½ cups sugar
- 4 eggs
- 1½ teaspoons vanilla extract
- 2 cups all-purpose flour
- 1½ teaspoons baking powder
- ½ teaspoon salt
- 2 cups fresh or frozen cranberries
- ½ cup chopped pecans

DRIZZLE
- 2 cups confectioners' sugar
- 3 tablespoons 2% milk

1. In a large bowl, cream the butter, cream cheese and sugar until light and fluffy. Add eggs, one at a time, beating well after each addition. Beat in vanilla. Combine the flour, baking powder and salt; stir into creamed mixture just until moistened. Fold in cranberries and pecans.

2. Fill greased or paper-lined muffin cups three-fourths full. Bake at 350° for 20-25 minutes or until a toothpick inserted near the center comes out clean. Cool muffins for 5 minutes before removing from pans to wire racks.

3. Combine confectioners' sugar and milk; drizzle over muffins.

For a **sweet treat**, use **white chocolate chips** instead of pecans in the muffin recipe. For a **hint of citrus**, add a little finely grated **orange peel**.

Moist and packed with colorful berries, these marvelous muffins are a seasonal specialty. They are light and tasty, and they freeze very well.
—**LEONARD KESZLER** BISMARCK, NORTH DAKOTA

CREAM CHEESE CRANBERRY MUFFINS

General Recipe Index

Alphabetical Recipe Index